ESTATES
and
FUTURE INTERESTS

IN A NUTSHELL

By

LAWRENCE W. WAGGONER
Lewis M. Simes Professor of Law
University of Michigan

SECOND EDITION

St. Paul, Minn.
WEST PUBLISHING CO.
1993

COPYRIGHT © 1981, 1993 By LAWRENCE W. WAGGONER

ISBN 0-314-02770-X

1st Reprint–1997

ESTATES IN LAND
and
FUTURE INTERESTS

IN A NUTSHELL

PREFACE

The objective of this book is to help law students understand estates in land and future interests. First year property students and second or third year students who are taking courses covering wills, trusts, and future interests are the intended audience.

It is fitting that the Nutshell Series includes *Estates in Land and Future Interests* in its inventory of titles. It was in the future interests area that putting a body of law into a nutshell first appears to have emerged. The case was Van Grutten v. Foxwell, [1897] App. Cas. 658, 670-71 (H.L.). In the course of his opinion in *Van Grutten*, Lord Macnaghten referred to Lord Thurlow's statement about the Rule in Shelley's Case as one that put "the case in a nutshell."* Far from

---

* Lord Thurlow, it should be noted for the sake of accuracy, never himself undertook to put the Rule in Shelley's Case into a nutshell. His statement about the rule was contained in a letter he wrote to Francis Hargrave. The letter is published in 3 Francis

glorifying the idea of putting a case like *Shelley's* into a nutshell, however, Lord Macnaghten added that "it is one thing to put a case like *Shelley's* into a nutshell and another thing to keep it there." By this he meant that an oversimplified exposition of a body of law does little good and might do considerable harm. This warning is particularly apt, not just to the Rule in Shelley's Case, but to the whole subject of estates in land and future interests. This is a hard technical subject, possibly as hard as any you will encounter as a law student. Lord Macnaghten's warning notwithstanding, however, it is believed possible to present a succinct exposition of a body of law, even one as technically difficult as this one, without oversimplifying it. *Estates in Land and Future Interests in a Nutshell* seeks to achieve this objective.

Portions of this *Nutshell* have been adapted from Lawrence W. Waggoner et al., *Family Property Law: Cases and Materials on Wills, Trusts, and Future Interests* (1991).

LAWRENCE W. WAGGONER

June 1993

Hargrave, Jurisconsult Exercitations 360 (1813). Lord Thurlow's letter does not even purport to state the rule in any formal way, much less put it into a nutshell.

IV

OUTLINE

OUTLINE

OUTLINE

OUTLINE

OUTLINE

OUTLINE

OUTLINE

OUTLINE

OUTLINE

TABLE OF ABBREVIATIONS

Restatement 2d of Property	Restatement (Second) of Property (Donative Transfers) (1983, 1986, 1988, 1992)
Restatement of Property	Restatement of Property (1936, 1940, 1944)
Restatement 2d of Trusts	Restatement (Second) of Trusts (1959)
Scott on Trusts	Austin W. Scott, The Law of Trusts (William F. Fratcher ed., 4th ed. 1987-91)
Simes on Future Interests	Lewis M. Simes, Handbook of the Law of Future Interests (2d ed. 1966)
Simes & Smith on Future Interests	Lewis M. Simes & Alan F. Smith, Law of Future Interests (2d ed. 1956)
UPC	Uniform Probate Code (1990; amended slightly in 1991 and 1993)

TABLE OF ABBREVIATIONS

Uniform Rule	Uniform Statutory Rule Against Perpetuities (promulgated in 1986; amended slightly in 1990)

TABLE OF CASES
References are to Pages

TABLE OF CASES

TABLE OF CASES

TABLE OF CASES

TABLE OF CASES

ESTATES IN LAND
and
FUTURE INTERESTS

IN A NUTSHELL

Chapter 1

INTRODUCTION TO ESTATES IN LAND AND FUTURE INTERESTS

§ 1.1. Fragmentation of Ownership

Our legal system, like many others in the world, permits outright ownership of property. Outright ownership is called ownership in *fee simple absolute* if land and *absolute ownership* if personalty. Outright ownership of property carries with it several rights (called incidents of ownership). Two important incidents of ownership are the right to possess the property (the nearly unrestricted right to use it and to exclude others from using it) and the right to transfer ownership to another (the right to sell it and the nearly unrestricted right to give it away by either inter-vivos gift or testamentary devise).

Our legal system also permits ownership to be divided or fragmented. Derived from the English common law, fragmentation of ownership is an ingenious concept. To understand what the concept means, it is important to understand what it does not mean: The concept does not mean dividing property itself into tangible segments or parcels. Division of property into tangible segments, each one owned by a different person, is also possible under our legal

1

system, but that is hardly an ingenious concept. The ingenuity of fragmentation is that it allows two or more persons to have simultaneous interests in the property as a whole. Fragmentation of ownership involves an abstract allocation of the incidents of ownership among the owners. The manner of allocation depends to a great extent on the form of fragmentation.

There are three basic forms of fragmentation. First, ownership can be fragmented into *concurrent* interests of various types; these are the familiar tenancy in common, joint tenancy, and tenancy by the entirety (spouses only). Secondly, ownership can be fragmented into *legal* and *equitable* interests; this arises when property is placed in trust. Finally, ownership can be fragmented sequentially into *present* and *future* interests; a future interest in property is a nonpossessory interest that might or will become possessory at some future time.

§ 1.2. Basic Terminology

One of the frustrating features of this subject area is the terminology. Some words or phrases are used interchangeably and other words or phrases are used inconsistently. Many courts and textwriters and the Restatement of Property use the terms "present estate,"[1] "present interest,"[2] "possessory estate," "possessory interest," "present possessory interest," and "present possessory estate" interchangeably. They also use the terms "future interest" and "future estate" interchangeably. In this *Nutshell*, the term *present estate* or *possessory estate* is generally used when referring to a present (possessory) estate in land[3] and the term *interest* is generally used when referring to a future interest.

Do not be confused by the terms *present* interest and *future* interest. The words "present" and "future" seem to distinguish between interests that are currently created and interests that are to be created in the future. This is not the distinction. *Both present and future interests are already created. A present interest is a possessory interest or estate; a future interest is an interest or estate in which the right to possession is postponed.* In the disposition *"to A for*

---

[1] The Restatement defines the word *estate* to mean an interest in land that is or might become possessory and is ownership measured in terms of duration. See Restatement of Property § 9.

[2]   The Restatement defines the word *interest* to mean either (1) varying aggregates of rights, privileges, powers and immunities or (2) any one of them. See Restatement of Property § 5.

[3]   The term *possessory estate* is more apt when referring to an interest in land, whereas the term *present interest* is more apt when referring to the income interest of a trust beneficiary, for that beneficiary has a present right to the income generated by the trust property, but not a present right to possession of the trust property.

life, remainder to B," *A* has an estate in the property that is possessory and *B* has an interest that is nonpossessory. Because *B*'s interest is just as much a present interest as *A*'s is, *B* can transfer his or her interest to another and *B*'s creditors can attach it. Thus the word "future" in the term "future interest" refers to the time when the right to *possession* arises, not to the time when the interest is *created*. Consequently, although *B*'s right to possession will arise in the future (when the life tenant dies), *B*'s *interest* in the property does not arise in the future. *B* received her *interest* in the property (her future interest) at the same time that *A* received his interest in the property (his possessory life estate).

§ 1.3. The Importance of Present and Future Interests

Although the law of present and future interests developed in the context of *legal* interests in *land*, such interests are not commonly created today. Today's combination of present and future interests mainly affects trusts of personal property, typically securities. Trusts combine two types of fragmentation of ownership: Legal title to the trust property is held by the trustee and equitable title is held by the trust beneficiaries, and the equitable title is subdivided in terms of time, i.e., between income beneficiaries and corpus beneficiaries. Thus the common life estate and future interest today are *equitable* interests in *personal* property.

Trusts of personal property are mainstays of

modern estate planning practice. Estate planning lawyers should therefore know something about present and future interests. In recent years, trusts have been proliferating. There are no reliable statistics regarding the number of trusts currently in existence, or regarding their aggregate value. However, the federal government compiles statistics about trusts in which the trustee is a federally insured commercial or savings bank. According to these annual compilations, there were 1.4 million personal trusts at the end of 1987 having an aggregate market value of $422.5 billion, as compared with 520,326 personal trusts in 1968 having an aggregate market value of slightly over $99 billion. Thus this two-decade period saw the number of trusts administered by federally insured commercial or savings banks nearly triple and the aggregate market value more than quadruple (unadjusted for inflation).

§ 1.4. A Word About the Hypothetical Examples Used in This Book

Hypothetical examples are used throughout this book to supplement and illustrate the text. These hypothetical examples are structured as follows:

(a) Words of Inheritance Generally Used for Possessory Estates but not for Future Interests. In line with modern law, the dispositive language for future interests dispenses with words of inheritance. Under the earlier common law, a conveyance "to *A*" gave *A* only a life estate; to give *A* a fee simple interest required "words of inheritance"—"to *A* and

his heirs."[4] But words of inheritance are no longer necessary, except in perhaps a very few states. This change has been accomplished by statute in the vast majority of states (see Restatement of Property § 39) and by judicial decision in many of the remaining states (see Restatement of Property, Introductory Note to Chapter 3, at p. 49). Consequently, the hypotheticals in this book read "to *A* for life, remainder to *B*" rather than "to *A* for life, remainder to *B* and his/her heirs." The dispositive language for possessory fee simple estates generally includes words of inheritance. Thus a fee simple determinable will commonly appear in the form of "to *A* and her heirs so long as . . ." rather than "to *A* so long as . . ." even though the latter form would be sufficient under modern law to give *A* a fee simple rather than a life estate.

(b) *Examples Built Around Legal Interests in Land*. The hypothetical examples usually involve *legal* interests in *land*. This has been done to simplify the wording. As pointed out earlier (§ 1.3), such interests are not commonly created today; estates and future interests are more commonly in trusts of securities. Nevertheless, the process of classification

---

[4] Occasionally the language of a disposition will say "*A or* his heirs." While not recommended, the substitution of the "or" for the orthodox "and" will probably not make any difference. The Restatement of Property § 27 cmt. e states that, in the absence of evidence of a contrary intention, "or his heirs" will be treated as words of inheritance.

is easier to understand if illustrated by examples that say "*G* transferred land to *A* for life, remainder to *B*," rather than the wordier "*G* transferred securities to the Faithful Bank, in trust, to pay the income to *A* for life, and at *A*'s death to deliver the trust assets to *B*."

(c) Word "Transfer" Used to Cover Conveyances and Devises. Whether the transfer was a conveyance (inter-vivos transfer) or a devise (testamentary transfer) makes no difference in most of the examples. The generic word "transfer" is used in those cases. If the type of transfer makes a difference, the term "conveyance" or "devise" is used, as appropriate.

(d) Transferor Originally Owned the Property in Fee Simple Absolute. Unless otherwise stated, you should assume that *G* owned the property in fee simple absolute when *G* made the transfer.

(e) Examples Double as Review Questions. The examples serve two functions. They aid initial understanding by illustrating the principles stated abstractly in the text. They also aid exam preparation by serving as review questions. Each example is arranged so that the facts and solution are given in separate paragraphs. This allows you to test your ability to answer each problem by covering up the solution, and then to check your answer without flipping back and forth between problems and answers given several pages apart.

(f) Charting the Facts. It will help you understand the examples if you make a linear chart of the facts

as they develop over time. Starting with horizontal lines depicting the lifetimes of the transferor and transferees, insert in the horizontal lines the following symbols: ⊗ to indicate a person's death; ↓ to indicate the time and direction of a transfer; and | to indicate the time when an interest or estate of a living person changes into another interest or estate. To illustrate this technique, take a devise of land by *G* "to *A* for life, remainder to *B*." If *B* survived *A*, the case can be charted as follows:

G→⊗
A→↓←(life estate)——→⊗
B→↓←(vested rem)→|←(fsa)→

Your chart shows that when the life tenant, *A*, died, *B*'s remainder became a fee simple absolute.

To take a more complex example, suppose that *G* devised land "to *A* for life, then to *B* if *B* survives *A*, but if not to *C*." If *B* predeceased *A* but *C* survived *A*, the case can be charted as follows:

G→⊗
A→↓←(l/e)————————————→⊗
B→↓←(cont rem)→⊗
C→↓←(cont rem)→|←(vested rem)→|←(fsa)→

Your chart shows that when *B* died, *C*'s contingent remainder became a vested remainder (see infra § 8.1), and when *A* died, *C*'s vested remainder became a fee simple absolute.

PART I

CLASSIFICATION OF ESTATES IN LAND AND FUTURE INTERESTS

Chapter 2

THE IMPORTANCE AND PROCESS OF CLASSIFICATION

§ 2.1. In General

Classification is a process of identification, of fixing the proper label or labels to a property interest. The study of estates in land and future interests was at one time dominated by—some would say obsessed with—the study of classification. The preoccupation with classification was appropriate, though tedious, as long as important legal consequences turned on classification. Today, few legal consequences turn on classification. Why, then, study classification at all? Unfortunately, classification is still important in solving some legal problems, such as applying the Rule Against Perpetuities. A contingent remainder, for example, is subject to the Rule Against Perpetuities, but a vested remainder is not. Additionally, you need to be familiar with the terms associated with classification to understand the legal literature and communicate with others in practice. Before discussing the various rules of law that turn on classification, we deal with the process of classification in detail.

The hierarchy of estates is a refined, artificial structure that took centuries to develop fully. If it had been designed in one fell swoop, the flexibility it provides estate planners and clients could surely have been achieved by a system of much greater simplicity. A proposal for a simplified system is noted later. See infra § 8.2.

The complexity and artificiality in the current system was not so much designed as evolved, step by step over a fairly long period of time, from the struggles of competing interest groups. The owners of the great landed estates, assisted by ingenious lawyers, sought to avoid the estate taxes of the day and to safeguard their estates through generations and generations. As one loophole was plugged, their lawyers found another. The result was that great distinctions were drawn on the basis of slight variations in dispositive language. Through classification, different ways of saying the same thing were accorded different legal consequences. Form controlled over substance. In classification, form still controls over substance. Form controls legal consequences less than before, however, because the legal consequences that depend upon classification have gradually diminished.

As we study the current system, bear in mind also that the system of classification, which was originally developed in feudal times mainly for legal interests in land, has been transposed today to the classification of the beneficial interests in the modern trust. See Olin L. Browder, Jr., Trusts and the Doctrine of Estates, 72 Mich. L. Rev. 1507 (1974).

Quantum of Estates. According to the hierarchy of

estates, the possessory estates are ordered by "quantum." In descending order of quantum, the groupings are: (1) the fee simple estates (all fee simple estates are of the same quantum); (2) the fee tail; (3) the life estate; (4) the term of years; (5) the estate from period to period; (6) the estate at will; and (7) the estate at sufferance.

Freehold and Nonfreehold Estates. Feudal law in England distinguished between "freehold" and "nonfreehold" estates. The freehold estates are: (1) the fee simple estates; (2) the fee tail; and (3) the life estate. The nonfreehold estates are: (1) the term of years; (2) the estate from period to period; (3) the estate at will, and (4) the estate at sufferance.

Particular Estate. The term *particular estate* is a term of art denoting any estate that is less than a fee simple—a fee tail, a life estate, a term of years, and so on.

Chart. The following chart of the hierarchy of estates is presented here partly as a point of departure but mainly as a point of retrospection for use as you work your way through the succeeding text.

THE HIERARCHY OF ESTATES AND FUTURE INTERESTS[1]

Possessory Estates	Possible Combinations of Future Interests	
	Nonreversionary (created in a transferee)	Reversionary (retained by transferor)
Fee Simple Absolute	None permissible	None Permissible
Defeasible Fee Simple:		
Fee Simple Determinable[2]	When none created	Possibility of Reverter
	Executory Interest	If Any, Possibility of Reverter
Fee Simple Subject to a Condition Subsequent[3]		Right of Entry (Power of Termination)
Fee Simple Subject to an Executory Limitation[4]	Executory Interest	

[1] Although the chart is believed to be substantially accurate and complete, it does not purport to depict all the combinations of future interests that possibly could follow each possessory estate. A remainder following a life estate might, for example, be in fee simple determinable, in which case the transferor might retain a possibility of reverter in addition to, or instead of, a reversion.

[2] "Fee simple determinable" is the most common name employed to describe this estate. Other names are "base fee," "qualified fee," and "fee simple on a special limitation."

[3] The "fee simple subject to a condition subsequent" and the "fee simple subject to an executory limitation" are created by the same language. The distinction between the two is based on the nature of the future interest following it. If such an estate is followed by both an executory interest and a right of entry, the possessory estate could properly be called a fee simple subject to an executory limitation and a condition subsequent. It may be noted further that the "fee simple subject to an executory limitation" is sometimes called a "fee simple subject to a conditional limitation."

[4] Supra note 3.

THE HIERARCHY OF ESTATES AND FUTURE INTERESTS

Possessory Estates	Possible Combinations of Future Interests	
	Nonreversionary (created in a transferee)	*Reversionary (retained by transferor)*
Fee Tail[5]	. . . Same as with Life Estate . . .	
Life Estate	When no remainder created	Indefeasibly Vested Reversion
	Contingent Remainder (subject to a condition precedent); If any, Alternative Contingent Remainder	Reversion Vested Subject to Defeasance (may be merely technical)
	Remainder Vested Subject to Defeasance (conditional); If any, Executory Interest	If any, Possibility of Reverter
	Remainder Vested Subject to Defeasance (limitational);	If any, Reversion either Vested Subject to Defeasance or Indefeasibly Vested Remainder
	Remainder Vested Subject to Open; Executory Interest in unborn class members	None permissible
	Indefeasibly Vested Remainder	None permissible

[5] The fee tail estate, though still permissible in a handful of states, has faded from importance.

THE HIERARCHY OF ESTATES AND FUTURE INTERESTS

Possessory Estates	Possible Combinations of Future Interests	
	Nonreversionary (created in a transferee)	*Reversionary (retained by transferor)*
Life Estate Subject to a Special Limitation[6]	. . . Same as with Life Estate . . .	
Life Estate Subject to a Condition Subsequent		Reversion and Right of Entry (otherwise, same as with Life Estate)
Life Estate Subject to an Executory Limitation	Remainder and Executory Interest (otherwise, same as with Life Estate)	
Term of Years	. . . Same as with Life Estate . . .	

§ 2.2. The Process of Classification

Classifying possessory estates and future interests may appear at first to be a daunting task, especially in view of the complexity shown in the chart above; but, while intricate, classification is really not that difficult if the steps outlined in the subsequent chapters of this book are followed.

---

[6] Another name for this interest is "determinable life estate."

Chapter 3

POSSESSORY ESTATES

§ 3.1. The Estates in Fee Simple

Although there are four fee simple estates, they can be divided into two general categories—fee simple absolute and fee simple defeasible.

(a) Fee Simple Absolute.

☞ *The estate in* FEE SIMPLE ABSOLUTE *is an estate in land that is not subject to termination; it is unlimited in duration.*

The personal-property counterpart of the fee simple absolute is called absolute ownership. The fee simple absolute is not subject to any special limitations, conditions subsequent, or executory limitations. A fee simple absolute is never followed by a future interest.

> *EXAMPLE 3-1.* G conveyed land "to A and his heirs."
>
> A has a fee simple absolute; no future interest follows it. The words "and his heirs" are "words of limitation," meaning words defining the estate granted to A, not "words of purchase," meaning words granting a property interest to A's heirs.

(b) Defeasible Fee Simple. The defeasible fee simple estates terminate upon the happening of an event specified in the grant. There are three defeasible fee simple estates: (1) the fee simple determinable; (2) the fee simple subject to a condition subsequent; and (3) the fee simple subject to an executory limitation. Distinguishing among these estates requires an understanding of the concept of defeasance.

Defeasance means that the holder of the estate will lose that estate upon the happening of a specified event. Defeasance is a broad term that encompasses two categories: condition and limitation. A possessory estate that is subject to defeasance is subject to either a condition subsequent or a limitation. See Restatement of Property § 16 cmt. b.

Possessory estates that are subject to a "condition subsequent" terminate by being cut short or divested upon the happening of the specified event. Language in a grant that signifies a "condition subsequent" are such words as "on condition that" or "provided that," followed by such words as "but if" or "and if." (In some grants, only the "but if" or "and if" language will appear.)

Possessory estates that are subject to a "limitation" terminate naturally or by their own terms. Language in a grant that signifies a "limitation" are such words as "during," "until," "while," "so long as," "for so long as," or simply "for [a designated period]," followed by such words as "at," "upon," or "then." A "special" limitation subjects an estate to possible termination in addition to that normally characteristic of the estate; thus a special limitation describes an event that is not certain to happen. See Restatement of Property § 23.

(1) Fee Simple Determinable.

☞ *The FEE SIMPLE DETERMINABLE is a fee estate that is subject to a special limitation.*

This means that it automatically terminates or expires if the specified event happens; the terminating event is an event that is not certain to happen. The future interest following the estate in fee simple determinable is a possibility of reverter (if reversionary) or an executory interest (if nonreversionary).

EXAMPLE 3-2. *G* conveyed land "to *A* and her heirs so long as *A* does not allow liquor to be sold on the land; upon *A*'s allowing liquor to be sold on the land, the land reverts to me."

A has a fee simple determinable. *G* has a possibility of reverter.

EXAMPLE 3-3. *G* conveyed land "to *A* and her heirs so long as *A* does not allow liquor to be sold on the land; and upon *A*'s allowing liquor to be sold on the land, the land goes to *B*."

A has a fee simple determinable. *B* has an executory interest.

Note that the limitation regarding selling liquor applies only to *A* and not to *A*'s successors in interest. Therefore, *B*'s executory interest is valid under the

Rule Against Perpetuities because it must vest or fail within A's lifetime.

(2) Fee Simple Subject to a Condition Subsequent.

☞ *The* FEE SIMPLE SUBJECT TO A CONDITION SUBSEQUENT *is a fee estate that is subject to divestment in favor of a reversionary future interest called a right of entry (also called a power of termination).*

The happening of the specified event does not automatically divest the estate; rather, it empowers the grantor or his or her successor in interest to divest the estate by exercising the right of entry.

> EXAMPLE 3-4. G conveyed land "to A and his heirs on condition that A not allow liquor to be sold on the land, and if A allows liquor to be sold on the land, then the grantor is to have the right to re-enter and take possession."
> A has a fee simple subject to a condition subsequent. G has a right of entry.

(3) Fee Simple Subject to an Executory Limitation.

☞ *The* FEE SIMPLE SUBJECT TO AN EXECUTORY LIMITATION *is a fee estate that is subject to divestment in favor of a nonreversionary future interest called an executory interest.*

The happening of the specified event divests the estate.

> ***EXAMPLE 3-5.*** *G* conveyed land "to *A* and her heirs, but if *A* allows liquor to be sold on the land, the land goes to *B*."
>
> *A* has a fee simple subject to an executory limitation. *B* has an executory interest.

§ 3.2. Fee Tail

☞ *The FEE TAIL ESTATE is subject to termination if and when the line of the tenant in tail's issue fails.*

That is, the estate terminates upon the death of the tenant in tail's last living descendant.

The fee tail estate has an interesting history (see Restatement of Property Ch. 5; Bergin & Haskell on Estates in Land and Future Interests 28-34), but its present is no longer very important and its future even less so. In almost all states, the fee tail estate is abolished. Language purporting to create it—"to *A* and the heirs of his body"—has different consequences in different states. The most predominant results are that it creates a fee simple absolute in *A* or that it creates a life estate in *A*, with a remainder in fee in *A*'s issue.

§ 3.3. Life Estates

☞ *LIFE ESTATES are estates that expire naturally (by their own terms) on the death of the measuring life.*

Unless the life estate is a life estate pur autre vie (see below), the measuring life is the life tenant. Life estates are by definition defeasible estates because they are subject to a limitation ("to *A for* life;" "to *A so long as A* lives;" "to *A until A*'s death;" "to *A during A*'s lifetime"). See Restatement of Property § 16 cmt. b.

The phrase "equitable life estate" is sometimes used to describe the interest of a trust beneficiary who has the right to the income from a trust for his or her lifetime.

By adding a special limitation or a condition subsequent to the grant, life estates can be made prematurely defeasible, so that they might end before the life tenant's death.

> *EXAMPLE 3-6. G* transferred land "to *A* for life or until *A* remarries."
> *A*'s estate is called a "life estate subject to a special limitation." Another name for it is "determinable life estate."

> *EXAMPLE 3-7. (1) G* transferred land "to *A* for life, remainder to *B*; but if *A* remarries, to *B* immediately."
> *A*'s estate is called a "life estate subject to an executory limitation."
> *(2) G* transferred land "to *A* for life on condition

that *A* not remarry; and if *A* remarries, *G* is to have the right to re-enter and take possession."

A's estate is called a "life estate subject to a condition subsequent."

A life estate need not be measured by the life of the one in possession, but can be measured by the life of another. This type of estate is called a *life estate pur autre vie*.

> *EXAMPLE 3-8. G* transferred land "to *A* for the life of *B*." *A* predeceases *B*. *A*'s will devises her entire estate to *X*.
>
> *A* has a life estate pur autre vie. Unlike a life estate that terminates on the life tenant's death, *A* can devise the remaining portion of her life estate to *X*. After *A*'s death, *X* has a life estate pur autre vie—for the life of *B*.

§ 3.4. Term of Years

☞ *TERMS OF YEARS are estates that expire naturally (by their own terms) on the expiration of the term.*

Terms of years are defeasible estates because they are subject to a limitation ("to *A for* 10 years").

The phrase "equitable term" is sometimes used to describe the interest of a trust beneficiary who has the right to the income from a trust for a term. Equitable terms are used most frequently in charitable lead trusts, but they are also used in trusts that give

the right to the income to a family member until he
or she reaches a specified age.

By adding a special limitation or a condition
subsequent to the grant, terms of years can be made
prematurely defeasible, so that they might end before
the expiration of the term.

> *EXAMPLE 3-9. G* transferred land "to *A* for 10
> years or until *A* remarries."
>
> *A*'s estate is called a "term of years subject to a
> special limitation." Another name for it is
> "determinable term of years."

> *EXAMPLE 3-10. (1) G* transferred land "to *A* for 10
> years, remainder to *B*; but if *A* remarries, to *B*
> immediately."
>
> *A*'s estate is called a "term of years subject to an
> executory limitation."
>
> *(2) G* transferred land "to *A* for 10 years on
> condition that *A* not remarry; and if *A* remarries, *G* is
> to have the right to re-enter and take possession."
>
> *A*'s estate is called a "term of years subject to a
> condition subsequent."

***Digression on Historical Distinction Between
Freehold and Nonfreehold Estates***. Historically,
because a term of years is a nonfreehold estate (supra
§ 2.1), a grant "to *A* for 10 years, then to *B*" was not
characterized as a term of years in *A followed by* a
remainder in *B*. Rather, *B* was characterized as
owning the land in fee simple absolute *subject to A*'s
term of years.

Today, the distinction between freehold and nonfreehold estates has little continuing importance. Characterizing *B* as owning the land subject to a term of years in *A* may still be appropriate regarding a commercial transaction, such as where *B*, as lessor, leases the land to *A*, as lessee, for 10 years. In the setting of noncommercial transactions, however, the ancient characterization was abolished in the Restatement of Property § 157 cmt. e & illus. 9. Cmt. e states:

> The creation of a remainder in land does not require . . . that the estates preceding the future interest be freehold estates . . . . Historically, an interest created subsequent to a non-freehold estate was not a remainder. If it was not subject to a condition precedent, it was a present interest. If it was subject to a condition precedent, it was a springing executory interest. Modern usage has broadened the inclusiveness of the word remainder in the manner stated in this Comment.

Accord, Am. L. Prop. § 4.31. This *Nutshell* follows the modern usage as described in the Restatement and the American Law of Property.

Chapter 4

REVERSIONARY AND NONREVERSIONARY FUTURE INTERESTS

Classifying a future interest requires identifying its type, labeling it in terms of vesting, and identifying the type of possessory estate it might or will later become.

There are five types of future interests: (1) remainders; (2) executory interests; (3) reversions; (4) possibilities of reverter; and (5) rights of entry (also called powers of termination). Executory interests are further divided into springing and shifting executory interests.

There are four vesting categories: (1) indefeasibly vested; (2) vested subject to complete defeasance; (3) vested subject to open (i.e., subject to partial defeasance); and (4) contingent.

Regarding the type of possessory estate the future interest will become if and when it becomes possessory, the range of interests is the same as it is for interests that start out as possessory estates: (1) fee simple absolute; (2) fee simple subject to a condition subsequent; (3) fee simple determinable; (4)

fee simple subject to an executory limitation; (5) fee tail; (6) life estate; and (7) term of years. We ignore the fee tail in this book because that estate is turned into some other estate by statute in almost all states.

The first step is to identify the future interest by type. Once you have done this you can then go on to classify it in terms of vesting and in terms of the type of possessory estate it might or will become. Preliminary to identifying a future interest by type, you must determine whether it is reversionary or nonreversionary.

Three of the five future interests are reversionary interests: the reversion, the possibility of reverter, and the right of entry. The other two—the remainder and the executory interest—are nonreversionary. Accordingly, if a future interest is reversionary, it must be a reversion, a possibility of reverter, or a right of entry, and if a future interest is nonreversionary, it must be a remainder or an executory interest.

☞ *Rule 1: To be* REVERSIONARY, *a future interest must be retained by (or created in) the transferor.*

☞ *Rule 2: To be* NONREVERSIONARY, *a future interest must be created in a transferee (someone other than the transferor).*

The classification of an interest as reversionary or nonreversionary is fixed at the time of creation. A post-creation transfer of a reversionary interest to a transferee does not change the interest into a nonreversionary interest. Conversely, a post-creation transfer of a nonreversionary interest to the transferor does not change the interest into a reversionary interest. It makes no difference whether the post-creation transfer was inter vivos, testamentary, or resulted from intestate succession.

EXAMPLE 4-1. G conveyed land "to *A* for life." Later *G* conveyed all his interest in the land to *B*.

When *G* made the second conveyance, he no longer owned the life estate he had previously conveyed to *A*; *G* owned only a reversionary interest (a reversion in this case). Consequently, the second conveyance constitutes a conveyance of *G*'s reversion to *B*. This conveyance does not change the reversion into a nonreversionary interest (a remainder). *A*'s life estate is still followed by a reversion, but the reversion is now held by *B*.

EXAMPLE 4-2. G conveyed land "to *A* for life." *G* later died leaving a will that did not mention the land but contained a residuary clause devising and bequeathing all her property not otherwise disposed of to *B*. *G* was survived by *A* and *B*.

At *G*'s death, *B* took *G*'s reversion.

EXAMPLE 4-3. G conveyed land "to *A* for life." *G* later died intestate, i.e., without a valid will. *G* was survived by *A* and by his sole heir, *B*.

At *G*'s death, *B* took *G*'s reversion.

Distinguishing a reversionary from a nonreversionary interest is easy if the interest was originally created during the transferor's lifetime, as in the examples above. When *G* carved out and conveyed a life estate to *A*, *G* retained what he did not transfer—i.e., a reversion.

If *G* still owned the property at the time of his death, however, and devised a life estate in the property to *A*, would the future interest be originally created in *G* or in a transferee? Common sense suggests that a dead transferor cannot retain anything. But the law views the situation differently. When *A*'s life estate is created in a will, the nature of the future interest depends upon whether it also passes under *G*'s will or passes to the transferor's heirs by intestacy. If by intestacy, the future interest is reversionary.

> *EXAMPLE 4-4*. *G*'s will devised land "to *A* for life." *G*'s will contained no residuary clause. Thus the residue of *G*'s estate passed by intestacy to *G*'s sole heir, *B*.
> *B* takes a reversion, not a remainder.

If the future interest passes under the residuary clause in the will, however, there is a split of authority in the cases.

> *EXAMPLE 4-5*. *G*'s will devised land "to *A* for life," and devised the residue of her estate to *B*.
> Most courts and other authorities would hold that *B*

takes a remainder; a few courts would say it is a reversion.

If the will expressly creates the future interest, rather than allowing it to pass under the residuary clause, the interest is nonreversionary.

> *EXAMPLE 4-6*. *G*'s will devised land "to *A* for life, and upon *A*'s death, the land goes to *B*."
>
> Or, clause 1 of *G*'s will devised land "to *A* for life;" clause 2 states that "Upon *A*'s death, the land goes to *B*."
>
> *B* takes a remainder in both cases.

Chapter 5

THE REVERSIONARY FUTURE INTERESTS: REVERSIONS, POSSIBILITIES OF REVERTER, AND RIGHTS OF ENTRY

§ 5.1. Conventional Definitions

If a future interest is reversionary, it is either a reversion, a possibility of reverter, or a right of entry. It cannot be a remainder or an executory interest.

How do you differentiate among reversions, possibilities of reverter, and rights of entry?

☞ *REVERSIONS are future interests retained by transferors when they transfer out an estate or estates of less quantum than they originally had.*

Because a particular estate (a possessory estate other than a fee simple) is an estate of less quantum than a fee simple estate (supra § 2.1), a property owner retains a reversion when he or she transfers out a particular estate and (1) does not create a nonreversionary future interest to follow it or (2) creates one or more nonreversionary future interests

33

that do not exhaust all possible post-transfer events.

☞ *POSSIBILITIES OF REVERTER are future interests retained by transferors when they transfer out an estate or estates of the same quantum as they originally had.*

Because all fee simple estates are of the same quantum (supra § 2.1), a property owner retains a possibility of reverter when he or she transfers out a fee simple determinable and (1) does not create an executory interest or (2) creates one or more executory interests that do not exhaust all possible post-transfer events.

☞ *RIGHTS OF ENTRY[1] are future interests created in transferors when they transfer out an estate subject to a condition subsequent (i.e., subject to divestment).*

Whether the quantum of the estate is the same as or lesser than that of the transferor's original estate is unimportant. The most common example is that of an owner of property in fee simple absolute who transfers out a fee simple subject to a condition subsequent, who expressly creates in himself or

---

[1] Rights of entry go by other names: rights of re-entry, rights of entry for condition broken, powers of termination. These terms are interchangeable.

herself a right to re-enter and retake the premises if and when the condition is broken, and who (1) does not create an executory interest or (2) creates one or more executory interests that do not exhaust all possible post-transfer events.

§ 5.2. Reversionary Interests Where No Future Interests Created

We are now ready to illustrate each of the reversionary future interests.

EXAMPLE 5-1. *G* conveyed land "to *A* for life." Or, *G* conveyed land "to *A* for 10 years."

Because *G* did not create a remainder interest following *A*'s particular estate, *G* retained a reversion. Note that *G*'s reversion was not expressly stated, but rather arose because *G* transferred an estate of less quantum than he owned (a particular estate is an estate of less quantum than a fee simple estate) and therefore retained what he did not convey. It would not change the analysis, however, if *G*'s reversion had been expressly stated. For example, if the first conveyance had said: "to *A* for life, and upon *A*'s death, to return to me," *G* would still have retained a reversion.

EXAMPLE 5-2. *G* conveyed land "to *A* and her heirs so long as *A* does not allow liquor to be sold on the land[, and upon *A*'s allowing liquor to be sold on the land, the land is to revert to the grantor]."

Because *G* did not create an executory interest following *A*'s fee simple determinable, *G* retained a possibility of reverter. The words contained in the brackets are not necessary to create a possibility of reverter. Possibilities of reverter need not be expressly stated because, like reversions, they constitute an undisposed-of interest remaining in the transferor. See Simes & Smith on Future Interests § 286. In practice, however, it is common expressly to state the possibility of reverter, and a small minority of decisions has held (erroneously) that, without the bracketed words, *A* takes a fee simple absolute. See, e.g., In re Copps Chapel Methodist Episcopal Church (Ohio 1929).

EXAMPLE 5-3. G conveyed land "to *A* and his heirs on condition that *A* never allow liquor to be sold on the land[, but if *A* allows liquor to be sold on the land, the grantor is to have the right to re-enter and take possession]."

G's right of entry is not exactly like any other future interest. It is like an executory interest in one sense only—it takes effect in possession by cutting short or divesting the preceding estate. But, unlike the executory interest, it does not take effect in possession automatically upon the happening of the event named in the condition. The happening of the specified event—*A*'s allowing liquor to be sold on the land—authorizes *G* to elect to divest *A*'s estate and take a possessory estate.

This points to another feature that distinguishes rights of entry from reversions and possibilities of reverter. A right of entry is not the undisposed-of interest retained by the transferor when she transfers out other interests. It is a newly created future interest in the transferor. Does this mean that a right of entry *must* be *expressly* created? Theoretically, no. The transfer of a fee simple subject to a condition subsequent *by itself* causes a right of entry to arise in the grantor. Omission of the bracketed portions of the above disposition would not necessarily prevent *G* from having a right of entry. See Simes & Smith on Future Interests § 247. On the other hand, the law recognizes a strong constructional preference against forfeitures. Thus it is quite possible, perhaps even likely, that the omission of the bracketed portions would result in a court concluding that *G* had no right of entry. See infra § 5.7(e).

§ 5.3. Reversionary Interests Where Future Interests Were Created

We are now ready to look at a few examples in which the transferor created one or more future interests in transferees. There will still be a reversionary future interest if all possible post-transfer events have not been exhausted by the contingencies attached to these nonreversionary future interests.

> *EXAMPLE 5-4. G* transferred land "to *A* for life, remainder to *B* if *B* survives *A*, but if not, to *C* if *C* survives *A*."
> The contingencies upon which the remainders following *A*'s life estate depend do not exhaust all possible post-transfer events. Because both *B* and *C* might predecease *A*, *G* retained a reversion.

EXAMPLE 5-5. G transferred land "to A and her heirs so long as A does not allow liquor to be sold on the land, and upon A's allowing liquor to be sold on the land, the land is to go to B if B is then living, and if B is not then living, to C if C is then living, and if neither B nor C is then living, the land is to revert to the grantor."

G has a possibility of reverter because of the possibility of A's allowing liquor to be sold on the premises after B and C have both died.

EXAMPLE 5-6. G transferred land "to A and his heirs on condition that A never allow liquor to be sold on the land, but if A allows liquor to be sold on the land, the land is to go to B if B is then living, and if B is not then living, to C if C is then living, and if neither B nor C is then living, the grantor is to have the right to re-enter and take possession."

G has created in himself a right of entry. Note also that A's possessory estate falls into two categories. It is both a fee simple subject to a condition subsequent and a fee simple subject to an executory limitation. See supra pp. 20-21.

EXAMPLE 5-7. G transferred land "to A for life, remainder to B, but if B fails to survive A, the land is to return to me."

G's reversionary interest is not a reversion. The Restatement of Property § 154 cmt. e & illus. 2 states that it is a possibility of reverter rather than a right of entry. For the explanation, see below.

> *EXAMPLE 5-8. G* transferred land "to *A* for life, remainder to *B* if *B* survives *A*, but if not, the land is to return to me."
>
> *G*'s reversionary interest is a reversion.

How have we arrived at the conclusions stated? In *5-7*, *G* has in effect conveyed a fee simple (by virtue of the combination of *A*'s life estate and *B*'s vested remainder in fee simple), which is an estate of the same quantum as *G* originally owned. Thus *G*'s reversionary interest is not a reversion. In *5-8*, the same analysis might be applied, but for the fact that *B*'s remainder in fee simple is contingent. As explained in Am. L. Prop. § 4.18 at 435-36: "Here the only vested estate transferred is a life estate which is a lesser estate than the fee simple which the grantor had. Hence a reversion . . . is created." This also explains why *G*'s interest is a reversion in Example *7-5*, infra.

§ 5.4. Effect of the Failure of the Future Interest Created in the Transferees

A nonreversionary future interest can fail for any variety of reasons. The beneficiary might predecease the testator or predecease a subsequent time to which survival is required by the terms of the disposition; the future interest might be disclaimed; it might violate the Rule Against Perpetuities; and so on.

In Examples *5-5* and *5-6*, we already noted that *G* retained a reversionary interest because of the possibility that both *B* and *C* would predecease the time when their interests would become possessory. The question addressed in this section is what would be the effect in Examples 5-5 and 5-6 if the executory interests of *B* and *C* failed for some reason. On this point, the courts have treated dispositions like 5-5 and 5-6 differently. If the possessory estate is a fee simple determinable, as in 5-5, the grantor is held to have retained a possibility of reverter entitled to become possessory in the place of the failed executory interest or interests. But if the possessory estate is a fee simple subject to an executory limitation, as in 5-6, the grantor is not held to have created a right of entry in herself; instead, the failure of the executory interest is deemed to render the possessory estate a fee simple absolute.

EXAMPLE 5-9. G transferred land "to the Zion Church so long as the land is used for church purposes. If church use ever ceases, the land shall go to *B* and his heirs." *B*'s executory interest violates the Rule Against Perpetuities and is therefore void.

G has a possibility of reverter. The church's interest is still a fee simple determinable. See First Universalist Soc'y v. Boland (Mass. 1892). But cf. Restatement 2d of Property § 1.5 cmt. b.

EXAMPLE 5-10. G transferred land "to the Zion Church on condition that the land be used for church purposes. If church use ever ceases, the land shall go to *B* and her heirs." *B*'s executory interest violates the Rule Against Perpetuities and is therefore void.

G does not have a right of entry. The invalidity of

B's executory interest causes the church's fee simple to become a fee simple absolute, not a fee simple subject to a condition subsequent. See Proprietors of the Church in Brattle Square v. Grant (Mass. 1855). In justification of this result, it is sometimes said that the condition is not really part of the church's possessory estate, but rather is a condition precedent attached to *B*'s interest; when *B*'s interest failed, the condition was also stricken.

The Restatement 2d of Property § 1.5 cmts. b & c assert a different position, by suggesting that it might be appropriate to hold that the invalidity of an executory interest following a fee simple determinable as well as a fee simple subject to an executory limitation renders the fee estate absolute.

§ 5.5. Technical Reversions

If the grantor creates more than one nonreversionary future interest, one of which is certain to become possessory in fee simple absolute, it would seem to be obvious that there can be no reversionary future interest. There is, however, the special case of the "technical" reversion: When the transferor creates more than one *contingent remainder,* the transferor has a reversion even when all post-transfer possibilities are exhausted by the contingencies attached to the remainders. In such a case, the reversion is said to be merely technical because by the terms of the grant it can never become possessory.

EXAMPLE 5-11. G transferred land "to A for life, remainder to B if B survives A, but if not, to C."

G has a technical reversion.

EXAMPLE 5-12. G transferred land "to A for life, remainder to B, but if B fails to survive A, to C."

G does not have a reversion, not even a technical one. Technical reversions only arise when there are contingent remainders; here, B has a vested remainder subject to divestment and C has an executory interest.

What explains the reversion in Example *5-11*? The possibility of a forfeiture at early common law may be at the root of the problem. At an earlier time, there were various circumstances that would cause a life tenant to forfeit the life estate. A forfeiture would occur, for example, if the life tenant made a "tortious feoffment" (an attempt to convey a greater estate than owned). If A's life estate was forfeited before A's own death, there would be no need for a reversion in Example *5-12* because B's remainder would become possessory, subject to being divested in favor of C if B predeceased A. But in Example *5-11,* B's remainder, being contingent on B's surviving A, would not become possessory; nor would C's remainder become possessory because it was contingent on B's not surviving A. There had to be a reversion to fill the gap. Thus under the earlier law, the reversion in Example *5-11* was not merely technical.

Nowadays, a life estate cannot be terminated before

the death of the life tenant by forfeiture. Nevertheless, the existence of a reversion, albeit technical, in cases like *5-11* is probably still recognized. Today a technical reversion may still serve a function with respect to the doctrine of destructibility of contingent remainders. See infra Chapter 10.

§ 5.6. Reversionary Future Interests Following Particular Estates Subject to Premature Termination

Sections 3.3 and 3.4 explained that a life estate or term of years may be subjected to possible termination before the life tenant's death or the expiration of the term. This additional event may be stated either in the form of a limitation or in the form of a condition subsequent. In either case, the transferor has a reversion.

If the additional event is expressed as a condition, the particular estate is called a life estate (or a term of years) subject to a condition subsequent. In such cases, the transferor, if he or she so provides, has created a right of entry in addition to his or her reversion.

> *EXAMPLE 5-13. G* transferred land "to *A* for life on condition that *A* not remarry, but if *A* remarries, the grantor has the right to re-enter and take possession."
>
> *G* has both a right of entry and a reversion. Her reversion takes effect in possession upon *A*'s death if *A* never remarries. If *A* remarries, *G*'s right of entry

permits *G* to divest *A* of the remaining portion of his life estate. Cf. Example 5-3.

If the additional event is expressed as a limitation, the particular estate is called a life estate (or term of years) subject to a special limitation. By the better view, the transferor has not retained a possibility of reverter in addition to his or her reversion.

> *EXAMPLE 5-14.* *G* transferred land "to *A* for life or until *A* remarries."
>
> *G* has only a reversion, which takes effect in possession upon the earlier of *A*'s death or remarriage. Cf. Examples 5-7 and 5-8.

Some scholars have said that *G*'s interest that may take effect in possession upon *A*'s remarriage is a possibility of reverter, but such scholars disagree about whether the possibility of reverter merges into *G*'s reversion. See Bergin & Haskell on Estates in Land and Future Interests 58-59; Ralph E. Boyer, Survey of the Law of Real Property 105 (3d ed. 1981). It is believed to be more accurate, however, to say that this interest is a reversion, not a possibility of reverter. The reason is that *G* (who is assumed to have owned the property in fee simple absolute prior to the transfer) conveyed an estate of lesser quantum than he originally had; a life estate, whether or not subject to a special limitation, is an estate of lesser quantum than a fee simple. Thus *G*'s interest fits the definition of a reversion given earlier in § 5.1. See Am. L. Prop. § 4.18; 2A Powell on Real Property ¶ 271; Restatement of Property § 154 cmts. d and e. A possibility of reverter properly arises only when *G* conveyed an estate of the same quantum as he originally owned. The standard example is where *G* owning the property in *fee simple* absolute transfers out a *fee simple* determinable. Another example is where *G* owning only a *life estate* in the property transfers out a *life estate* pur autre vie subject to a special limitation. In these latter two examples, *G* has retained a possibility of reverter but not a reversion.

A life estate customarily arises from the inclusion of words expressly limiting the duration of the estate to a lifetime ("to *A for life* "). But a life estate can also be indicated implicitly. See Restatement of Property § 108. Thus if the phrase "for life" is omitted from the language of a disposition containing a special limitation, it may be unclear in a given case whether the transferee takes a life estate subject to a special limitation or a fee simple determinable. The question is whether the special limitation itself manifests an intent that the estate must terminate at the transferee's death in all events.

> EXAMPLE 5-15. *H* devised land "to *W* during widowhood."
> Most but not all decisions have held that *W*'s estate is a life estate subject to a special limitation because she ceases being a widow upon her death even if she never remarried. A devise "to *A* so long as he

occupies the land" would probably be similarly construed.

> **EXAMPLE 5-16.** W devised land "to H so long as he remains unmarried."
> W's devise will likely but not certainly be held to give H a fee simple determinable, which will become a fee simple absolute upon his death if he never remarries. See Saunders v. Saunders (Or. 1971).

Note that the absence of words of inheritance is not a factor in resolving the issue. See supra § 1.4. On the other hand, if words of inheritance had been included in either of these examples, their inclusion would have been a factor making it more certain that H took a fee simple determinable in 5-16 and perhaps tipping the scale in 5-15 in favor of the fee simple determinable classification. See infra § 7.9.

§ 5.7. Ambiguous Language: Possibility of Reverter or Right of Entry?

The dispositive language in Examples 5-2, 5-3, 5-5, and 5-6 is unambiguous. Language clearly granting A a fee simple determinable is followed by language clearly describing a possibility of reverter, and language clearly granting A a fee simple subject to a condition subsequent is followed by language clearly describing a right of entry.

In practice, unfortunately, the language of an actual disposition may be quite ambiguous. In such cases courts often assert that forfeitures are disfavored in the law. Thus a forfeiture will be avoided entirely if the language admits of some other construction, and if not, then at least the less drastic type of forfeiture incident to a right of entry will be preferred to the automatic forfeiture incident to a possibility of reverter. These constructional preferences gain strength as the amount of consideration paid by the grantee rises in relation to the value of a fee simple absolute in the land at the time of the grant. Nevertheless, these are tendencies only, and as the following discussion demonstrates, the result reached in any given case may be quite unpredictable. In other words, the results are not always in accord with these constructional preferences. The drafting lesson should be obvious: To avoid litigation about the nature of the estate granted, lawyers must be careful to use standard language and to couple reverters with limitations and rights of entry with conditions. Sadly, though, there are rare cases when a court has not given proper effect to unambiguous language. See, e.g., Schoolcraft Community School District v. Burson (Mich. 1959) (grantor held to have created a right of entry in himself by virtue of a conveyance to a school district "so long as the land is used for a school and no longer").

Cases of ambiguous language frequently fall into one of the following categories.

(a) Words of Condition Plus Reverter Clause. A deed or will may grant or devise a possessory fee simple estate "on condition that" the land be used in a particular way (or on some other condition), and

provide further that if the condition is violated the land is to "revert" to the grantor.

> EXAMPLE 5-17. G transferred land "to A and her heirs on condition that A never allow liquor to be sold on the land, but if A allows liquor to be sold on the land, the property is to revert to the grantor."

Under the structure of estates, of course, a possibility of reverter cannot follow a fee simple subject to a condition subsequent. Some courts have held that A takes a fee simple determinable and that G's interest is a possibility of reverter. The Restatement of Property § 45 cmt. m, however, takes the position that G's language manifests an intent to grant A a fee simple subject to a condition subsequent and to create in himself a right of entry, presumably on the theory that the nature of the future interest depends on the nature of the possessory estate. Some court decisions that have reached this same conclusion have relied on the preference for the less drastic type of forfeiture of a right of entry over the automatic forfeiture incident to a possibility of reverter.

(b) Statement of Purpose Plus Reverter Clause. The language of a deed or will sometimes states that the land is to be "used" for a particular purpose, and also includes a "reverter" clause.

> EXAMPLE 5-18. G transferred land to the School District "to be used for school purposes and ceasing to be used for school purposes, it shall revert to the

grantor."

It would seem that the ambiguity in the language describing the School District's possessory estate would be resolved in favor of the fee simple determinable classification because of the fact that the language describing the future interest is unambiguously in the form of a possibility of reverter. And some courts have so held. On the other hand, the tendency to adopt the construction leading to the less drastic type of forfeiture, and possibly other factors as well, has led some courts to the conclusion that the School District has a fee simple subject to a condition subsequent and that *G* has a right of entry.

(c) Statement of Purpose Only. If the language of the deed or will contains only a statement of purpose, the predominant construction has been that the possessory estate is a fee simple absolute.

> *EXAMPLE 5-19.* *G* transferred land to the School District "to be used for school purposes."
>
> It would probably be held that *G* has neither a right of entry nor a possibility of reverter, and that the School District has a fee simple absolute. See Restatement of Property § 45 cmt. o; Town of Nahant v. United States (D. Mass. 1968). At least one case, however, Weber v. Ford Motor Co. (Mich. 1928), held that the possessory estate was a fee simple subject to a condition subsequent, with a right of entry in the grantor.

(d) Words of Limitation Only. If the language only contains words of limitation ("to the School District so long as used for school purposes"), the result ought to and probably would be that a fee simple determinable was created in the transferee, leaving a possibility of reverter in the grantor. See Example 5-2. In one case, however, Schoolcraft Community School District v. Burson (Mich. 1959), the court inexplicably held that the grantor's interest was a right of entry.

(e) Words of Condition Only. As indicated in Example 5-3, it is not theoretically necessary that a right of entry be expressly created, and if the possessory estate is unambiguously in the form of a fee simple subject to a condition subsequent, it may be held to be exactly that and if so the transferor's interest is a right of entry. See, e.g., Hughes v. Cook (Ind. Ct. App. 1955). However, the courts' dislike of a forfeiture has led to the statement that no provision will be construed as creating a condition subsequent if the language will bear any other possible interpretation. See, e.g., Templeton v. Stong (Tenn. 1945). Indeed, in the absence of an express right of entry clause, the courts sometimes construe rather unambiguous language of condition as not subjecting the possessory estate to a condition subsequent. Any one of the following constructions is possible—the grantee has a fee simple absolute: subject to a contractual obligation in favor of the grantor; subject to a trust obligation in favor of the grantor; subject to an equitable charge or lien; or subject to no legally

enforceable obligation at all. See Restatement of Property § 45 cmt. n. The examples below illustrate these alternate constructions.

> *EXAMPLE 5-20. G*'s deed states: "Provided always, and these presents are upon this express condition, that the aforesaid premises shall not, nor shall any part thereof, or any buildings thereon erected or to be erected, be at any time hereafter used or occupied as a tavern or public house of any kind." Held, not a conveyance upon a condition subsequent, but a covenant for the benefit of the grantor's adjoining lot, which covenant was extinguished by the union in one person of the title to the two parcels. See Post v. Weil (N.Y. 1889). This is an attractive construction where the language indicates that the grantor wanted to control the use to which the land is put.

> *EXAMPLE 5-21. G*'s deed states: "Provided always that the several tracts or parcels of land thus granted to the Town of Cape Girardeau and the Citizens thereof shall remain forever affected and appropriated to the public uses to which they are respectively intended, and that they nor any part of them, shall never become private property." Held, the effect of this language was to create a trust, not an estate on a condition subsequent. The reasons cited were that conditions subsequent are not favored, and there was no expression of intention for a reverter. See United States v. Certain Land in City of Cape Girardeau (E.D. Mo. 1948). A trust is an attractive construction where the grant was for a charitable purpose.

EXAMPLE 5-22. G's deed states: "I hereby give, devise and bequeath unto my son S the following described real estate . . . on condition that he pay to my children, J, A, and N the sum of $3,825 to each one of said children within one year after my death." Held, title vested absolutely in S subject to a charge in favor of the other named children. See Spangler v. Newman (Ill. 1909). This is an attractive construction where the obligation relates to the payment of money.

EXAMPLE 5-23. G conveyed to a Board of School Trustees and their successors "upon condition that the same shall be held and possessed by the party of the second part only so long as the said property shall be used for school purposes." Held, this created an absolute fee, not a fee on a condition subsequent. The court said, "And where the language in the deed merely expresses the motive and purpose which prompted the conveyance, without reservation of power of termination or right of re-entry for condition broken, an unqualified fee will pass." Washington Board of Education v. Edgerton (N.C. 1956).

§ 5.8. Certain Legal Incidents of Possibilities of Reverter and Rights of Entry

(a) Enforcement. A fee simple determinable terminates automatically if and when the terminating event happens; the right to possession is instantly shifted to the holder of the possibility of reverter. Possibilities of reverter become possessory automatically upon the happening of the terminating event.

In the case of a right of entry, however, the rule is different: Rights of entry do not automatically become possessory if and when the specified event happens; the right to possession arises upon the grantor's later exercise of the right to re-enter (or upon exercise by the grantor's successors in interest, as described in (b) below). In other words, the happening of the specified event does not divest the possessory estate; it merely authorizes the grantor or the grantor's successors to divest the possessory estate.

The above difference between possibilities of reverter and rights of entry, while theoretically valid, may have less practical importance than it may seem. The early common-law rule was that a right of entry could be exercised only by a physical entry on the land. In most states now, however, the commencement of an action to regain possession satisfies the requirement of an election to divest the possessory estate, and the holder of a possibility of reverter often must institute a similar action in order to enforce his or her "automatic" interest. In addition, after the stipulated event has occurred, the time allowable under the law of many states for bringing an action to enforce a possibility of reverter is the same as that for making an election under a right of entry. The statute of limitations in several states explicitly begins running upon the occurrence of the specified event against both a possibility of reverter and a right of entry; in other states the statute has been so interpreted; and in still others, the statute is open to such an interpretation. The two interests may thus be in alignment on the question of adverse possession. Finally, although the statute of limitations in some states is held not to begin running until an election under a right of entry has been effected, the courts, drawing an analogy to the equitable doctrine of laches, have required that an election be made within a "reasonable time" after the breach of the condition; and there is authority that the period of the statute of limitations constitutes a "reasonable time."

(b) The Rule Against Perpetuities and Statutory Restrictions on Duration. It is assumed that possibilities of reverter and rights of entry, probably for mostly historical reasons, are exempt from the Rule Against Perpetuities, and all American courts that have decided the question have so held. It should be noted, however, that in many states the question has not been decided.

In response to the inapplicability or supposed inapplicability of the Rule Against Perpetuities to these interests, a number of states have statutes that impose a cut off of possibilities of reverter and rights of entry after a certain period of time. The statutes vary in detail, but they generally state that these interests cease to exist if the event upon which they are predicated has not occurred within a certain period of time—ranging from twenty to fifty years. The effect of their ceasing to exist is to render the possessory estate *absolute*, whether it was a fee simple determinable or a fee simple subject to a condition subsequent. For a more detailed discussion of these statutes, see William F. Fratcher, A Modest Proposal for Trimming the Claws of Legal Future Interests, 1972 Duke L.J. 517, 529-31.

Chapter 6

THE NONREVERSIONARY FUTURE INTERESTS: REMAINDERS AND EXECUTORY INTERESTS

§ 6.1. Conventional Definitions

If a future interest is nonreversionary, it is either a remainder or an executory interest. It cannot be a reversion, a possibility of reverter, or a right of entry.

How do you differentiate remainders from executory interests?

☞ *REMAINDERS*[1] *are future interests created in a transferee that become possessory if at all upon the natural termination of the preceding vested estate.*

The preceding vested estate must (1) have been created when the future interest was created, (2) be a possessory estate, and (3) be a "particular" estate. (A "particular" estate is a possessory estate other than

---

[1] The term "remainder" was derived from the idea of an interest that "remained out" after the termination of a prior estate.

a fee simple.)

☞ *EXECUTORY INTERESTS*[2] *are future interests created in a transferee that become possessory if at all by cutting short or divesting the preceding vested estate or interest.*

The preceding vested estate or interest (1) need not have been created when the future interest was created, (2) can be a possessory estate or a future interest, and (3) can be a fee simple estate or a particular estate.

In trying to work through these definitions, we consider first the situation in which a possessory estate is succeeded by only one future interest. We then consider the situation in which there are two or more future interests.

§ 6.2. Remainders and Executory Interests Differentiated When a Possessory Estate is Followed by a Single Nonreversionary Future Interest

When a possessory estate is succeeded by a single nonreversionary future interest, the following rules apply:

___

[2] The term "executory interest" was derived from the effect of the Statute of Uses in 1536 in "executing" springing and shifting uses.

☞ *Rule 1: If the possessory estate is a fee tail, a life estate, or a term of years, the future interest is a remainder.*

☞ *Rule 2: If the possessory estate is a fee simple subject to defeasance, the future interest is an executory interest.*

EXAMPLE 6-1. G transferred land "to A for life, and upon A's death, the land goes to B."

Or, G transferred land "to A for 10 years, and at the expiration thereof, the land goes to B."

B has a remainder in both cases, not an executory interest.

EXAMPLE 6-2. G transferred land "to A and her heirs on condition that A never allow liquor to be sold on the land, but if A allows liquor to be sold on the land, the land goes to B." (The disposition might omit the "on condition that" phrase, and simply say: "to A and her heirs, *but if* A allows liquor to be sold on the land, the land goes to B.")

B has an executory interest, not a remainder.

Special Case—Executory Interest Succeeds Fee Simple Determinable. In one special case, an executory interest does not "cut short" or "divest" the preceding vested estate, but takes effect on its "natural termination." Because a remainder cannot follow a fee simple estate, a fee simple must always be followed by an executory interest, even when the fee simple is subject to a special limitation.

EXAMPLE *6-3*. *G* transferred land "to *A* and her heirs as long as *A* never allows liquor to be sold on the land, and upon *A*'s allowing liquor to be sold on the land, the land goes to *B*."

B has an executory interest, not a remainder.

§ 6.3. Nonreversionary Future Interests Following Particular Estates Subject to Premature Termination

A life estate or a term of years is sometimes subject to termination before the life tenant's death or the expiration of the term certain. If this terminating event is stated in the form of a limitation, the particular estate is called a life estate subject to a special limitation (sometimes called a determinable life estate) or a term of years subject to a special limitation. The word "special" is added to differentiate such estates from an ordinary life estate or term of years, since life estates or terms of years are already subject to a regular limitation ("*for* life;" "*for* X years").[3] The future interest that follows such estates is a remainder.

EXAMPLE *6-4*. *G* transferred land "to *A* for life or until *A* remarries, and upon *A*'s death or remarriage,

---

[3] The word "special" also indicates that the terminating event is an uncertainty, and thus the fee simple determinable is sometimes called by another name—a fee simple subject to a special limitation. See Restatement of Property § 23.

to *B*."

Technically, *B* has two interests, both remainders. But it is common to say simply that *B* has a remainder.

> *EXAMPLE 6-5.* *G* transferred land "to *A* for 10 years or until *A* remarries, whichever sooner occurs, and upon the expiration of 10 years or *A*'s earlier remarriage, the land goes to *B*."
> Like Example *6-4*, *B* has a remainder.

If the terminating event is stated in the form of a condition, the particular estate is called a life estate (or a term of years) subject to an executory limitation. Both a remainder and an executory interest follow such estates.

> *EXAMPLE 6-6.* *G* transferred land "to *A* for life, and upon *A*'s death the land goes to *B*; but if *A* remarries, the land goes to *B* immediately."
> *B* has both an executory interest and a remainder. Her executory interest takes effect in possession only if *A* remarries. Her remainder interest takes effect in possession upon *A*'s death if *A* never remarried.

> *EXAMPLE 6-7.* *G* transferred land "to *A* for 10 years, and at the expiration thereof, to *B*; but if during this 10-year period *A* remarries, the land goes to *B* immediately."
> As in Example *6-6*, *B* has both an executory interest and a remainder.

§ 6.4. Remainders and Executory Interests Differentiated When a Possessory Estate is Followed by More than One Future Interest

When a *defeasible fee simple* is followed by more than one nonreversionary future interest, only one of which can become possessory, all the future interests are executory interests. Because a remainder cannot follow a fee simple estate (see supra § 6.2), the future interests are executory interests because they cannot be anything else.

> *EXAMPLE 6-8.* *G* transferred land "to *A* and his heirs, but if *A* allows liquor to be sold on the land the land goes to *B* if *B* is then living, and if *B* is not then living the land goes to *C*."
> *B* and *C* have executory interests.

When a *particular estate* is followed by more than one nonreversionary future interest, only one of which can become possessory, the *first future interest will always be a remainder*. See supra § 6.2. The other or subsequent future interests might be remainders or executory interests. In determining which they are, the following rules apply:

☞ *Rule 1: If the first future interest is a contingent (nonvested) remainder, the other future interests will also be contingent remainders.*

☞ *Rule 2: If the first future interest is a vested remainder subject to divestment, the other future interests will be executory interests.*

> ***EXAMPLE 6-9.*** *G* transferred land "to *A* for life, remainder to *B* if *B* survives *A*, but if not, to *C*."
> Because *B* has a contingent remainder, *C* has a contingent remainder. For convenience, *B* and *C*'s interests are called *alternative contingent remainders.*

> ***EXAMPLE 6-10.*** *G* transferred land "to *A* for life, remainder to *B* if *B* survives *A*, but if not, to *C* if *C* survives *A*, and if neither *B* nor *C* survives *A*, to *D*."
> Because *B* has a contingent remainder, *C* and *D* have contingent remainders. As in *6-9*, all three interests are alternative contingent remainders.

> ***EXAMPLE 6-11.*** *G* transferred land "to *A* for life, remainder to *B*, but if *B* fails to survive *A*, to *C*."
> Because *B* has a vested remainder subject to divestment, *C* has an executory interest.

> ***EXAMPLE 6-12.*** *G* transferred land "to *A* for life, remainder to *B*, but if *B* fails to survive *A*, to *C* if *C* survives *A*, and if neither *B* nor *C* survives *A*, to *D*."
> Because *B* has a vested remainder subject to divestment, *C* and *D* have executory interests.

§ 6.5. Springing and Shifting Executory Interests
Historically, executory interests are divided into two categories: springing and shifting. The distinction between the two turns on whether the executory

interest potentially divests an estate retained by the grantor or an estate conferred by the grantor on another.

SHIFTING EXECUTORY INTERESTS potentially divest an estate or interest conferred by the grantor on another.

EXAMPLE 6-13. G transferred land "to A and her heirs, but if A allows liquor to be sold on the premises, the land goes to B."

B's executory interest is a shifting executory interest.

SPRINGING EXECUTORY INTERESTS potentially divest an estate or interest retained by the grantor.

EXAMPLE 6-14. G transferred land "to B to take effect in possession or enjoyment upon his marriage."

B's executory interest is a springing executory interest.

EXAMPLE 6-15. G transferred land "to A for life, and one day after A's death, to B if B is then living."

B's executory interest is a springing executory interest. B's interest is not a remainder because it cannot take effect in possession on the natural termination of A's life estate. When A dies, G's retained interest becomes a possessory estate in fee simple subject to divestment one day later in favor of B if B is then living.

FUTURE INTERESTS DIFFERENTIATED IN TERMS OF VESTING

Future interests are subject to an additional level of classification—classification in terms of vesting. There are four categories here: indefeasibly vested, vested subject to (complete) defeasance, vested subject to open (partial defeasance), and contingent (nonvested).

§ 7.1. Indefeasibly Vested

☞ *A future interest is INDEFEASIBLY VESTED if it is not subject to any conditions or limitations.*

In other words, the future interest must be certain to become a possessory fee simple absolute at some time in the future. See Restatement of Property § 157 cmt. f. Only remainders and reversions can be indefeasibly vested.

> *EXAMPLE 7-1.* *G* transferred land "to *A* for life, remainder to *B*."
> *B*'s remainder is indefeasibly vested. It is certain to

become possessory because *A* is bound to die. When *A* dies, *B*'s remainder will become a possessory fee simple absolute.

Note that *B* might not be alive when *A* dies. Except as otherwise provided by a statute such as UPC § 2-707,[1] *B*'s interest is not subject to a condition of survival of *A*. Therefore, the possibility of *B*'s death before *A* does not affect the classification of *B*'s interest. If *B* dies before *A*, *B*'s indefeasibly vested remainder will pass to *B*'s successors in interest—*B*'s devisee or, if *B* died intestate, *B*'s heirs.

EXAMPLE 7-2. *G* conveyed land "to *A* for life."

G's reversion is indefeasibly vested. The discussion of *B*'s remainder in Example *7-1* apply to *G*'s reversion in this example.

EXAMPLE 7-3. *G* conveyed land "to *A* for life, remainder to *B* for 10 years."

G's reversion is indefeasibly vested. Ten years after *A*'s death, it is certain to become a possessory fee simple absolute.

B's remainder is not indefeasibly vested. Although it is certain to become possessory upon *A*'s death (a certain event), it will not become a fee simple

---

[1] UPC § 2-707 (1990) creates a rebuttable rule of construction that all future interests in trust are subject to a condition of survival and creates a substitute gift to the descendants of a beneficiary who fails to satisfy that condition of survival. The statute is discussed in Edward C. Halbach, Jr. & Lawrence W. Waggoner, The UPC's New Survivorship and Antilapse Provisions, 55 Alb. L. Rev. 1091 (1992).

absolute. *B*'s remainder is vested subject to defeasance (in the limitational sense). See infra § 7.2(b).

§ 7.2. Vested Subject to Defeasance

☞ *A future interest is* VESTED SUBJECT TO DEFEA-SANCE *if it is subject to either one or more conditions subsequent or one or more limitations.*

The term "vested subject to complete defeasance" is sometimes employed in order to distinguish such an interest from one that is vested subject to open. Defeasible future interests, like defeasible possessory estates, can be subject to either a condition subsequent (divestment) or a limitation.

(a) Vested Subject to Divestment. A future interest that is subject to a condition subsequent can be classified as vested subject to defeasance or as vested subject to divestment. The term "vested subject to divestment" is preferred because the use of that term distinguishes such a future interest from one that is vested subject to a limitation. Only remainders and reversions can be vested subject to divestment.

A remainder is vested subject to divestment if it is subject to a condition that is stated in condition-subsequent form. A *reversion* is vested subject to divestment if it is subject to a condition, regardless of whether the condition is stated in condition-precedent or condition-subsequent form. The reason for the difference is that a *remainder* that is subject to a condition may be either contingent or vested subject to divestment, whereas a *reversion* subject to a condition cannot be contingent. Reversions are always vested.

> *EXAMPLE 7-4.* *G* transferred land "to *A* for life, remainder to *B*, but if *B* fails to survive *A*, to *C*."
>
> *B*'s remainder is vested subject to divestment because the condition of surviving *A* is stated in condition-subsequent form—"to *B*, but [not] if *B* fails to survive *A*."
>
> *C*'s executory interest is subject to the condition that *B* not survive *A*. This condition is stated in the form of a condition precedent—"if *B* fails to survive *A*, to *C*." *C*'s executory interest is contingent.
>
> *G* retained no reversion.

> *EXAMPLE 7-5.* *G* conveyed land "to *A* for life, remainder to *B* if *B* survives *A*, but if not, to return to me."
>
> *B*'s remainder is contingent because the condition of surviving *A* is stated in the form of a condition precedent—"to *B* if *B* survives *A*."
>
> *G*'s reversion is subject to the condition that *B* not survive *A*, and so *G*'s reversion cannot be indefeasibly vested. This condition is stated in the form of a condition precedent ("if [*B* does not survive *A*], to return to me"). Nevertheless, *G*'s reversion is classified as vested subject to divestment because the rule that reversions are always vested overrides all other rules.
>
> This analysis also applies to the more common way of expressing this disposition (where *G*'s reversion is not expressly stated): "to *A* for life, remainder to *B* if

B survives *A*."

EXAMPLE 7-6. *G* conveyed land "to *A* for life, remainder to *B* if *B* survives *A*, but if not, to *C*."

B's remainder is contingent because the condition of surviving *A* is stated in the form of a condition precedent—"to *B* if *B* survives *A*."

C's remainder is also contingent because the condition that *B* not survive *A* is stated in the form of a condition precedent—"if [*B* does not survive *A*], to *C*.".

G retained a technical reversion. There is always a reversion when a particular estate is followed by contingent remainders. In a case such as this example, the contingencies stated with respect to the interests of *B* and *C* exhaust all the post-creation possibilities; hence the reversion is said to be merely "technical." See supra § 5.5. The reversion is classified as vested subject to divestment because it cannot be indefeasibly vested and because it must be vested.

(b) Vested Subject to a Limitation (Defeasance). A future interest that is subject to a limitation can be classified as vested subject to defeasance or as vested subject to a limitation. Although the term "vested subject to defeasance" is used more commonly, the term "vested subject to a limitation" serves to distinguish such a future interest from one that is vested subject to divestment, which is also often called "vested subject to defeasance." Only remainders and reversions can be vested subject to a limitation (defeasance).

EXAMPLE 7-7. G transferred land "to A for life, then to B for life, then to C."

B's remainder is vested subject to a limitation (defeasance). It is sometimes referred to simply as a vested remainder for life. Note that B must survive A in order for his interest to become possessory. This implicit requirement of survival is *not* regarded as a "condition" of survival. (If it were, it would mean that B's remainder was either contingent or vested subject to divestment, the choice between the two depending on whether the condition of surviving A was deemed to be a condition precedent or a condition subsequent. In fact, one court, *in dictum,* did refer to a remainder for life as contingent [see Brugh v. White (Ala. 1957)] and another, *again in dictum*, referred to such a remainder as vested subject to divestment [see Lufburrow v. Koch (Ga. 1885)]. Since the classification was not relevant to resolving either case, however, these cases are not properly regarded as setting forth a view contrary to the one stated herein.) Rather, B's interest is regarded as terminating naturally upon his death, whether he dies before or after A's death. In other words, B's interest is a life estate just like A's interest is a life estate, except that B's life estate does not become possessory until A dies and therefore may never become possessory.

C's interest is a remainder because B's interest is subject to a limitation and because it is an estate less than a fee simple. C's remainder is indefeasibly vested because it is not subject to any condition or limitation.

EXAMPLE 7-8. *G* conveyed land "to *A* for life, then to return to me for life, then to *C*."

This is the same as Example *7-7* except that the future interest subject to a limitation (defeasance) is a reversion in *G* rather than a remainder in *B*.

EXAMPLE 7-9. *G* transferred land "to *A* for life, then to *B* for 10 years, then to *C*."

B's remainder is vested subject to a limitation (defeasance). In this case, the time of *B*'s death is irrelevant. If *B* dies while *A* is still alive, *B*'s remainder will pass to her devisees or, if she dies intestate, to her heirs. If *B* dies after *A*'s death but before the 10th anniversary of *A*'s death, whatever amount of time is left of *B*'s 10-year term will pass to her devisees or, if she dies intestate, to her heirs.

§ 7.3. Vested Subject to Open

☞ *A remainder is VESTED SUBJECT TO OPEN if it is subject to no conditions precedent and is created in a class that contains at least one living member and that is still "open," i.e., where it is possible for additional persons to become class members (typically through birth or adoption).*

Older labels for this type of interest are (1) *vested subject to partial divestment* or (2) *vested in quality but not in quantity*. These older terms are descriptive of the phenomenon that each time a new member is added to the class, the shares of the existing class members are reduced. Whichever label is used, it is important to note that the existing class member or members are the ones who are regarded as having a vested remainder. The interests of the unborn (or unadopted) class members are contingent on being born (or adopted). They are executory interests because upon birth (or adoption) they partially divest the interests or shares of the living class members.

> *EXAMPLE 7-10.* G transferred land "to A for life, remainder to A's children." When the transfer was made, A had two children, X and Y.
>
> X has a vested remainder subject to open in an undivided half of the property, and Y has a vested remainder subject to open in the other undivided half.
>
> Suppose a third child, Z, is born after the transfer occurred. Upon birth, Z's executory interest becomes a vested remainder subject to open in an undivided third of the property, and X and Y's interests become vested remainders subject to open in the other two undivided thirds.
>
> Note that there is no requirement that A's children survive A. The interest of a child who dies before A would pass to the child's successors in interest—her devisee or, if she dies intestate, her heirs.

At their inception, only remainders can be vested subject to open. The executory interest, the only other nonreversionary future interest, can be created in a class that is subject to open, but because executory interests are normally contingent,[2] they cannot be *vested* subject to open.

None of the reversionary interests can be subject to open at their inception because the reversionary interests are, by definition, retained by the transferor when created. See supra Chapter 4. Even if a future interest was reversionary because it was originally "retained by" the transferor's successors in interest (see Example *4-4*), which might be a group of people (the transferor's heirs), the membership of this group of takers is determined once and for all at the transferor's death. That is, it is not a class that is subject to open to allow in more members later.

After their inception, however, reversionary future interests might be transferred to a class that contains at least one living member and that is subject to open. If the nonreversionary future interest is a possibility of reverter or a right of entry, it would still not become *vested* subject to open because such interests are, probably, regarded as contingent (see infra § 7.4). Reversions, however, are vested, and if such a subsequent transfer occurs, the reversion would become vested subject to open.

> *EXAMPLE 7-11. G* conveyed land "to *A* for life." *G* later died (while *A* was alive), devising her indefeasibly vested reversion to *A*'s children. Two children of *A* were living at *G*'s death.

---

[2] For the abnormal case of the executory interest without contingencies, see infra § 7.9.

A's two children receive vested reversions subject to open and *A*'s unborn children receive executory interests.

Suppose that *A* had no children at *G*'s death. Would this cause *G*'s reversion to become contingent because it is created in unborn persons? No. The situation at *G*'s death would probably be viewed as follows: *G* carved springing executory interests (created in *A*'s unborn children) out of her indefeasibly vested reversion. *G*'s indefeasibly vested reversion would thus become vested subject to divestment, and would pass to her residuary devisees or her heirs, depending on the situation.

§ 7.4. Contingent (Nonvested)

☞ *A future interest is* CONTINGENT *(nonvested)[3] if it is subject to a condition precedent.*

A condition precedent may be explicit or implicit. An explicit condition precedent exists where the language of the disposition declares that the interest is to become possessory *if* some event occurs. Implicit conditions precedent exist when the future interest is created in unborn or unascertained persons.

Remainders can be contingent but need not be.

---

[3] The traditional term is "contingent," but the Restatement 2d of Property adopts the term "nonvested."

Executory interests are normally contingent.[4] Reversions cannot be contingent but possibilities of reverter and rights of entry are regarded as contingent.

>   *EXAMPLE 7-12.* *G* conveyed land "to *A* for life, remainder to *B* if *B* survives *A*."
>
>   *B*'s remainder is contingent because the condition of surviving *A* is stated in the form of a condition precedent—"to *B* if."
>
>   *G*'s reversion appears to be subject to the condition precedent that *B* not survive *A*, but *G*'s reversion is classified as vested subject to divestment because of the rule that reversions are always vested. This means that *B*'s remainder acts like an executory interest in that it potentially divests *G*'s reversion. Nevertheless, it is a remainder because its predominant feature is that it takes effect in possession, if at all, on the natural termination of *A*'s life estate.

>   *EXAMPLE 7-13.* *G* transferred land "to *A* for life, remainder to *A*'s children." When the transfer was made, *A* had no children.
>
>   *A*'s unborn children have contingent remainders. Their remainders are implicitly contingent on being born (or adopted), not on surviving *A*.

---

[4] For the abnormal case of the executory interest without contingencies, see infra § 7.9.

EXAMPLE 7-14. G transferred land "to A for life, remainder to A's heirs."

The remainder to A's heirs is contingent because it is created in unascertained persons. The persons who are A's heirs cannot be determined or ascertained until A's death.

Nevertheless, any person who would be an heir of A if A were to die now is called an heir apparent or an heir expectant. Those persons are regarded as having contingent remainders during A's lifetime rather than mere expectancies. Thus it is sometimes said that they take by purchase rather than by succession. Their remainders are of course implicitly contingent on their actually being A's heirs when A dies.

EXAMPLE 7-15. G transferred land "to A for life, remainder to B, but if B fails to survive A, to C."

B's remainder is vested subject to divestment because it is subject to a condition subsequent—"to B, but [not] if B fails to survive A." C's executory interest is contingent because it is subject to the condition precedent that B not survive A—"if B fails to survive A, to C."

EXAMPLE 7-16. (1) G transferred land "to A and his heirs on condition that A never allow liquor to be sold on the land, but if A allows liquor to be sold on the land, the land is to go to B."

(2) G transferred land "to A and his heirs for as long as A never allows liquor to be sold on the land, and upon A's allowing liquor to be sold on the land, the land goes to B."

B's executory interest is contingent in both cases

because it is subject to the condition precedent that *A* allow liquor to be sold on the land.

> *EXAMPLE 7-17*. *(1)* *G* conveyed land "to *A* and her heirs on condition that *A* never allow liquor to be sold on the land, but if *A* allows liquor to be sold on the land, the grantor shall have the right to re-enter and take possession."
>
> *(2)* *G* conveyed land "to *A* and her heirs for as long as *A* never allows liquor to be sold on the land, and upon *A*'s allowing liquor to be sold on the land, the land is to revert to the grantor."

G's right of entry in Variation *(1)* and *G*'s possibility of reverter in Variation *(2)* would appear to be contingent because both are subject to the condition precedent that *A* allow liquor to be sold on the land. Most authorities do in fact classify these interests as contingent (Am. L. Prop. §§ 4.6, 4.12; Simes & Smith on Future Interests §§ 281, 1238). The Restatement of Property § 154 cmt. e, at 531, classifies possibilities of reverter as contingent but does not classify rights of entry in terms of vesting. It is believed that both interests are properly classified as contingent.

§ 7.5. Assessing the Distinction Between Contingent Remainders and Vested Remainders Subject to Divestment

The following examples, as well as many of the previous examples, reveal that the distinction between a contingent remainder (§ 7.4) and a vested remainder subject to divestment (§ 7.2(a)) does not rest on substance.

EXAMPLE 7-18. *G* transferred land "to *A* for life, remainder to *B* if *B* survives *A*, if not to *C*."

B's remainder is contingent because the condition of surviving *A* is stated in the form of a condition precedent—"to *B* if *B* survives *A*."

EXAMPLE 7-19. *G* transferred land "to *A* for life, remainder to *B*, but if *B* fails to survive *A*, to *C*."

B's remainder is vested subject to divestment because it is subject to a condition subsequent—to *B*, but [not] if *B* fails to survive *A*."

There is no differences in substance between *G*'s conveyance in *7-18* and *7-19*. In both cases, *G* wants to subject *B*'s right to possession to the requirement or condition that *B* outlive *A*. *G* also wants possession to go to *C* if *B* does not outlive *A*. Classification of *B*'s interest turns on the *form* in which the condition is *stated* rather than on the substance or nature of the condition.

B's right to possession in both *7-18* and *7-19* is subject to a condition of surviving *A*. This condition of survival is *stated* in the form of a condition *precedent* in *7-18* ("to *B* if . . . "), whereas in *7-19* the same condition is *stated* in the form of condition *subsequent* ("to *B, but [not] if . . . .*").

This means that *the* difference between a contingent remainder and a vested remainder subject to divestment is:

☞ *A* *CONTINGENT* *REMAINDER* *is subject to a condition precedent.*

☞ *A* *VESTED* *REMAINDER* *SUBJECT* *TO* *DIVESTMENT* *is subject to a condition subsequent.*

Furthermore, the distinction between a condition precedent and a condition subsequent is artificial because it rests on the form of stating the condition. The very same condition can always be stated either way.

Despite the artificiality of the distinction, many legal consequences, such as the applicability of the Rule Against Perpetuities, turn on the distinction. These legal consequences are discussed infra Part II.

The artificiality of the distinction is felt most heavily in cases such as *7-18* and *7-19*, where the conditional event *cannot* occur *after* the life tenant's death (or after the expiration of a term certain). Such is the nature of the condition in these examples—a condition of survival. In fact, conditions of survival are the most frequently used conditions in actual practice. But conditions of a different type can of course be imposed.

If the condition *can* and *does* occur *after* the termination of the particular estate, the difference between a condition precedent and a condition subsequent becomes substantive. Take, for example, the following two dispositions:

EXAMPLE 7-20. *G* transferred land "to *A* for life, remainder to *B* if he lives to age 21."

EXAMPLE 7-21. *G* transferred land "to *A* for life, remainder to *B*, but if he dies before age 21, to *C*."

In these dispositions, the conditional event might happen after the preceding life estate terminates. If *B* is under 21 when *A* dies, *B*'s interest in *7-20* would not become possessory unless and until he reaches 21. In *7-21*, however, *B*'s interest would become possessory immediately upon *A*'s death, subject to being lost if he later dies under 21. This result seems justified, but not because the interest is technically vested in *7-21* and contingent in *7-20*. Rather, the choice between precedent and subsequent language is helpful, and in most cases probably decisive, in determining the transferor's intent. Nevertheless, for other purposes, the condition precedent-condition subsequent distinction is still artificial regarding these two illustrations. For example, during *A*'s lifetime the verbal difference does not justify the rule in some states that *B*'s interest is inalienable in *7-20* but alienable in *7-21*. See infra § 9.2.

Historically, distinguishing between conditions precedent and conditions subsequent may have been necessitated by the now-defunct forfeiture doctrine. At an earlier time, there were various circumstances that would cause a life tenant to forfeit the life estate. See supra § 5.5. A forfeiture would occur, for example, if the life tenant made a "tortious feoffment" (an attempt to convey a greater estate than owned). The forfeiture of *A*'s life estate before *A*'s own death had different consequences if the remainder interest was subject to a condition precedent rather than a condition subsequent. If the condition was a condition subsequent of survival, for example, the remainder would become possessory as soon as *A*'s life estate was forfeited, subject of course to divestment if *B* died before *A*. But if the condition of survival were a condition precedent, the remainder could not become possessory until *A*'s death. Indeed, under the earlier law, the contingent remainder would never become possessory because it would be destroyed. See infra Chapter 10. The forfeiture of a life estate is no longer recognized, but the same question can still arise now because it is possible for a life tenant voluntarily to renounce or disclaim the life estate.

§ 7.6. Future Interests Belong To More Than One Category

Often a future interest will be subject to open but the phrase "subject to open" will not appear in its classification because it is contingent (see supra § 7.4) or might not appear in its classification because it is vested subject to complete defeasance (see supra § 7.2). This does not mean that the interest is not actually subject to open; it merely means that the fact that it is subject to open is not expressed or might not be expressed as part of its classification.

EXAMPLE 7-22. *G* transferred land "to *A* for life, remainder to *A*'s children who survive *A*; but if none of *A*'s children survives *A*, to *B*."

The remainders in *A*'s children are contingent. They are also subject to open, but recognition of this fact by using the phrase "contingent subject to open" is not permissible in the classificatory scheme.

EXAMPLE 7-23. *G* transferred land "to *A* for life, remainder to *A*'s children, but if none of *A*'s children survives *A*, to *B*." *A* was alive and had living children when the transfer occurred.

The remainders in *A*'s living children are vested subject to (complete) divestment. They are also subject to open. The Restatement of Property § 157 cmt. c would classify such interests as "vested subject to (complete) divestment" and leave it at that. Nevertheless, it is permissible to classify the interests as "vested subject to (complete) divestment and to open" because, unlike the interests in Example 7-22, the interests are vested.

It should be noted that the condition subsequent of survival imposed on the interests of *A*'s children in this example is not the same in substance as the condition precedent of survival imposed on *A*'s children in Example 7-22. In Example 7-22, if at least one of *A*'s children survives *A* but some predecease *A*, only the ones who survive *A* take. But in this example, as long as at least one child survives *A*, courts can be expected to hold that the interests of those children who predecease *A* are not divested. See Restatement of Property § 254 cmt. a, illus. 2.

§ 7.7. Summary

It may be helpful at this point to set forth the table (opposite) as a way of summarizing the categories of vesting that are permissible for each of the five future interests at their inception.

Future Interest	*Permissible Categories of Vesting at Inception*
Remainders	Indefeasibly Vested Vested Subject to Defeasance (Divestment or Limitation) Vested Subject to Open Contingent
Executory Interests	Contingent
Reversions	Indefeasibly Vested Vested Subject to Defeasance (Divestment or Limitation)
Possibilities of Reverter	Contingent
Rights of Entry	Contingent

§ 7.8. The Law Favors the Vesting of Estates

The law traditionally prefers vested interests to contingent interests. See Restatement of Property § 243 & cmts. As the court colorfully stated in Roberts

v. Roberts (K.B. 1613), "the law always delights in vesting of estates, and contingencies are odious in the law, and are the causes of troubles, and vesting and settling of estates, the cause of repose and certainty." The law delights "in preventing of contingencies, which are dangerous. . . ."

The source of the preference for vested interests is complex, but it is commonly claimed that the desire to avoid certain common-law rules, such as the destructibility rule and the Rule Against Perpetuities, to promote alienability, to promote completeness of the disposition, and to promote equality of distribution among different lines of descent all played important roles.

In general, it can be said that the courts will construe a provision as not imposing a condition precedent if they can do so without contradicting the express language of the instrument, i.e., where there is sufficient ambiguity in the language to permit what might be called an even choice.

The situations in which this problem arises generally fall into one of the following categories.

(a) Condition Stated Both as a Condition Precedent and as a Condition Subsequent. When a particular estate is followed by a remainder that is subject to a condition and when the reversion is not expressly stated, then the condition will probably be stated only in condition-precedent form; if so, the remainder is clearly contingent. "To *A* for life, remainder to *B* if *B* survives *A*" is the standard example. See supra § 6.2. But when *two or more*

nonreversionary future interests are created following a particular estate (see supra § 6.4), and when the condition attached to the first one is stated in condition-precedent form, it will ordinarily be possible to identify later language in the disposition as stating the same condition in the form of a condition subsequent. This is the situation presented in the three examples below. Whether the fact that the condition is stated both ways will lead to the remainder being classified as vested subject to divestment depends on a variety of factors. It is believed that very few courts will give the preference for vested interests sufficient weight by itself to classify the first remainder as vested subject to divestment rather than contingent in all cases—that is, in all cases except those where they are forced to classify the first remainder as contingent because it is created in an unborn or unascertained person or persons (as in Example *7-25* below). In one type of case, however, where a "gap in possession" would occur if the interest were held to be contingent, the courts seem inclined to hold the remainder to be vested subject to divestment. This is Example *7-26*, below.

EXAMPLE *7-24*. *G* transferred land "to *A* for life, remainder to *B* if *B* survives *A*, *but if not*, to *C*.

The Restatement of Property § 278 adopts the rule that the classification of *B*'s interest is governed by the form in which the condition is stated the first time it is stated. Most courts follow this approach, and hold

B's remainder to be contingent. See, e.g., Quilliams v. Koonsman (Tex. 1955). Indeed, this is the classification assumed in many of the preceding examples. See Examples *6-9, 6-10,* and *7-6.*

A very few decisions, however, have said that the condition of surviving *A* is stated twice, once as a condition precedent ("to *B* if") and once as a condition subsequent ("to *B* . . . , but [not] if"). Because the law favors the vesting of estates, these decisions classify *B*'s remainder as vested subject to divestment rather than contingent. See, e.g., Safe Deposit & Trust Co. v. Bouse (Md. 1943).

EXAMPLE 7-25. *G* transferred land "to *A* for life, remainder to *A*'s children who survive *A*, but if none survives *A*, to *C*." *A* has no children at the time of the transfer.

The fact that the remainder created in *A*'s children is in favor of an unborn class would force all courts to hold the reminder in *A*'s children to be contingent, including the courts that would otherwise be inclined to classify *B*'s remainder in Example *7-24* as vested subject to divestment.

EXAMPLE 7-26. *G* transferred land "to *A* for life, remainder to *B* if he lives to age 21, but if not, to *C*." At *A*'s death, *B* was 17 years old.

An early English case, Edwards v. Hammond (C.P. 1683), held *B*'s interest to be vested subject to divestment in favor of *C* should *B* die before reaching 21. Most American courts would probably follow *Edwards*. This approach prevents a gap between the termination of *A*'s life estate and the happening of the condition attached to the future interest following it. If the court allowed such a gap to occur by classifying *B*'s remainder as contingent, the gap would have to be filled somehow, in all likelihood by determining that *G*'s reversion became possessory until *A* either reached 21 or died before reaching that age.

An additional reason for classifying *B*'s remainder as vested rather than contingent would be to prevent the destruction of *B*'s remainder under the destructibility rule. See infra Chapter 10. *Edwards*, however, was not a case involving the destructibility rule because the subject matter of the disposition in that case (a copyhold) was not land.

For more extensive discussion of conditions stated both ways, see Simes & Smith on Future Interests §§ 148, 149.

(b) Remainders for Life. In addition to the rule of *Edwards*, another manifestation of the preference for vested interests is the rule that remainders for life are vested subject to defeasance (subject to a limitation, not to a condition precedent or subsequent). See supra Example 7-7. Remainders for life present an even choice because they could have been classified as contingent (on surviving the primary life tenants).

Suppose, however, that the language of the disposition *expressly* conditions a remainder for life on surviving the primary life tenant, and that the express condition is stated in the form of a condition precedent.

EXAMPLE 7-27. G transferred land "to A for life, remainder to B for life if B survives A."

Does the inclusion of the phrase "if B survives A" remove this case from the even-choice category, and force a court to classify B's remainder as contingent? A very small number of courts have held that it does, but most courts have ignored the language of condition as mere surplusage and have classified B's remainder as vested despite of the conditional language. Cases are collected in Simes & Smith on Future Interest § 142.

(c) Remainders Subject to a Power. Frequently someone will be given a power to divert the property to someone other than the beneficiary of the remainder interest. In these cases, the remainder is subject to a condition, but the condition is not clearly stated as a condition precedent. The preference for vested estates tips the scale in favor of treating the condition as a condition subsequent.

EXAMPLE 7-28. G transferred land "to A for life, empowering A to sell, consume, or otherwise dispose of the land or any part as may be necessary for A's support and maintenance; at A's death the land or such part of the proceeds of any sale as may remain unexpended is to go to B."

B's remainder is vested subject to divestment in whole or in part by the exercise of the power by A. The same result would be reached in the case of a remainder interest in a trust where the settlor retained a power to revoke the trust or where the settlor conferred upon someone else (typically the trustee or the income beneficiary) a power to invade the corpus on behalf of the income beneficiary.

> *EXAMPLE 7-29. G* transferred land "to *A* for life, remainder to the persons *A* shall by will appoint, and in default of appointment, to *B*."
>
> *B*'s remainder is vested subject to divestment by the exercise of the power by *A*. It could be argued that this case is different because the language expressly imposes a condition precedent on *B*'s remainder—that *A* will not exercise the power. This argument has not been accepted, however, because the idea that remainders subject to a power are vested subject to divestment is too well entrenched.

(d) Remainders Subject to a Charge or Lien. Transferors occasionally appear to condition a future interest on payment of sum of money to a designated person. Most courts hold that the remainder is vested and that the taker is entitled to possession on the termination of the prior interest, but subject to a charge or a lien on the property in the designated amount. See, e.g., Miller v. Miller (Neb. 1976); Estate of Marra (N.Y. Sur. Ct. 1987); cf. Spangler v. Newman (Ill. 1909) (Example *5-22*). Contra, Allison v. Wilson (S.C. 1991).[5]

---

[5] In *Allison*, the named remainderperson predeceased the life tenant. The court held that the remainder was contingent on timely payment of the required amount by the named remainderperson. Timely tender of the payment by the

EXAMPLE 7-30. G transferred land "to A for life, remainder to B if B pays C \$5,000 within one year of A's death." B had not paid C the \$5,000 by the one-year deadline.

By the prevailing view, if B does not pay the \$5,000 to C within a reasonable time, C can enforce the charge or lien in that amount against the land. This construction accomplishes G's objective because it assures that C will get the money and that the land will go to B upon A's death. Had the court held that B's remainder was contingent on paying the money, B would lose the land and C would not receive the money. Avoiding this result is supported by and coupled with the general preference for vested interests that by itself might not have been enough to counteract what appears from the language to have been an express condition precedent.

§ 7.9. Executory Interests Without Contingencies

The typical executory interest is subject to a condition precedent and is classified as contingent (nonvested). See supra §§ 7.4, 7.7. In rare cases, an executory interest is created without contingencies, so that it is certain to become possessory in fee simple absolute. Normally a future interest that is certain to become possessory in fee simple absolute is classified as indefeasibly vested. But in §§ 7.1 and 7.7, we learned that the only nonreversionary future interest that can be indefeasibly vested is a remainder. Why,

remainderperson's successors in interest did not satisfy the condition.

therefore, is the type of interest under consideration here not an indefeasibly vested remainder rather than an executory interest? One way to answer this question is to say that it is, *if* the preceding possessory estate is a particular estate—a life estate or a term of years. The circumstance that causes the future interest to be an executory interest is that the preceding possessory estate is a fee simple; as we learned supra § 6.2, remainders cannot follow fee interests. Consequently the reason this type of interest is an executory interest is that it takes effect upon the termination of a possessory fee estate.

The initial question, therefore, is whether the possessory estate is a fee or a particular estate. If it is a particular estate, the situation poses no problem of classification: The future interest is an indefeasibly vested remainder. But if the possessory estate is a fee, the future interest must be an executory interest, and the problem arises: Can we call such an executory interest indefeasibly vested, or must we still call it contingent despite the fact that it is not contingent on anything?

First we consider the situation where the possessory estate was retained by the transferor, and then consider the case where the possessory estate is conveyed to a transferee.

EXAMPLE 7-31. *(1)* G conveyed land "to B to take effect in possession 25 years from now."

(2) G conveyed land "to B to take effect in possession upon my death."

The language of these deeds does not clearly express *G*'s intent. If the transfer had been "to *B*, the grantor reserving a term of 25 years [or a life estate] in the land," there would be little doubt about the classification of the interests. *G*'s estate would be a particular estate—a term of years or a life estate—and *B*'s interest would be an indefeasibly vested remainder. As one of the many consequences, *G* would be under a duty to *B* not to waste the property. Also, *B*'s interest would not be subject to the Rule Against Perpetuities, for this Rule applies only to contingent nonreversionary future interests.

In the absence of a clear expression of *G*'s intent, however, the prevailing though not universal assumption is that *G* did not wish to expose himself or herself to a potential liability for waste, that *G* intended to maintain the status quo regarding his or her rights and duties with respect to the land. See Simes & Smith on Future Interests § 223. The only way to give effect to such an intention is to classify *G*'s estate as a defeasible fee simple, not a term of years or a life estate. See Restatement of Property § 46 cmt. i.

If *G*'s estate is a defeasible fee simple, *B*'s interest is a springing executory interest. This raises two problems: (1) can there be a fee simple that is bound to terminate; and (2) if so, how is *B*'s executory interest to be classified in terms of vesting? The answer to the first question is yes, for while it normally is said that a fee simple must be an interest of potentially infinite duration (see supra § 3.1(a)), an exception is made in the case we are dealing with now, i.e., where the fee simple is retained by the transferor. The answer to the second question is clouded, but the Restatement of Property § 370 cmt. h, and the commentators suggest that, while it might not be possible directly to classify such an executory interest as indefeasibly vested, at least the Rule Against Perpetuities ought not be applicable. See Simes & Smith on Future interests § 1236; Am. L. Prop. § 24.20; 5 Powell on Real Property ¶ 779. See also Restatement 2d of Property § 1.4 cmt. m, illus. 18 (declaring such an executory interest to be "vested," and hence not subject to the Rule Against Perpetuities). Some commentators even suggest that such executory interests should be treated like indefeasibly vested remainders for all purposes, including the right to hold *G* liable for waste. See J.J. Dukeminier, Jr., Contingent Remainders and Executory Interests: A Requiem for the Distinction, 43 Minn.L.Rev. 13, 51 (1958). Such a view, of course, defeats the reason for classifying *G*'s retained interest as a fee simple in the first place, and should not be accepted. See Restatement of Property § 194 cmt. b; Simes & Smith on Future Interests § 1664. *G* should be under no greater duty with respect to waste than he or she would be if a conventional defeasible fee simple were retained, i.e., one that was *uncertain* to terminate.

It should be recognized that the classificatory problems just discussed would not arise if *B*'s interest were conditioned on survival or on some other event.

"To *B* to take effect in possession 25 years from now if she is then living" or "to *B* to take effect in possession upon my death if he survives me" would grant to *B* a conventional (i.e., contingent) executory interest and the possessory estate retained by *G* would be a conventional fee simple subject to defeasance.

Does the analysis change when, instead of retaining the possessory estate, the transferor conveys it to someone else? The answer is unclear.

> *EXAMPLE 7-32. (1)* G transferred land "to *A* and his heirs for 25 years, then to *B*."
>
> *(2)* G transferred land "to *A* and his heirs but upon *A*'s death, to *B*."

The first thing to be noticed about these cases is the inclusion of words of inheritance. In the absence of the phrase "and his heirs," it would be clear that *A* would take a term of years in Variation *(1)* and a life estate in Variation *(2)*, and that *B*'s interest in both variations would be an indefeasibly vested remainder. But the inclusion of the words of inheritance may be taken as an expression that *G* intended that *A* have the same rights with respect to the land that an owner in fee simple would have—in particular, freedom from liability for waste. If this is accepted as *G*'s intent, and if such an intention can validly be carried out, it would mean that *B*'s interest is an executory interest of the same peculiar type encountered in Example *7-31*, except that here it is a shifting rather than a springing executory interest.

Somewhat surprisingly, and without explanation, the Restatement of Property § 46 cmt. i, takes the position that no matter how clearly *G*'s intent is expressed, it is not possible to create a *shifting* executory interest on an event that is bound to occur. Thus the Restatement would classify *B*'s interest in the above cases as an indefeasibly vested remainder, and *A*'s interest as either a term of years or a life estate. Simes & Smith on Future Interests § 223 disagree. Because it would be possible for *G* to have expressly given *A* a term of years or a life estate "without impeachment for waste," it would seem that Simes & Smith have the better of the argument, and that *B*'s interest should be an executory interest that is exempt from the Rule Against Perpetuities because it is bound to become possessory but that *B* should have no greater rights against *A*'s wasting the property than she would have if her interest had been a conventional (i.e., contingent) executory interest. The situation is far from settled.

Chapter 8

PERMISSIBLE CHANGES IN CLASSIFICATION DUE TO SUBSEQUENT EVENTS

It was pointed out in Chapter 4 that reversionary future interests do not become nonreversionary by virtue of a post-creation transfer to a transferee and that nonreversionary future interests do not become reversionary by virtue of a post-creation transfer to the transferor.

§ 8.1. Post-Creation Changes in Classification

Some changes in classification due to post-creation events are permissible, however. Specifically, executory interests can become remainders, contingent remainders can become vested remainders, and (if the destructibility rule is not in force in the jurisdiction or if in force does not apply for some reason) remainders can become executory interests.

EXAMPLE 8-1. *G* transferred land "to *A* for life, remainder to *B*, but if *B* fails to survive *A*, to *C*." *B* predeceases *A*.

At creation, *B*'s interest is a vested remainder subject to divestment and *C*'s interest is an executory interest.

At B's death, B's vested remainder is divested and C's executory interest becomes an indefeasibly vested remainder. It is as if the disposition changes to read: "to A for life, remainder to C." This points up the misleading nature of a statement that is unfortunately often repeated by courts: that an executory interest cannot vest until it vests in possession. The statement, as just illustrated, ignores the fact that an executory interest can vest before becoming possessory by changing into a remainder.

EXAMPLE 8-2. G transferred land "to A for life, remainder to B if B survives A, but if not, to C." B dies while A is still alive

At creation, B and C's interests are alternative contingent remainders.

At B's death, her contingent remainder is defeated, G's technical reversion is divested, and C's contingent remainder becomes an indefeasibly vested remainder.

EXAMPLE 8-3. G transferred land "to A for life, remainder to B if B lives to age 21." The destructibility rule has been abolished by statute in the jurisdiction.

If B reaches 21 while A is still alive, B's contingent remainder becomes indefeasibly vested and G's reversion is divested.

If B is younger than 21 when A dies, B's contingent remainder becomes an executory interest. G's reversion takes effect in possession upon A's death, as a fee simple subject to defeasance in favor of B if and when B later reaches 21.

EXAMPLE 8-4. G transferred land "to *A* for life, remainder to *A*'s children, but if none of *A*'s children survives *A*, to *B*." When the transfer was made, *A* had no children. Subsequently, a child, *X*, was born to *A*. Thereafter, but still during *A*'s lifetime, *X* died. The destructibility rule has been abolished by statute in the jurisdiction.

At creation, despite the exclusive use of condition-subsequent language, *A*'s unborn children have contingent remainders, *B* has an alternative contingent remainder, and *G* has a technical reversion.

When *X* was born, *X* took a vested remainder subject to divestment and subject to open, *B*'s interest and the interests of *A*'s unborn children change into executory interests, and *G*'s technical reversion is divested.

When *X* died, *B*'s interest and the interests of *A*'s unborn children do not change back into alternative contingent remainders because *X* does not lose his vested remainder. See supra Example *7-23. X*'s vested remainder, which remains subject to complete divestment (if *A* leaves *no* children surviving her) and subject to partial divestment (if *A* has additional children), passes through his estate to his successors in interest.

§ 8.2. Is All This Complexity Necessary?

In a word, No. Without sacrificing the slightest degree of flexibility in the planning of family property transactions, classification and the structure of estates could be vastly simplified and the artificiality in the present system could be eradicated. A proposal for a simplified system of estates, in which classification is based on the substance of the disposition rather than the form of its wording, has been put forward in Lawrence W. Waggoner, Reformulating the Structure of Estates: A Proposal for Legislative Action, 85 Harv. L. Rev. 729, 755-56 (1972):

[T]he [proposed] reformulated structure is based on the premise that the only appropriate distinctions are between certainty and uncertainty as to the termination of possessory interests and between certainty and uncertainty as to the ultimate possession of future interests. Possessory interests, by the terms of the particular transfer, either will not terminate (fee simple absolute), will terminate (life estate or term of years), or will possibly terminate (defeasible interest). Future interests either will become possessory (indefeasibly vested), will become possessory but with a now uncertain number of takers (vested subject to open), or will possibly become possessory (contingent). The reformulated structure is shown in the accompanying chart. . . .

POSSESSORY INTERESTS	FUTURE INTERESTS
Fee Simple Absolute	None permissible
Defeasible Fee Simple	Contingent
Life Estate (may or may not be defeasible)	Contingent (not certain to become possessory); Alternative Contingent Future Interest
	Vested Subject to Open; Contingent (in unborn class members)
	Indefeasibly Vested
Term of Years	Same as with Life Estate

PART II

CONSEQUENCES OF CLASSIFICATION

With the discussion of classification completed, attention can be trained on some of the consequences of classification.

Classification in all its fine detail is far less important today than it once was. This is partly because some of the rules that turned on classification have been widely abolished and partly because many of those rules applied, in any event, only to legal future interests in land, which are less often created today. Ironically, the reduced importance of classification has played a roll in keeping the complex and artificial structure in force, by reducing the pressure to reexamine and reformulate it.

At the same time, the importance of certain aspects of classification has not disappeared altogether. Part II explores some of the rules that turn on classification. We should distinguish between two types of consequences. Some consequences are directly linked to a certain classification. The most important consequence of this type is the inalienability of contingent future interests at common law. See infra Chapter 9. Inalienability flows directly and automatically from contingency where this rule is still followed. Most consequences of classification are only possible consequences. The interest's classification makes it subject to a certain rule. Contingent future interests, for example, are subject to the common-law Rule Against Perpetuities but do not necessarily violate it. Contingent remainders are subject to the common-law destructibility rule but are not necessarily destroyed.

Chapter 9

ALIENABILITY OF FUTURE INTERESTS

Alienation of future interests must be divided into transferability at death (by intestacy or will) and transferability by inter-vivos transfer.

§ 9.1. Transferability at Death: by Intestacy and Will

(a) Descendibility. All future interests are "descendible" (capable of passing by intestacy). At one time, the course of descent for future interests in land was different from that of possessory estates, however. Descent of the reversionary future interests was traced from the last person seized and of the nonreversionary future interests from the last purchaser. The details of this process need not trouble us here. They are described in Simes & Smith on Future Interests § 1882; Am. L. Prop. § 4.73. The divergent course of descent for future interests was abolished by statute in England in 1897, and today in the United States it is everywhere held that reversions, remainders, and executory interests descend according to the same rules as are applicable to possessory estates. Everywhere except South Carolina, possibilities of reverter and rights of entry

also descend according to the same rules as are applicable to possessory estates.

(b) Devisability. Soon after the Statute of Wills of 1540 authorized the transfer of land by will, reversions, remainders, and executory interests became devisable by will in England. In the United States, such interests are also devisable. It is also generally held that possibilities of reverter and rights of entry are devisable. In some states this conclusion is based on statutes so providing. There is a little authority and a few statutes to the contrary. See Simes & Smith on Future Interests § 1903.

(c) Descendibility and Devisability of Contingent or Defeasible Interests. A future interest that is either contingent or vested subject to defeasance is descendible and devisable only if the condition precedent or subsequent is such that the beneficiary's death does not extinguish the interest.

EXAMPLE *9-1. G* transferred land "to *A* for life, remainder to *B*, but if *B* fails to survive *A*, to *C*." *C* dies, then *B*, then *A*.

C's executory interest is contingent on *B*'s not surviving *A*, but not on *C* surviving *A*. Consequently, *C*'s executory interest was not extinguished by his death before *A*, and it is descendible and devisable.

B's vested remainder subject to divestment was, however, extinguished by her death before *A*, and so *B*'s remainder is neither descendible nor devisable.

§ 9.2. Voluntary Alienability During Life

(a) Inter-Vivos Alienability of Reversions, Remainders, and Executory Interests. Reversions and vested remainders (even if defeasible) are alienable inter vivos at common law, but contingent remainders and executory interests are inalienable. Contingent remainders were at first likened to an expectancy—not an interest but the possibility of an interest arising in the future. Lifetime, but not death time, transferability of such a possibility would violate the rules against champerty and maintenance, and was not permitted. When executory interests were later recognized, they were regarded as sufficiently analogous to contingent remainders to warrant the same treatment.

Despite the inalienability of contingent remainders and executory interests, the common law recognizes two ways of transferring these "inalienable" interests *in effect*, and equity recognizes still another. (It may be noted that these three methods of transferring inalienable future interests are also available for transferring non-existent interests such as expectancies.)

☞ *Contract to Convey. A purported transfer, if for adequate consideration, is treated in equity as a contract to convey.* The contract becomes specifically enforceable if and when all conditions precedent are satisfied, so as to give the transferor an alienable interest.

☞ *Estoppel By Deed*. *Even without adequate consideration—indeed, without any considerations at all—when a purported transfer is made by a deed that contains a covenant of warranty, the title inures at law by estoppel to the grantee if and when the conditions precedent are later satisfied.*

☞ *Release*. *At law, an inalienable future interest can be released to the holder of the interest that would be defeated by the satisfaction of the conditions precedent attached to the released interest.* For example, in a disposition "to *A* for life, remainder to *B*, but if *B* fails to survive *A*, to *C*," a release of *C*'s executory interest to *B* would be enforceable at law. Releases do not have to be contained in a warranty deed, nor is consideration necessary. A writing under seal was, however, required at common law, but today where the significance of seals is abolished any instrument capable of transferring an interest in land would probably be sufficient.

Today, contingent remainders and executory interests are no longer regarded as mere possibilities of receiving an interest in the future. Rather, they are present interests in which the right to possession is postponed and uncertain. See Restatement of Property § 157 cmt. w. Even so, the states take various approaches to the inalienability rule.

In about seven states, the common-law rule of inalienability is still followed. In these states, the equitable contract to convey, the estoppel by deed, and the release methods of transferring inalienable interests are also recognized. Therefore, the inalienability rule followed in these few states in effect boils down to this: Purported transfers for inadequate consideration by quit claim deed to someone other than a person in whose favor the interest could have been released are ineffective.

In a small number of states, the inalienability rule is probably not followed, at least not strictly. By statute or case law in a few states, remainders and executory interests that are contingent as to person (interests created in unborn or unascertained persons) are still inalienable, but those that are contingent as to event are alienable.

> *EXAMPLE 9-2*. G transferred land "to A for life, remainder to B if B survives A; if not, to B's heirs."
>
> B's remainder is contingent as to event, and under this rule would be alienable. The remainder in B's heirs, however, is contingent as to person and would be inalienable.

In the vast majority of states, however, mostly by statute but occasionally by common-law decision, *all* contingent future interests are said to be alienable—even those that are contingent as to person. How can this be? How can a future interest that is contingent as to person be alienable? The answer is that these interests are not *truly* alienable. Although the law typically authorizes a specially appointed fiduciary called a guardian ad litem to represent the interests of unborn or unascertained persons in litigation, the law seldom authorizes this fiduciary to join in a transfer of a property interest on behalf of these persons.

>   *EXAMPLE 9-3. G* transferred land "to *A* for life, remainder to *A*'s children."
>   If *A* is childless, no one is authorized to transfer the remainder interest on behalf of *A*'s unborn children.
>   If *A* has living children, they can transfer their interests. But, no one is authorized to transfer the executory interests on behalf of *A*'s unborn children. The most that *A*'s living children can transfer is a remainder that is subject to open (partial divestment).

What, then, does it mean to say that in the vast majority of jurisdictions even future interests that are contingent as to person are alienable. The proposition refers to future interests that are created in unascertained persons, rather than to those that are created in unborn persons as in Example *9-3*.

>   *EXAMPLE 9-4. G* transferred land "to *A* for life, remainder to *B*'s heirs." *B* is alive, but if *B* died now, *B*'s sole heir would be *B*'s child, *C*.
>   In states in which contingent-as-to-person future interests are alienable, *B*'s heir apparent (*C*) would have a transferable interest, not merely an expectancy, in the subject matter of *G*'s disposition. See Am. L. Prop. § 4.67 n. 10 & accompanying text. If *C* should transfer her interest, her transferee would, however,

receive an interest that is contingent on *C*'s actually qualifying as *B*'s heir. See Restatement of Property § 162 cmt. c. It is thus clear that no one, not even *C*, can transfer the remainder interest that follows *A*'s life estate. The remainder interest is not truly alienable, notwithstanding *C*'s ability to transfer her interest. (Be careful not to confuse the notion that *C* has a property interest *in the subject matter of the disposition* with the notion that *C*, as *B*'s heir apparent, merely has an expectancy *in B's own property*.)

(b) Inter-Vivos Alienability of Possibilities of Reverter and Rights of Entry. The courts are divided on the alienability of possibilities of reverter. In some states there are statutes making all future interests alienable, which should include possibilities of reverter. In Illinois this interest is by statute expressly made inalienable.

In the absence of statute, rights of entry are inalienable inter vivos. Statutes in a number of states provide otherwise, either expressly covering these interests or by provisions making all future interests alienable. It is generally held that both interests are releasable.

(c) Effect of Attempt to Alienate Rights of Entry. Several American courts have held that an attempt to convey a right of entry inter vivos extinguishes the right of entry. No rational justification has been offered for this result. The rule has been repudiated in Iowa and Oklahoma and abolished by statute in Michigan. The Restatement originally adopted the rule, but rejected it in 1948. The rule was rejected in

Pickens v. Daugherty (Tenn. 1966).

§ 9.3. Involuntary Alienability: Creditors's Rights

Statutes in the various states provide creditors with the right to impound their debtors's assets prior to judgment and the right after judgment to subject their assets to sale for its satisfaction. These statutes purport to specify the types of assets that are subject to these procedures, but the statutory language is usually so general that it is within the power of the courts to determine the extent to which the debtor's future interests can be affected.

(a) General Principle. The general principle followed by the courts under these statutes is that if the future interest is voluntarily alienable, it is also subject to the claims of creditors. Indefeasibly vested remainders and reversions, since they are voluntarily alienable, are automatically available to creditors in the satisfaction of their claims. The same is true of remainders and reversions that are vested subject to defeasance.

Contingent remainders and executory interests are not subject to the claims of creditors in the minority of states in which they are not voluntarily alienable. The fact that the equitable contract to convey, the estoppel by deed, and the release methods are available in these states does not change the result. Conversely, in states in which contingent remainders and executory interests are voluntarily alienable (the vast majority of states), courts rather routinely hold such interests to be subject to creditors's claims. See, e.g.,

Everson v. Everson (Pa. 1981). See also Restatement of Property §§ 166, 167.

(b) The "Sacrificial" Sale Problem. A judgment sale of a future interest that is subject to conditions will undoubtedly bring a low purchase price. The sale might not substantially benefit the creditor, and might do serious harm to the debtor by depriving him or her of the possibility of gaining property of much higher value. The "winner" in such situations is neither the debtor nor the creditor, but the purchaser at the sale. (There is, of course, the possibility that the purchaser may be the creditor.)

Does this justify departing from the general principle that a future interest that is voluntarily alienable is also subject to the claims of creditors? With respect to legal future interests, the Restatement of Property §§ 166, 167 take the position that it is not, but bow to the Trusts Restatement with respect to equitable future interests. The Restatement 2d of Trusts § 162 states:

> [I]f the interest of the beneficiary of a trust is so indefinite or contingent that it cannot be sold with fairness to both the creditors and the beneficiary, it cannot be reached by his creditors.

Although there would seem to be no supportable distinction between legal and equitable interests regarding this issue, the few instances of departure from the general principle have involved equitable interests. The form of the departure varies, however.

One form, as suggested by the Trusts Restatement, is simply to deny creditors access to future interests subject to remote contingencies.

> *EXAMPLE 9-5.* G transferred property to a trustee, in trust, to pay the income to A for life, then to B for life, corpus to be paid on the death of B if he survives A to B's then-living issue; if B survives A but is not survived by issue, corpus on B's death to be paid to C if C survives B.
>
> C's remainder is contingent on B's surviving A, B's dying without surviving issue, and C's surviving B. C's remainder cannot be actuarially valued. In such circumstances, the court in Clarke v. Fay (Mass. 1910), operating with statutory support, denied C's creditor access to the contingent remainder.

Rather than deny access, there is precedent for a more imaginative solution: Refuse to order an immediate judgment sale of such interests, but impose a lien on the future interest until the contingencies are satisfied, if ever.

> *EXAMPLE 9-6.* G transferred property to a trustee, in trust, to pay the corpus and accumulated income to A if he lives to age 25; if not, to B upon A's death under 25.
>
> A's creditors sought by creditors' bill to reach his contingent remainder in the corpus and accumulated income. In Meyer v. Reif (Wis. 1935), the court suggested imposing a lien on A's interest in the trust, and an order directing the trustee to satisfy the

creditor's judgment if *A* should reach 25 out of the trust fund before paying over the remaining corpus to *A*. The court said:

> To grant the relief above suggested would protect the [creditor] and be fairer to the [beneficiary, *A*] than to sell his interest in the fund. A sale as ordinarily made on execution or pursuant to judgment would carry the interest in the fund and thus carry the whole fund when [*A*] arrived at the age of twenty-five, if he reached that age. The uncertainty of his arriving at that age would prevent the bidding of an amount at all commensurate with the amount of the fund, and such a sale would be likely to work injustice to [*A*] through carrying the amount of the fund in excess of the amount due on the [creditor's] judgment.

Two points should be noted about *Meyer*. First, a lien can only be imposed in equity. As the court noted:

> The case is in equity, and equity "has . . . never placed any limits to the remedies which it can grant, either with respect to their substance, their form, or their extent; but has always preserved the elements of flexibility and expansiveness, so that new ones may be invented, or old ones modified, in order to meet the requirements of every case."

Consequently, the imposition of a lien is possible only when the contingent interest is equitable rather than legal. In this limited respect, therefore, there is a supportable distinction between legal and equitable interests.

The second point about *Meyer* is that the condition attached to the future interest—living to age 25—is one that would certainly make the interest subject to valuation and is one that is likely to be fulfilled. The *Meyer* court was not concerned with these points, but rather with the fact that the amount that the future interest might bring on a sale would not be commensurate with the amount of the corpus of the trust fund. Since it is unrealistic to think that any future interest, even one that is indefeasibly vested, would bring a sale price equal to the value of the trust fund, the possibility exists that this more imaginative form of relief might not be limited to equitable future interests that are subject to contingencies, let alone those subject to remote contingencies.

(c) Creditors's Rights Against the Estate of a Deceased Debtor. When the owner of a future interest dies, his or her interest may be transmitted by will even if it was not alienable inter vivos. It may well be argued that the decedent's creditors should be satisfied at this time from such assets, for otherwise they will be deprived of all chance of payment. There appears to be little law on the subject. Some statutes governing the payment of claims against decedents' estates answer the matter by equating the creditors's

rights to property that the decedent could have alienated inter vivos. Text writers and the Restatement of Property § 169 indicate that the same result will probably be reached in situations in which the controlling statute is not so explicit.

(d) Creditors's Rights Under the Federal Bankruptcy Law. In federal bankruptcy proceedings, the rights of creditors are far-reaching. The Bankruptcy Reform Act of 1978, 11 U.S.C.A. § 541, treats "all legal or equitable [property] interests" owned by the debtor as part of the bankrupt's estate, "notwithstanding any provision in . . . applicable nonbankruptcy law . . . that restricts . . . transfer of such interest by the debtor. . . ." This language is broad enough to include all types of future interests, even those that are immune from the claims of creditors under state law.

Chapter 10

THE DESTRUCTIBILITY OF CONTINGENT REMAINDERS

§ 10.1. Statement of the Destructibility Rule

The common-law destructibility rule provides:

☞ *A legal contingent remainder in land is destroyed if it does not vest by the time the preceding freehold estate terminates.*

The destructibility rule is a rule of law, not a rule of construction, which means that it is intent-defeating rather than intent-effecting.

§ 10.2. Legal Theory Underlying the Destructibility Rule

Conventional instrumentalist accounts attribute the destructibility rule to the common-law courts's desire to promote alienability of land. In this respect, the rule can be viewed as a precursor of the Rule Against Perpetuities. The rule was also the product, however, of elaborate conceptual structures.

In part, the destructibility rule reflected a particular conception of conveyancing, which in turn reflected a particular conception of ownership. Under assumptions derived from feudal tenure on "held" land, one was not spoken of as "owner." Holding land was a matter status more than of right, and having that status depended on having possession. In other words, the right to possession was not fully separated from possession in fact. "Seisin," the word for it, implied possession under a claim to a freehold estate. Seisin was transferred by a transaction called a "feoffment," which required a ritual called "livery of seisin," whereby the parties would go onto the land and the conveyor would express his intent to convey and hand the conveyee a stick, stone, or clod of dirt as symbolizing the transfer of the land itself.

Within this conception of conveyancing, the common-law courts could not imagine a conveyance to take effect in possession at a future date or a conveyance that would shift seisin at a future date from one person to another.

Common-law courts did, however, permit conveyances for life, with remainder, vested or contingent, to another. The courts manipulated the concept of seisin by creating the fiction that the life tenant took the seisin for himself and for the remainderman or the reversioner. Strangely enough, this kind of automatic shift in seisin apparently did not stimulate the common-law courts to design others—not until the Statute of Uses wrought its far-reaching effects upon the structure and conceptions of estates and the modes of conveyancing. In short, the type of future interest that could not be imagined was the executory interest. One of the consequences of the seisin concept was the destruction of legal contingent remainders in land.

At early common law, no naked future interest could be created that would take effect in possession in the future, and none could be created that would divest a fee simple interest. These rules provided the technical explanation for the destructibility rule: A remainder needed a freehold estate to "support" it. When the supporting freehold estate terminated, there was no problem if the remainder was then entitled to become possessory; seisin passed to the remainderman from the life tenant. But if the remainder was not yet entitled to become possessory—if, for example, a condition precedent remained unsatisfied—seisin passed to the reversioner whose interest, always regarded as vested (see § supra 7.2(a)), thereupon became possessory. Note that the reversioner did not and could not (since his interest was a fee simple interest) take seisin from the life tenant on behalf of himself and the remainderman. He took it only on his own behalf. Lacking support, the remainder could no longer exist as a future interest, and so it was destroyed.

Seisin is now defunct in England, and accordingly the destructibility rule has long been abolished there by statute. Nevertheless, despite the fact that seisin was never given more than token recognition even in early America (Moynihan on Real Property 91), the destructibility rule was received in at least some states as part of our common law.   As noted above, the destructibility rule developed when remainders were the only type of legal future interest that could be created in transferees. One of the consequences of the Statute of Uses, enacted in 1535, was to change that. Prior to the Statute of Uses, the equity courts enforced "springing" and "shifting" uses. A springing use was a naked future interest in a transferee that would take effect in possession in the future and a shifting use was a future interest in a transferee that would divest a fee simple estate.

Then came the Statute of Uses, which provided that equitable interests were executed, i.e., changed into legal interests. The common-law courts recognized executed uses as valid future interests, bringing executory interests (springing and shifting) into the scheme of common-law estates. Because seisin could automatically transfer to the holder of an executory interest upon the happening of a future event, executory interests, not needing a "supporting" freehold, were held to be indestructible. See Pells v. Brown (1620).

§ 10.3. Interests Subject to the Destructibility Rule

(a) Only Contingent Remainders. Only contingent remainders are subject to destruction. Vested remainders, even vested remainders subject to divestment, cannot be destroyed. Executory interests, though contingent, cannot be destroyed. See Pells v. Brown (1620). The reversionary interests—reversions, possibilities of reverter, and rights of entry—are not subject to destruction. These rules

are still followed today where the destructibility rule is in force.

Consequently, classification of the interests both by type and in terms of vesting is the crucial first step, but it is only that—a first step. Destructibility is one of the possible consequences of classification, not one of its automatic consequences.

(b) Only Contingent Remainders in Land. Because the destructibility rule was rooted in the concept of seisin, a concept that is inapplicable to personal property, the destructibility rule only applies to contingent remainders in land. This rule is still followed today in states where the destructibility rule is in force.

(c) Only Legal Contingent Remainders. Similarly, an equitable contingent remainder, whether in land or personalty, could not be destroyed because seisin remained in the trustee throughout the continuance of the trust. This rule is still followed today where the destructibility rule is in force.

(d) Prior Estate Must be a Freehold. Because of its roots in the concept of seisin, the destructibility rule only applies if the particular estate is a freehold. Because we are dealing with contingent remainders, the prior possessory estate will always be a particular estate. See supra § 6.1. (A particular estate is any estate of less quantum than a fee simple.) The only particular estates that are freeholds are fees tail and life estates. Thus a contingent remainder following a term of years is not destructible. Since we are ignoring the fee tail estate, the succeeding discussion

deals only with contingent remainders following life estates.

(e) Inter-Vivos and Testamentary Transfers. No distinction is drawn between inter-vivos and testamentary transfers. The destructibility rule applies to both types of transfer, if the other requirements of the rule are met.

§ 10.4. Destruction by Merger, Forfeiture, and Time Gap

A legal contingent remainder in land was destroyed at common law in three basic situations—merger, forfeiture, and time gap. Destruction by merger and by forfeiture were within the control of one or more of the parties and therefore can properly be called methods of intentional destruction. Some commentators, looking at the situations from a slightly different perspective, have utilized the name of *artificial destruction* for these methods because, under both, the destruction results from an artificial termination of the life estate. An artificial termination occurs (or perhaps more accurately, is engineered) during the life tenant's lifetime.

Destruction by time gap is sometimes called *natural destruction* because here the destruction results from events existing at the natural termination of the life estate, i.e., at the life tenant's death. The events causing a natural destruction are typically outside the lawful control of the parties, and consequently this situation is not a method of intentional destruction.

(a) Time Gap Occurring at the Natural Termina-

tion of the Supporting Freehold. In most cases the condition precedent attached to a contingent remainder *must* be resolved one way or the other at or before the life tenant's death. The typical example is the remainder subject to a condition precedent of surviving the life tenant. Contingent remainders of this sort are not subject to natural destruction—destruction caused by a time gap. Sometimes, however, a contingent remainder is subject to a condition precedent that can be fulfilled after the life tenant's death. If the condition is not fulfilled when the life tenant dies, a time gap or gap in possession arises. The time gap causes the remainder to be destroyed. Be careful to note that the type of time gap that causes a natural destruction is one that was not certain to occur; it must be one that might or might not have occurred. The significance of this point is brought out more fully in (*b*), below. See infra pp. 129-31.

> *EXAMPLE 10-1.* (*1*) *G* transferred land "to *A* for life, remainder to *B* if *B* lives to age 21." At *A*'s death, *B* is under 21.
>
> (*2*) *G* transferred land "to *A* for life, remainder to the heirs of *B*." At *A*'s death, *B* is still living and hence his heirs have not yet been ascertained.
>
> Whether the destructibility rule is in force or not, *G*'s reversion takes effect in possession at *A*'s death in both of these cases. If the destructibility rule is in force, *B*'s contingent remainder in Variation (*1*) and the one in *B*'s heirs in Variation (*2*) are destroyed. As a result, *G*'s reversion becomes possessory in fee

simple *absolute*.[1]

In Variation *(1)*, if B had already reached 21 when A died or in Variation *(2)* if B had predeceased A, the contingent remainders would have become vested before the termination of the life estate, would have avoided destruction, and would have become possessory in fee simple absolute upon A's death.

(1) The Rule of Purefoy v. Rogers. The indestructibility of executory interests (see supra § 10.3) afforded an opportunity to save contingent remainders from destruction. The law courts merely had to accept the proposition that contingent remainders could change into executory interests whenever the supporting freehold terminated before the contingent reminder vested. Acceptance of this proposition would have indirectly abolished the destructibility rule. Upon failure of the supporting freehold (whether this occurred naturally or artificially), contingent remainders would always change into an

---

[1] If the destructibility rule were not in force, the contingent remainders in these two cases would not be destroyed. As noted above, G's reversion would still take effect in possession at A's death as a fee simple estate. But, as we know, a remainder cannot follow a fee estate. See supra § 6.2. Consequently we now have contingent remainders that have not been destroyed, but that cannot continue to be contingent remainders. So, what happens? They turn into springing executory interests, and G's reversion takes effect in possession at A's death, not as a fee simple absolute, but as a fee simple subject to defeasance. See Example *8-3*; cf. supra § 7.8(a).

interest that did not need a supporting freehold. But this was not to be. In Purefoy v. Rogers (K.B. 1670), the court prevented the demise of the destructibility rule by laying down this proposition:

> [F]or where a contingency is limited to depend on an estate of freehold which is capable of supporting a remainder, it shall never be construed to be an executory devise, but a contingent remainder only, and not otherwise.

In short, a contingent remainder cannot avoid destruction by changing into an executory interest.

(2) The Rule of In re Lechmere and Lloyd. A formalistic qualification of the rule of Purefoy v. Rogers was established in In re Lechmere and Lloyd (Ch. 1881). The disposition was "to *A* for life, remainder to such of his children as shall *before or after A's* death attain 21." At *A*'s death, some of *A*'s children were 21 or older but some were not, and the question was whether the interests of the ones not yet 21 had been destroyed. The court per the Master of the Rolls, Sir George Jessel, held that they were not destroyed because they were executory interests *from their inception;* the theory was that

> here we have two distinct classes as the objects of the devise, the one being children living at the death of the tenant for life and attaining twenty-one . . . before the death, and the other being children living at the death and attaining

twenty-one . . . after the death . . . But to enable the second class to participate it is necessary to read the gift to them as an executory [interest]. The rule is that you construe every limitation, if you possibly can, as a remainder, rather than as an executory [interest]. It is a harsh rule: why should I extend it? Why should a gift which cannot possibly take effect as a remainder not take effect as an executory [interest]? I see no good reason why it should not. The result is, in my opinion, that the devise in this case could not take effect as a remainder in respect of those children who survived the tenant for life but had not attained twenty-one at her death, and must, therefore, in order to let in those children, be construed as an executory [interest].

It is quite clear, as Jessel, M.R., conceded, that the result would have been different if the disposition had been "to *A* for life, remainder to such of *A*'s children as shall attain 21." The phrase "before or after *A*'s death" allowed the court to avoid classifying the interests of all of *A*'s children, including those who were under 21 when *A* died, as contingent remainders. This phrase is implicit in the disposition even when not express, and so the substance of the disposition is the same either way. Yet, the court made it clear that the *Lechmere* principle would not be applied without the "before or after" phrase.

Although the future interests in *Lechmere* were class gifts, the principle ought to apply to a gift created in an ascertained individual. Suppose in Example *10-1*, the disposition had read: "to *A* for life, remainder to *B* if before or after *A*'s death he lives to the age of 21." While here there are not two distinct classes, it would not be stretching *Lechmere* very far to say that *B* received two interests, one a contingent remainder ("to *B* if before *A*'s death he lives to age 21"), the other an executory interest ("to *B* if after *A*'s death he lives to age 21"). This analysis is supported by Miles v. Harford (Ch. 1879) (Jessel, M.R.), a case involving the separability doctrine under the Rule Against Perpetuities (a doctrine we will study infra § 13.10), but the question does not seem to have been raised in a destructibility case.

(b) Termination of the Supporting Freehold by Merger. The *natural* destruction of a contingent remainder is only possible when the condition precedent is of a certain type—one that might remain unsatisfied at the life tenant's death. *Any* contingent remainder, however, is susceptible to *artificial* destruction, even when the condition precedent cannot be satisfied after the life tenant's death. The artificial destruction of a contingent remainder is made possible by the premature termination of a life estate. One way of causing a premature or artificial termination of a life estate is by merger.

☞ *The DOCTRINE OF MERGER provides that if a life estate and a successive vested future interest in fee come into the hands of the same person, the life estate terminates by being merging into the other interest*.

See Simes & Smith on Future Interests § 197.

> **EXAMPLE 10-2.** *(1)* G devised land "to A for life, remainder to B if B survives A." G's will contains no residuary clause, and G's sole heir at law is R.
>
> *(2)* G devised land "to A for life, remainder to B if B survives A, but if not, to C." G's will contains no residuary clause, and G's sole heir at law is R.
>
> R has a reversion in both cases, albeit merely a technical one in Variation *(2)*. See supra § 5.5. If R conveys his reversion to A, A's life estate will merge into the reversion, gives A a fee simple. Because the merger destroys B's contingent remainder in both cases and also destroys C's contingent remainder in Variation *(2)*, and because Purefoy v. Rogers prevents their transformation into executory interests (§ 10.4(a)(l)), A's fee simple is a fee simple *absolute*. B's contingent remainder (and C's in Variation *(2)*) could also be destroyed by the same process if A conveyed his life estate to R or if both A and R conveyed their estates to a third person. The person who ends up with both the life estate and the reversion gets a fee simple absolute.[2]
>
> If A, not R, were G's sole heir, A would begin with

---

[2] Were the destructibility rule not in force, the merger of the life estate and the reversion would produce a fee simple defeasible, not a fee simple absolute, and B's contingent remainder (and C's in Variation *(2)*) would become an executory interest.

both the life estate and the reversion. Would the two merge in the hands of *A*, causing *B*'s contingent remainder (and *C*'s in Variation *(2)*) to be destroyed? No. It was held that a life estate and reversion created simultaneously in the same person do not merge if there is an intervening contingent remainder. See Bowles' Case (1615). However, the remainder could still be destroyed by *A*'s conveying the life estate and reversion to another person. Upon the subsequent conveyance, the two interests *would* merge and *B*'s contingent remainder (and *C*'s in Variation *(2)*) would be destroyed. See Purefoy v. Rogers.

The indestructibility of executory interests afforded conveyancers the means of avoiding the destructibility rule. One method was to interject an intentional and certain time gap between the natural termination of the life estate and the right to possession of the contingent future interest. For example, a slight modification of Variation *(1)* in Example *10-2* would give *B* an indestructible executory interest rather than a contingent remainder: "to *A* for life, and one day after *A*'s death, to *B* if *B* is then living." *B*'s interest is an executory interest at inception. See supra Example *6-15*. Thus a conveyance by *R* of his reversion to *A*, a conveyance by *A* of his life estate to *R*, or a conveyance by both *A* and *R* of their interests to a third person would not destroy *B*'s executory interest. A merger would indeed occur, but the resultant estate would *not* be a fee simple *absolute;* it would be a fee simple subject to defeasance in favor of *B* if *B* survives *A* by a day.

(c) Termination of the Supporting Freehold by Forfeiture. At common law, a life estate could be terminated before the life tenant's death by forfeiture. Under the feudal doctrine of seisin and disseisin, forfeiture occurred if the life tenant conveyed—by feoffment (livery of seisin), fine, or common recovery—a greater estate, a fee, than he owned. The conveyance gave the conveyee a "tortious fee," thus destroying any contingent remainder previously supported by the life estate. The conveyee's fee was held to be subject to a right of entry that arose in the person holding the next vested estate, typically the reversioner. See Archer's Case (1597); Chudleigh's Case (1595); Loddington v. Kime (1695). Although under the law of the time this right of entry was not alienable inter vivos (it was descendible, however), it could be released to the conveyee. See Moynihan on Real Property 90. These rules enabled the life tenant and the reversioner to transfer a fee simple absolute in the property, much in the fashion of, though in a different form from, the merger method as discussed above.

Forfeiture of a life estate is not recognized in the United States. If a life tenant purports to convey a fee, the transferee only receives a life estate. The principle we follow is that a person can convey no greater estate than he has. Consequently, this method of destroying a contingent remainder is not available even in those states that still adhere to the destructibility rule.

A life tenant can, however, renounce or disclaim

his or her life estate. Although disclaimer may appear to be the modern-day equivalent of forfeiture, the courts that have faced the question have not treated it that way.

> *EXAMPLE 10-3.* G devised land "to A for life, remainder to B if she lives to age 21." A files a disclaimer with G's executor as authorized by local law. B is 15 years old at G's death.

> B's contingent interest is not destroyed because it was an executory interest at its inception, not a contingent remainder. It is well-accepted that a person disclaiming a devise is treated as having predeceased the testator for purposes of the devolution of the disclaimed interest. Therefore the effect of A's disclaiming is that A is treated as having predeceased G; in other words, no life estate was ever created. It is as if G's will had devised the property "to B if she lives to age 21," creating an indestructible executory interest in B from the start. See Simes & Smith on Future Interests § 795.

§ 10.5. Present Status of the Destructibility Rule

The destructibility rule has been abolished by statute in over half of the states. ☺ The statutes are commonly retroactive. They apply to contingent remainders created though not destroyed before the effective date of the Act. The crucial date is the termination of the supporting freehold. These statutes have been held to be constitutional whenever challenged as effecting a deprivation of property without due process of law. A couple of statutes only apply to contingent remainders created after enactment. In about four states and the District of Columbia the statute abolishes artificial destructibility but not natural destructibility. The forfeiture method of artificial destruction is not recognized in the United States anyway.

In the remaining states, the question is largely open. The Restatement of Property § 240 takes the position that the rule is not part of our common law. A few courts have on their own openly rejected the rule. The New Hampshire court in effect rejected it by holding that the rule of Purefoy v. Rogers is merely a rule of construction (see Hayward v. Spaulding (N.H. 1908)) and the Massachusetts court did so by holding that the principle of *Lechmere & Lloyd* is applicable even when (as always is the case) the "before or after termination of the life estate" qualification is merely implicit in the disposition (see Bass River Savings Bank v. Nickerson (Mass. 1939)). Many but not all of the American decisions that accepted the rule are from states that subsequently abolished it by statute. Unless the rule is seen to be desirable as an instrument of social policy, it is doubtful that the rule would be accepted today in states in which the question is open, and the time may be ripe for the overruling of decisions that earlier accepted the rule in the other states, even without abolishing legislation. Recall also that if a condition is stated in both precedent and subsequent form, a court may be inclined to avoid the destructibility rule by holding that the remainder is vested rather than contingent; as noted before, however, this is much more likely in time gap cases than it is in other situations. See supra § 7.8(a).

§ 10.6. Destructibility Rule as an Instrument of Social Policy?

Is the destructibility rule a sound instrument of social policy? There is no doubt that legal contingent future interests prevent the free alienability of land. See William F. Fratcher, A Modest Proposal for Trimming the Claws of Legal Future Interests, 1972 Duke L.J. 517. Contingent future interests are often created in a class that is made up of or includes unborn or unascertained persons. Thus the destructibility rule can be seen as promoting the free alienability of property by destroying an interest that cannot be transferred. In the case of artificial destruction by merger, the rule enables the life tenant and reversioner to join in effecting a transfer of the property in fee simple absolute. In the case of natural destruction, the rule allows the reversioner to do so upon the life tenant's death. One can speculate that this view of the destructibility rule, as an instrument of social policy, accounted for the decision in Purefoy v. Rogers in the late 17th century. It was also about this time that the first seeds of the Rule Against Perpetuities began to emerge. Compare A.W.B. Simpson, An Introduction to the History of Land Law 205 et seq. (1961) with George L. Haskins, Extending the Grasp of the Dead Hand: Reflections on the Origins of the Rule Against Perpetuities, 126

U.Pa.L.Rev. 19 (1977).

Seen as an instrument of social policy, however, the destructibility rule is a very poor one. Its application is narrow (only legal contingent remainders in land following a freehold), and thus the rule is easily avoided by astute drafting. It also invariably requires litigation to apply it. In comparison, the Rule Against Perpetuities is a rule of much wider application, for it applies to executory interests as well as contingent remainders, to contingent interests in trust as well as legal interests, and to contingent interests in personalty as well as land. Yet, as we shall see, the Rule Against Perpetuities does allow property to be tied up for quite a long time, much longer than merely for a lifetime.

A possible solution to the problem of inalienable land is legislation that authorizes a life tenant, with court approval, to sell the property in fee simple absolute, and put the proceeds into a kind of trust whereby he or she is entitled to the income for life, with the corpus on the life tenant's death going to the persons entitled thereto. See Fratcher, supra, for other ideas for improvement of the law in this area.

Chapter 11

THE RULE IN SHELLEY'S CASE

§ 11.1. Statement of the Rule in Shelley's Case

The Rule in Shelley's Case provides:

☞ *A remainder interest in land in favor of the life tenant's heirs or the heirs of the life tenant's body is held by the life tenant if the remainder is of the same quality as that of the life estate.*

The Rule in Shelley's Case is a rule of law, not a rule of construction, which means that it is intent-defeating rather than intent-effecting.

The *name* of the rule derives from the case of Wolfe v. Shelley (K.B. 1581). The rule itself, however, was recognized in the early part of the 14th century. The classic historical statement of the rule comes not from the opinion of the court in Wolfe v. Shelley but from Lord Coke's winning argument for the defendant in that case:

It is a rule of law, when the ancestor by any gift or conveyance takes an estate in freehold, and in the same gift or conveyance an estate is limited mediately or immediately to his heirs in fee or in tail; that always in such cases "the heirs" are words of limitation of the [ancestor's] estate and not words of purchase.

As we shall see, the Rule has evolved in certain particulars since Lord Coke stated it, so that the statement in the first paragraph above is more accurate than Lord Coke's formulation.

§ 11.2.   Historical Development of the Rule in Shelley's Case

The rule known as the Rule in Shelley's Case was recognized two hundred years or more prior to Wolfe v. Shelley. Scholars have found 14th century cases in which the rule was applied or appears to have been applied.   See Provost of Beverley's Case (1366); Abel's Case (1324). Because remainder interests were probably not recognized as valid future interests until the latter part of the 13th century (after the Statute De Donis, 1285), and contingent remainders were not fully recognized until much later, some have speculated that the Rule may at first have been intent-effecting rather than intent-defeating. The idea is that a conveyance "to *A* for life, then to *A*'s heirs" could then only be given effect as a fee simple in favor of *A*. Nevertheless, the Rule evolved into a rule of law, not one of construction. Although this point was not finally settled until Perrin v. Blake (1769), Lord Coke's classic statement of the Rule (in his argument for the defendant in Wolfe v. Shelley) described it as a rule of law. The probable reason for its existence as a rule of law was made explicit even in the early *Provost of Beverley's Case*: By forcing the remainder to go to the life tenant, the land would pass to the life tenant's heirs *by descent* rather than by purchase. The feudal dues to the lord could be exacted only when land *descended* on the owner's death.

§ 11.3. Interests Subject to the Rule in Shelley's Case

(a) Only Remainders. Only remainders are subject to the Rule in Shelley's Case. The rule is inapplicable to executory interests, reversions, possibilities of reverter, and rights of entry. The limitation to remainders in land is still followed today where the Rule in Shelley's Case is in force.[1] See Restatement 2d of Property § 30.1(1) & cmt. e.

> *EXAMPLE 11-1*. *G* transferred land "to *A* for life, and one day after *A*'s death, to *A*'s heirs."
>
> The life tenant's heirs take an executory interest, not a remainder. See supra Example *6-15*. Shelley's Rule therefore does not apply: *A* takes a life estate only, and *A*'s heirs take the executory interest.
>
> If *G*'s transfer had been "to *A* for life, then upon *A*'s death, to *A*'s heirs," the future interest created in the life tenant's heirs would have been a remainder. Shelley's Rule would have applied, giving the

---

[1] In Texas, a state that has now abolished Shelley's Rule by statute, Darragh v. Barmore (Tex. Com. App. 1920) applied the Rule to an executory interest.

remainder to *A*; *A*'s life estate and remainder would have merged, giving *A* a fee simple absolute.

Consequently, classification of the future interest by type is the crucial first step, but it is only that—a first step. The Rule in Shelley's Case is one of the possible consequences of classification, not one of its automatic consequences.

(b) Only Remainders in Land. Because the Rule in Shelley's Case was tied to the feudal system and was developed by the law courts, only remainders in land are subject to the Rule. This limitation is still followed today in states where Shelley's Rule is in force.[2] See Restatement 2d of Property § 30.1(1) & cmt. b.

(c) Only Remainders in Favor of the Heirs (or Heirs of the Body) of the Life Tenant. For Shelley's Rule to apply, the transferor must be found to have intended that the remainder interest go either to the "heirs" of the life tenant or the "heirs of the body" of the life tenant in the technical sense of these terms. Unfortunately, *for purposes of Shelley's Rule*, the courts are not in agreement about the technical

[2] An apparent exception was North Carolina, where in Riegel v. Lyerly (N.C. 1965), the court applied the Rule to personal property. In 1987, North Carolina abolished Shelley's Rule by statute. See N.C. Gen. Stat. § 41-6.3. Another exception is Ohio, where in Society Nat'l Bank v. Jacobson (Ohio 1990), the Ohio Supreme Court in a muddled opinion applied the Rule to personal property in trust!

meanings of these terms. The existence of divergent views causes no problem when the transferor uses the term "heirs" or the term "heirs of the body" without any further qualification. In such cases, the transferor will almost certainly be deemed to have intended whatever technical meaning of the term is adopted by the particular court. That is to say, if *G* transfers land "to *A* for life, remainder to *A*'s heirs" or "to *A* for life, remainder to the heirs of *A*'s body," Shelley's Rule if in force will apply to give the remainder to *A* regardless of the jurisdiction. The divergent views affect the result only when the transferor's language is qualified in some manner.

(1) Majority American View: Definite Line of Succession. To explore these divergent views, we should begin with the technical meanings that present-day American courts would attribute to the terms "heirs" and "heirs of the body" in cases in which Shelley's Rule is *not* at issue. Suppose, for example, *G*'s will devises land outright to *G*'s own "heirs" or to the "heirs of *G*'s body." Who would take the property on *G*'s death? In the case of the devise to *G*'s own "heirs," the takers would presumptively be the persons who would have succeeded by intestate succession to *G*'s property had *G* died intestate: *G*'s actual heirs, in other words. Such persons, determined under the statute of descent in the jurisdiction, would potentially include *G*'s spouse, ancestors, and collaterals as well as *G*'s descendants. In the case of the devise to the "heirs of *G*'s body," the takers would presumptively be *G*'s

lineal descendants who under the statute of descent in the jurisdiction would have succeeded by intestate succession to G's property had G died intestate: G's actual heirs, in other words, but in the specialized sense of excluding G's spouse, ancestors, and collaterals, and including only G's lineal descendants. See Restatement of Property § 306. Both sets of takers—G's "heirs" and the "heirs of G's body"—would be determined once and for all at G's death and would include only persons who were living at that time. Predeceased persons and persons born later could not take. The label *definite line of succession* has been applied to "heirs" and "heirs of the body" when interpreted in the sense just described.

In cases in which the Rule in Shelley's Case *is* at issue, the majority American view adopts the definite line of succession concept of the terms "heirs" and "heirs of the body." See Restatement 2d of Property § 30.1 cmt. g.

(2) English and Minority American View: Indefinite Line of Succession. The English courts and a minority of American courts adopt a different view: the concept of an *indefinite line of succession*. An indefinite line of succession incorporates the idea of a continuum by which the heirs or heirs of the body succeed to a decedent's property at the decedent's death, the heirs or heirs of the body of these takers later succeed to the property on the death of the first takers, and so on indefinitely. The concept of "heirs" and "heirs of the body" as referring not

merely to the first takers on the decedent's death but also to all future takers is the more accurate conception of these terms as they were understood when the Rule in Shelley's Case was developed. At that time, in feudal England, the system of primogeniture was in force. Under this system, a decedent had only one heir: his eldest son (and if there were no sons, his daughters took collectively but were treated as a single heir). In this setting, the plural terms "heirs" and "heirs of his body" could not refer only to the first taker (singular). It had to refer to the first taker and all future takers. See Restatement 2d of Property § 30.1 cmt. f.

The system of primogeniture remained in force in England long after the feudal system was dismantled. Primogeniture was not abolished until 1925. Interestingly, the same piece of legislation—the Law of Property Act, 1925—also abolished the Rule in Shelley's Case in England. Thus throughout the entire existence of the Rule in Shelley's Case in England, the system of primogeniture was in force. Consequently, the English view of the technical meaning of the terms "heirs" and "heirs of the body" incorporated the notion of an indefinite line of succession. This is the view—the English view—that the minority of American courts adopted even though primogeniture had either long since been abolished in the state or was never accepted to begin with.

(3) Examples Illustrating the Divergent Views. With these two divergent views in mind—definite versus indefinite lines of succession—we should look

at a few examples in which they lead to different results.

EXAMPLE 11-2. *G* transferred land "to *A* for life, remainder to *A*'s heirs who are living at *A*'s death."

Because the group of people who would succeed to *A*'s property by intestate succession is determined at *A*'s death, and because only persons who survive a decedent can be counted among his or her heirs, *G*'s language requiring survival of *A* simply reinforces the notion that *G* intended to give the remainder to *A*'s heirs in the technical sense of the term as the majority conceives of the term. Shelley's Rule would therefore apply in jurisdictions following the definite line of succession interpretation of the word "heirs." See Porter v. Cutler (Ill. 1942).

But the language requiring that the takers be living at *A*'s death contradicts the idea of a continuum of succession from taker to taker. Consequently, in the minority of jurisdictions that define "heirs" as an indefinite line of succession, Shelley's Rule would not apply. See Finley v. Finley (Tex. Civ. App. 1958).

EXAMPLE 11-3. *G* transferred land "to *A* for life, remainder to the heirs of *A*'s body who are living at *A*'s death."

Like Example *11-2*, the qualifying language requiring the takers to be living at the life tenant's death corroborates the idea that *G* intended the technical meaning of heirs of *A*'s body, in the sense of a definite line of succession. Shelley's Rule would therefore apply in jurisdictions that adopt this technical meaning. But the same qualifying language contradicts the notion of an indefinite line of succession, and so Shelley's Rule would not apply in jurisdictions adopting the other definition. See Ortgiesen v. Ackerman (Ill. 1924).

Despite the divergent views in American law, both views have certain features in common. Consequently there are cases in which the transferor gives a remainder interest to the "heirs" or "heirs of the body" of the life tenant, but adds language that contradicts both technical meanings. In cases such as this, all jurisdictions would conclude that "heirs" or "heirs of the body" was used in a non-technical sense, and Shelley's Rule would not apply. Two illustrations are as follows.

EXAMPLE 11-4. G transferred land "to A for life, remainder to A's heirs (or the heirs of A's body) determined at my (G's) death."

Because A's heirs (or heirs of A's body) are not to be determined at A's death, G did not use the term "heirs" (or "heirs of the body") in either the definite or indefinite line of succession sense of the term. The Rule in Shelley's Case is inapplicable in both majority and minority view jurisdictions.

EXAMPLE 11-5. G transferred land "to A for life, remainder to A's heirs (or the heirs of A's body), but if A dies without children, to B."

The gift over to B on A's death without children indicates that G used the term "heirs" (or "heirs of the body") to mean children—a non-technical sense. The

Rule in Shelley's Case is inapplicable in both majority and minority view jurisdictions.

Shelley's Rule has been held to be inapplicable where the remainder is to the life tenant's heirs for life or for a term of years. See Simes & Smith on Future Interests § 1547. Thus a disposition "to A for life, remainder to A's heirs for their lives" would not trigger the Rule.

(4) Dispositive Language Not Using "Heirs" or "Heirs of the Body." Up to now, in exploring the meaning of the requirement that the remainder must be in favor of the life tenant's heirs or heirs of the body in the technical sense, we have concentrated on dispositions in which the terms "heirs" or "heirs of the body" appeared in the dispositive language. But Shelley's Rule has also been held to apply, especially in jurisdictions adhering to the definite line of succession concept, where the words used were the equivalents of these terms. Thus the Rule has been held to apply, even though the word "heirs" was not used, where the disposition said: "to A for life, remainder to the persons who on the death of A will inherit A's land." Similarly, despite the absence of the words "heirs of the body," the Rule has been held to apply where the disposition said: "to A for life, remainder to A's issue." The cases, which are collected in Simes & Smith on Future Interest § 1549, are not uniform. Some have held Shelley's Rule inapplicable to such dispositions. It is clear, though, that a disposition "to A for life, remainder to

A's children" would not trigger the rule even though it might turn out that *A*'s children are both *A*'s actual heirs and the actual heirs of *A*'s body. See Restatement 2d of Property § 30.1 cmt. g.

(d) Prior Estate Must Be Freehold. According to Lord Coke's statement of the Rule in Shelley's Case, the prior estate must be a freehold. This restriction is still followed. Thus Shelley's Rule does not apply to a remainder to the heirs or heirs of the body of a tenant for a term of years—"to *A* for 21 years, remainder to *A*'s heirs." Although at an early time contingent remainders could not follow a term of years, this old rule is no longer followed. See supra § 3.4; see also Am. L. Prop. § 4.31; Restatement of Property § 157 cmt. e & illus. 9. Accordingly, an often touted device for avoiding Shelley's Rule is to make the term of years much longer than *A*'s life expectancy *and* determinable on *A*'s death if *A* should die (as expected) before the term expires: "To *A* for 150 years or until *A*'s death, then to *A*'s heirs." See Restatement 2d of Property § 30.1 cmt. c.

Because the prior estate must be a freehold, and because the future interest must be a remainder, the prior estate must be either a life estate or a fee tail. Because the fee tail estate is abolished in the United States almost everywhere, and because no American decision on Shelley's Rule apparently exists in which the prior estate was a fee tail, the Restatement 2d of Property § 30.1 cmt. c takes the position that Shelley's Rule applies only when the prior estate is a life estate. The Restatement further states that

Shelley's Rule is applicable even though the life estate is determinable ("to *A* for life or until 150 years have expired, remainder to *A*'s heirs") or pur autre vie ("to *A* for *B*'s lifetime, remainder to *A*'s heirs"). There is, moreover, no requirement that the life estate be a possessory life estate; one in remainder will do. So, in the disposition "to *A* for life, remainder to *B* for life, remainder to *B*'s heirs," Shelley's Rule would apply, converting *B*'s remainder into a remainder in fee simple absolute.

(e) The Life Estate and Remainder Must Be of the Same Quality. Unlike the destructibility rule, the Rule in Shelley's Case applies to equitable as well as legal remainders. The only restriction is that the life estate and remainder must be "of the same quality." The reason for this restriction seems to have been lost in history, but it is followed nevertheless. See Restatement 2d of Property § 30.1(1) & cmt. h. To be "of the same quality," the life estate and remainder must both be legal interests or both be equitable interests. If one is legal and the other is equitable, Shelley's Rule does not apply.

It is easy to tell whether a life estate is legal or equitable: If it is in trust, it is equitable; if there is no trust, it is legal. There is also no difficulty in determining whether a remainder interest following a legal life estate is legal or equitable: It will be legal except for the unlikely case in which the property passes to a trustee on the life tenant's death. But if the life estate is equitable, there seems to be some mystery surrounding how to determine whether the remainder interest is legal or equitable.

Suppose, for example, *G* transfers land to a trustee, directing the trustee to pay the income to *A* for life, remainder at *A*'s death to *A*'s heirs. *A*'s life estate is clearly equitable, but is the remainder also equitable or is it legal? The answer depends on the extent of the trustee's legal title. A trustee takes only such legal title as is necessary to carry out the terms of the trust. See Restatement 2d of Trusts § 88. If the trustee's powers and duties require the trustee to own a legal fee simple absolute, then the remainder interest intended for *A*'s heirs must be an equitable remainder. A power in the trustee to sell the trust property or a duty to convey the property at the termination of the trust would be sufficient to make it necessary for the trustee to own a legal fee simple. See Restatement 2d of Property § 30.1 cmt. h. If, on the other hand, the trustee can adequately discharge the duties and exercise the powers by owning a legal life estate pur autre vie (for the life of *A*), then the remainder interest is legal.

(f) The Life Estate Must Have Been Originally Created in the Ancestor. Probably because Lord Coke's formulation of the Rule in Shelley's Case required that the ancestor take an estate of freehold and "in the same gift or conveyance" the life tenant's heirs or the heirs of the life tenant's body take a remainder, it is sometimes said that the Rule applies only if the life estate and the remainder were created in the same instrument. Stated in this form, it is not an independent requirement at all, but rather is

implicit in the restriction of the Rule's application to remainders. An interest cannot be a remainder unless it was created in the same instrument that created the life estate. See supra Chapter 6.

To say, however, that the life estate and the remainder interest must be created in the same instrument is in fact a loose statement of the requirement, and is not what Lord Coke said. The actual requirement is that the life estate *in the ancestor* must be created in the same instrument as the one that attempted to create a remainder interest in the life tenant's heirs or the heirs of the life tenant's body. See Restatement 2d of Property § 30.1(1) & cmt. i; Restatement of Property § 312 cmt. i. In short, the requirement is that the life estate must be originally created in the ancestor. Shelley's Rule does not apply if the life estate was originally created in someone else who later transferred it to the ancestor. Suppose, for example, a disposition "to *B* for life, remainder to the heirs of *A*." *B* subsequently assigns her life estate to *A*. Although the life estate and the remainder interest were created in the same instrument, Shelley's Rule is inapplicable because the life estate was not *originally* created in *A*.

(g) Contrary Intent Ineffective. Because Shelley's Rule is a rule of law, not a rule of construction, it applies despite a contrary intent. See Restatement 2d of Property § 30.1 cmt. j.

EXAMPLE 11-6. *G* transferred land "to *A* for life, remainder to *A*'s heirs." The instrument of transfer

stated: "This disposition shall not be construed to give
A a fee simple title, but only a life estate in said
lands."

G's intent could hardly be stated more clearly, but
it is disregarded. Shelley's Rule applies, giving the
remainder to *A* rather than to *A*'s heirs. *A*'s interest
then becomes a fee simple absolute as a result of the
merger of *A*'s life estate and remainder. See Finley v.
Finley (Tex. Civ. App. 1958).

(h) Inter-Vivos and Testamentary Transfers. No
distinction is drawn between inter-vivos and testamentary transfers. The Rule in Shelley's Case applies
to both types of transfer, if the other requirements of
the rule are met.

§ 11.4. The Rule in Shelley's Case in Operation

(a) Shelley's Rule and the Doctrine of Merger.
Lord Coke's classic formulation of the Rule in Shelley's Case (see supra § 11.1) seemed to suggest that
the Rule causes the life tenant to receive either a fee
simple absolute (in the case of a remainder to the life
tenant's "heirs") or a fee tail (in the case of a
remainder to the "heirs of the life tenant's body"). As
the Rule evolved, however, it became settled that the
import of the Rule is much narrower: *The Rule
merely gives the remainder interest to the life tenant.*
If the life tenant ends up with a fee simple absolute
or a fee tail, it is because of the merger of the life
estate and remainder interest. See Restatement 2d of
Property § 30.1 cmt. k.

EXAMPLE 11-7. G transferred land "to A for life, remainder to A's heirs."

Shelley's Rule applies to give the remainder intended for A's heirs to A.

The doctrine of merger says that, once in the hands of a single individual, a life estate and a vested remainder in fee merge to become a fee simple absolute.

EXAMPLE 11-8. G transferred land "to A for life, remainder to the heirs of A's body."

Shelley's Rule applies to give the remainder intended for the heirs of A's body to A.

The doctrine of merger says that, once in the hands of a single individual, a life estate and a vested remainder in tail merge to become a fee tail. In states that have a fee tail statute, A's fee tail would then be changed into whatever estate or interests the statute directs.

(b) Application of Shelley's Rule Need Not Cause a Merger. Shelley's Rule can apply even when no instantaneous merger occurs. Whether a merger occurs or not depends on whether the independent requirements of the doctrine of merger are met. Basically, for interests to merge they must be vested and successive. See supra § 10.4(b).

EXAMPLE 11-9. G transferred land "to A for life, then to B for life, then to A's heirs."

Although Shelley's Rule applies to give the remainder interest to A, the intervening life estate created in B prevents A's two interests from merging while *B* is alive. Should *B* predecease *A*, *B*'s death would cause *A*'s life estate and remainder to merge and become a fee simple absolute. See Restatement 2d of Property § 30.1 cmt. *l*, illus. 17. Should *B* survive *A*, *B*'s remainder for life would become possessory, and upon *B*'s death the right to possession of the property would shift to whomever succeeded to *A*'s remainder interest.

EXAMPLE 11-10. *G* transferred land "to *A* for life, remainder to *B* if *B* survives *A*; if not, to *A*'s heirs."

The interest intended for *A*'s heirs is a remainder, not an executory interest. The Rule in Shelley's Case therefore gives the remainder to *A*, even though it is contingent on *B*'s failing to survive *A*. No merger would occur upon creation, however, because contingent interests do not merge. See Restatement 2d of Property § 30.1 cmt. o. Nevertheless, if *B* should die during *A*'s lifetime, *B*'s death would cause *A*'s life estate and remainder to merge then. If *B* should survive *A*, *A*'s remainder would be defeated, and *B* would take the property in fee simple absolute. See *id.*, illus. 22.

(c) Fractional Interests. A relatively small number of cases have arisen in which the ancestor's life estate and the remainder interest were of an undivided fraction of the whole. Little difficulty arises when the fractions correspond.

EXAMPLE 11-11. *G* transferred land "to *A* and *B* equally for their respective lives, and on the death of each, *A*'s half to *A*'s heirs and *B*'s half to *B*'s heirs."

The Rule in Shelley's Case and the doctrine of merger combine to give *A* and *B* each an undivided half of the fee, probably as tenants in common rather than as joint tenants. See Restatement 2d of Property § 30.1 cmt. r, illus. 27.

Even when the fractions do not correspond, little difficulty should arise if the smaller fraction applies to the remainder rather than to the life estate.

> *EXAMPLE 11-12*. *G* transferred land "to *A* for life, remainder in half to *B* and in the other half to the heirs of *A*."
>
> The Rule in Shelley's Case and the doctrine of merger combine to give *A* an undivided half in fee simple absolute; the other half is held by *A* for life, with the remainder in that half going to *B*.

When the smaller fraction applies to the life estate, there is confusion about the proper result.

> *EXAMPLE 11-13*. *G* transferred land "to *A* and *B* equally for life, *and on the death of the survivor,* to the heirs of *A*."
>
> This much is clear: The Rule in Shelley's Case and the doctrine of merger combine to give *A* an undivided half in fee simple absolute. Equally clear is this: *B* has a life estate in the other undivided half. What is unclear is whether the remainder interest in the other half is held by *A* or by *A*'s heirs. In other words, does Shelley's Rule operate on the whole of the remainder interest, or only on the half in which *A*'s life estate attaches?

The Restatement of Property § 312 cmt. r, supported by what scant case authority exists, essentially takes the following position on the question. Because the remainder interest is not to take effect in possession until the death of the survivor of *A* and *B* (rather than half on the death of *A* and half on the death of *B*), it is likely that the disposition would be construed as conferring on *A* and *B* a *cross remainder* for life in each other's half. If so, then *A* has a possessory life estate in half and a remainder for life in the other half. If *A* survives *B*, thus succeeding to a life estate in the whole, Shelley's Rule operates on the whole remainder, not merely on the half, and the doctrine of merger gives *A* a fee simple absolute in the whole.

An alternative construction is that *A* and *B* take the life estate in joint tenancy. If this construction is adopted, the Restatement states that Shelley's Rule operates on the remainder in the whole, not merely in the half, regardless of whether *A* survives *B*. After application of the doctrine of merger, *A* has a fee simple absolute in the whole, but subject to an undivided half interest for life in *B*. The Restatement's position is based on the idea that in theory each joint tenant is seized of the whole, and so *A*'s life estate is in the whole. Professor Simes disagreed with this analysis. Simes argued that Shelley's Rule should apply only to half of the remainder even when the life estates are construed to be held by *A* and *B* as joint tenants. See Simes on Future Interest 54; Simes & Smith on Future Interests § 1559; Am. L. Prop. § 4.50 (written by Simes). (It must be noted, though, that Simes apparently misread the Restatement, for he erroneously cited the Restatement as supporting his position on the question.)

EXAMPLE 11-14. G transferred land "to A and B equally for life, *and on the death of each,* the decedent's half to the heirs of A."

Here A has only a life estate in half, with no possibility of succeeding to a life estate in the whole by surviving B. It should therefore be clear that Shelley's Rule operates only on the half in which A's life estate attaches. The doctrine of merger then gives A a fee simple in that undivided half. The Rule in Shelley's Case does not apply to the other undivided half—the half in which B has a life estate. See Restatement of Property § 312 cmt. r, illus. 26.

(d) Post-Creation Application of the Rule. The Restatement 2d of Property § 30.1 cmt. p and the Restatement of Property § 312 cmt. q take the position that even if the requirements of Shelley's Rule are not met when the instrument of transfer takes effect, the Rule can nevertheless apply if the Rule's requirements are subsequently satisfied and if the subsequent satisfaction comes about automatically in accordance with the terms of the original transfer. Professor Simes's distaste for the Rule itself led him to a contrary conclusion; Simes argued that if the Rule is inapplicable at the outset, its intrusive reach should not be unnecessarily extended. See Simes & Smith on Future Interest § 1562; Am. L. Prop. § 4.49 (written by Simes).

The Restatement's position is supported by the scant authority that exists on the problem, and more importantly has a policy reason to commend it: It removes to a great extent the artificiality of the distinction between contingent remainders and executory interests, as illustrated by the following example.

> *EXAMPLE 11-15.* G transferred land "to A for life, remainder to B, but if B fails to survive A, to A's heirs." B subsequently died survived by A.
>
> Shelley's Rule does not apply at the time of the transfer because the future interest in A's heirs is an executory interest. But when B died, the future interest became a remainder. See supra Example 8-1. Under the Restatement's position, Shelley's Rule would then apply, converting the remainder intended for A's heirs into a remainder in A. The doctrine of merger would give A a fee simple absolute.
>
> Suppose we change the form *but not the substance* of the original transfer. Suppose it said: "to A for life, remainder to B if B survives A; if not, to A's heirs." Shelley's Rule would apply because the future interest in A's heirs was initially a remainder. No merger would occur to give A a fee simple absolute, though, unless and until B predeceases A.
>
> The bottom line is this. If Shelley's Rule can come into operation subsequently as well as initially, as the Restatement avows, then regardless of the *form* in which the disposition is stated, the result will be the same: If B survives A, B takes a fee simple absolute upon A's death; if B predeceases A, A takes a fee simple absolute upon B's death. Since the *substance* of the disposition is the same either way it is stated (see supra § 7.5), the courts would do well to make the

result be the same also.

Such an approach has another feature to commend it. By preventing the alternative form of stating the same disposition from being used by knowledgeable attorneys as a manipulative device for avoiding Shelley's Rule, it might hasten additional legislative abolition of the Rule.

§ 11.5.   The Present Status of the Rule in Shelley's Case

In England, Shelley's Rule was abolished in 1925 by the Law of Property Act. In this country, the Rule apparently continues in force in a small number of states. In most states and in the District of Columbia, the Rule has been abolished by statute.[3] ☺ The Restatement 2d of Property § 30.1(3) states that the Rule "should be abolished by judicial decision to the extent it has not been abolished prospectively by statute."

Statutes abolishing Shelley's Rule are usually not retroactive, and so do not apply to pre-effective date instruments. This means that in those states in which the abolitionary statute was not enacted before the early part of this century, the Rule may still be a force to reckon with, since the question of the Rule's applicability frequently arises on the life tenant's death. Furthermore, in a few states, the statutes apply only to dispositions by will. Some of the statutes that

---

[3] For a state-by-state compilation of abolishing statutes, see Restatement 2d of Property, Statutory Note to § 30.1.

appear to be designed to abolish the rule are
ambiguous and subject to restrictive constructions that
could leave the Rule to operate in certain cases. See
Powell on Real Property ¶ 380; Simes & Smith on
Future Interests §§ 1563-69; Annot., 99 A.L.R.2d
1161 (1965).

§ 11.6. The Rule in Shelley's Case as an Instrument of Social Policy

Like the destructibility rule, the Rule in Shelley's
Case can be viewed as an instrument of social policy:
It promotes the free alienability of land by giving the
life tenant a fee simple absolute. In the absence of a
rule like Shelley's Rule, the land in the standard
disposition of "to A for life, remainder to A's heirs"
would be unmarketable. It is true that in most states
now, A's heirs apparent would have a transferable
interest. See supra § 9.2. But even if A and A's heirs
apparent agree to join in a conveyance, their combined interests do not add up to a fee simple absolute.
(It might be noted that under the destructibility rule,
A could join—not with his or her heirs apparent—but
with the reversioner in effecting a transfer in fee
simple absolute in this case.)

Seen as an instrument that promotes the free
alienability of land, however, the Rule in Shelley's
Case operates in an even narrower range than the
destructibility rule. The destructibility rule applies to
all contingent remainders in land, whereas Shelley's
Rule only applies to contingent remainders in the
heirs or heirs of the body of the life tenant. Beyond

this point, Shelley's Rule suffers from the same defects as the destructibility rule. The defects, along with a better solution to the problem of inalienable land, are set forth supra § 10.6. Suffice it to say that the Rule in Shelley's Case cannot be justified as an instrument of social policy.

Chapter 12

THE DOCTRINE OF WORTHIER TITLE

§ 12.1. Statement of the Worthier Title Doctrine

As followed in the majority of American jurisdictions, the doctrine of worthier title provides:

> ☞ *When a transferor, by an inter-vivos conveyance, purports to create a future interest in the transferor's heirs, the transferor is presumed to intend to retain the future interest rather than confer it on his or her heirs.*

The doctrine is a rule of construction, not a rule of law, which implies that it is intent-effecting. It will, however, yield to a contrary intention in individual cases.

§ 12.2. Evolution of the Worthier Title Doctrine From a Rule of Law to a Rule of Construction

It was said at an early time that taking title by descent (intestacy) was "worthier" than taking by purchase (by inter-vivos conveyance or by will). No one is sure why this was so, but, like the Rule in

161

Shelley's Case, it was probably related to the incidents of feudal tenure: The feudal dues to the lord could be exacted only when land passed by descent on the owner's death. A statute enacted in 1267, in fact, provided that a conveyance from a tenant to the tenant's eldest son (the tenant's heir-apparent) was void as against the lord. See Moynihan on Real Property 151-52. The doctrine of worthier title emerged not long after this statute was enacted.

In its original form, the doctrine of worthier title was closely allied to the Rule in Shelley's Case. Like Shelley's Rule, it was a rule of law; that is, it would not yield to a contrary intention of the transferor, no matter how strongly expressed. Moreover, like Shelley's Rule, it applied only to interests in land. Because, after the Statute of Wills of 1540, land could be transferred by devise as well as by conveyance, the doctrine split into two branches. The *inter-vivos branch* provided that a transferor could not, by an inter-vivos transfer, create a future interest in the transferor's own heirs; an attempt to do so was a nullity. An inter-vivos transfer of land, for example, "to *A* for life, then to my heirs," was read as if it said "to *A* for life." Because the transferor had parted with only a life estate, the transferor retained a reversion. Thus, in early England, the property almost certainly passed by intestacy to the transferor's heirs on death. The testamentary branch of the doctrine provided that if a *devise* of land were made to an heir of the same interest the heir would have taken by descent had there been no devise, the heir would be regarded as taking by descent.

(a) Testamentary Branch. The feudal system never became part of American law or society. The testamentary branch of the doctrine was not primarily directed to the question of who is entitled to take the property on the transferor's death, though it did make a slight difference because of the old rule that descent was traced from the last person seized. The main focus of the testamentary branch was on the question of the capacity in which the transferor's heir took. Because the capacity in which heirs take, as purchasers or by descent, is no longer very important, and because the old rule tracing descent from the last person seized is all but abrogated, the testamentary branch of the doctrine would seldom make any difference in result in the United States. Principally for this reason, the Restatement 2d of Property § 30.2(2) and the Restatement of Property § 314(2) provide that it is not the law here. Recently, in unusual cases in which it would have made a difference in result, the highest courts of Alabama and Iowa held that the testamentary branch would not be followed. See City Nat'l Bank v. Andrews (Ala. 1978); Matter of Campbell (Iowa 1982); Matter of Estate of Kern (Iowa 1979). It may be assumed that courts in other jurisdictions would also reject the testamentary branch, but confident predictions are hazardous on such matters. See Restatement 2d of Property § 30.2, Reporter's Note 6. Kansas abolished the testamentary branch by statute. A number of other states and the UPC abolish both the inter-vivos

and testamentary branches by statute. See infra §
12.7. For further discussion of the testamentary
branch, see Joseph W. Morris, The Wills Branch of
the Worthier Title Doctrine, 54 Mich. L. Rev. 451
(1956).

(b) Inter-Vivos Branch. The inter-vivos branch is
another matter altogether. This branch of the doctrine
can make a considerable difference in result quite
apart from the incidents of feudal tenure. Although
this branch was originally concerned with the
capacity in which the transferor's heirs succeeded to
the property on the transferor's death, it is obvious
that if the doctrine applies the transferor has the right
later to decide to give the property to someone other
than his or her heirs. Even if the transferor does not
specifically transfer the reversion, the reversion
would be covered by the residuary clause in the
transferor's will.

Had the case of Doctor v. Hughes (N.Y. 1919) not
arisen when it did, perhaps the worthier title doctrine
would eventually have met the fate of the Rule in
Shelley's Case and the destructibility rule: substantial
statutory abolition. But when Doctor v. Hughes came
to be decided by the New York Court of Appeals,
Judge Cardozo seized the opportunity to adjudge the
doctrine's future course. The grantor had conveyed
real property to a trustee, in trust, to pay the grantor
an annuity of $1500 for life, and upon his death, the
corpus of the trust was to go to the grantor's "heirs
at law." During the grantor's lifetime, judgment
creditors of the grantor's daughter sought to reach

her interest in the trust, arguing that she (as one of his heirs-apparent) had a property interest in the trust property. Judge Cardozo rejected their claim on the ground that the grantor's purported gift to his heirs at law amounted to the reservation of a reversion in himself, and so his daughter had nothing upon which her judgment creditors could execute. This result could have been reached by applying the rule-of-law version of the inter-vivos branch of the worthier title doctrine. But Judge Cardozo was disinclined to decide the case on such a traditional ground. Noting that the doctrine was a rule of law in England and that it had been abolished there by statute in 1833, Judge Cardozo wrote:

But in the absence of modifying statute, the rule persists to-day, at least as a rule of construction, if not as one of [law]. . . . We do not say that the ancient rule survives as an absolute prohibition limiting the power of a grantor. . . There may be times, therefore, when a reference to the heirs of the grantor will be regarded as the gift of a remainder, and will vest title in the heirs presumptive as upon a gift to the heirs of others. . . But at least the ancient rule survives to this extent, that to transform into a remainder what would ordinarily be a reversion, the intention to work the transformation must be clearly expressed. [Finding no such clear expression, he concluded:] No one is heir to the living; and seldom do the living mean to forego the power of disposition during life by the direction that upon death there shall be a transfer to their heirs. This grant . . . was . . . subject to destruction, as against the heirs at law, at the will of the grantor. They had an expectancy, but no estate.

From this time forward, the courts in New York and many other states viewed the inter-vivos branch of the worthier title doctrine as merely a rule of construction. The Restatement 2d of Property § 30.2(1) and the Restatement of Property § 314(1) also take this position. In only a very few jurisdictions is it still followed as a rule of law. Conversely, about twenty percent of the states (including New York) have abolished the doctrine altogether, mostly as the result of legislative action in fairly recent years. Section 2-710 of the UPC abolishes the doctrine as a rule of law and as a rule of construction. See infra § 12.7.

§ 12.3. Consequences of the Shift From a Rule of Law to a Rule of Construction

In shifting the inter-vivos branch of the doctrine to a rule of construction, Judge Cardozo may have desired to soften the old rule of law by allowing it to yield to the grantor's contrary intention. But shifting a rule of law to a rule of construction is not a natural evolutionary step in legal development. Rules of law and rules of construction are based on entirely different premises. Rules of law are intent-defeating; rules of construction are intent-effecting. Defeating intention is only justified to vindicate goals of sound public policy; the proper function of rules of law is therefore to prohibit individual choices that are deemed to be unduly harmful to society as a whole. Rules of construction, on the other hand, operate in areas in which society as a whole is indifferent to the result. The only public policy goal that rules of construction vindicate is giving effect to private intention in areas of societal indifference. Rules of construction seek to facilitate this intent-effecting goal by providing a presumptive meaning—one designed to accord with common intention—to words that have failed to express the actual intention of the parties clearly.

When the policy reasons that underlie a rule of law disappear, as they have with respect to the worthier title doctrine, the normal course is for the legislature to repeal the rule (as the English legislature did in 1833) or for the courts to abrogate it or at least to nibble away at its scope until it eventually ceases to operate. The shifting of the worthier title doctrine from a rule of law to one of construction is therefore not a normal step in the evolutionary process of law. It has done more harm than good.

(a) As a Rule of Construction, the Doctrine Makes Little Sense. Judge Cardozo's statement that "[n]o one is heir to the living; and seldom do the living mean to forego the power of disposition during life by the direction that upon death there shall be a transfer to their heirs" is an ingenious attempt to justify worthier title as a rule of construction. But

consider the content of this rule of construction: It declares that when a grantor says "then to my heirs" the grantor is presumed to have meant "reversion in myself;" the presumption is rebutted, though, if the grantor says "then to my heirs and I really mean it." This turns language on its head. Instead of taking unclear language and presumptively attributing common meaning to it (the normal function of a rule of construction), it takes clear language and presumptively attributes abnormal meaning to it.

(b) Expansion of the Doctrine's Scope. The shift to a rule of construction expanded rather than contracted the scope of the doctrine. Because of its feudal origins, the old rule applied only to land. As a rule of construction, there is no basis for so limiting it, and it now applies to both land and personalty. This is very important, since most modern future interests are created in trusts of personal property. Moreover, as a rule of construction rather than a rule of law, the doctrine is not restricted to remainders; it also applies to executory interests.

(c) Unpredictability of Result. As a rule of construction, the doctrine invites litigation and promotes unpredictability. This might not have occurred to the degree it did in New York and elsewhere had the courts insisted on adhering to Judge Cardozo's statement that the doctrine could be rebutted only by a clear expression of a contrary intent. But cases after Doctor v. Hughes reduced the presumption to a regular one under which the contrary intent can be

shown from the instrument as a whole or even from surrounding circumstances. See infra § 12.5.

§ 12.4. Interests Subject to the Worthier Title Doctrine

(a) Remainders and Executory Interests, Legal or Equitable, in Real or Personal Property. As noted supra § 12.3(b), the doctrine of worthier title as a rule of construction applies to all manner of future interests, remainders and executory interests in land or personalty. The doctrine also applies to equitable as well as legal interests. There is no requirement that the preceding interest and the future interest be of the same quality. Nor is there a requirement that the preceding interest be a freehold: Commonly it is a life estate, but it can be a term of years, a fee tail, or a defeasible fee simple.

(b) Inter-vivos Transfers Only. As noted supra § 12.2, the testamentary branch of the doctrine is probably defunct. The inter-vivos branch, which we are discussing, applies only to inter-vivos transfers.

(c) Future Interests Purportedly Created in the Grantor's Heirs or Next of Kin. For the worthier title doctrine to apply, the future interest must purportedly be created in those persons who would succeed by intestate succession to the grantor's property if the grantor died intestate: that is, the grantor's actual heirs with respect to land; the grantor's next of kin (sometimes called "distributees") with respect to personal property. The divergent concept of heirs as comprising an indefinite line of succession (see supra

§ 11.3(c)) does not appear to have crept into the worthier title doctrine. Thus the definite line of succession concept is the exclusive criterion for determining whether the future interest gives rise to the worthier title presumption. For example, it is usually held that if the heirs are to be determined at any time other than at the grantor's death, the presumption does not arise because the intended takers are not those who would take on intestacy. A future interest in the grantor's "children" or "descendants" does not trigger the worthier title doctrine, regardless of whether the grantor's children or descendants actually turn out to be his or her heirs at death.

§ 12.5.   Rebutting the Presumption

In exploring how the presumption is rebutted, keep in mind that we are talking about a confusing matter. To rebut the presumption, it must be established that the grantor really meant what he or she clearly said: "then to my heirs."

(a) Planning: Drafting A Clear Expression of a Contrary Intent. Future interests in the heirs of the grantor are rather commonly created, although they are seldom the principal or primary future interest. After the settlor of an inter-vivos trust has designated his or her first or second choices to take the corpus upon the trust's termination, the settlor might designate his or her heirs as the backstop takers just in case none of the first or second choices can take.

Regardless of the priority, it is virtually out of the question that any attorney-drawn trust would purport to create a future interest in the grantor's heirs when a reversion was actually intended. To avoid litigation, and to rebut the presumption, the attorney should expressly add to the term "heirs" a phrase such as *"such persons to take as purchasers, my intention being to create a remainder interest in my heirs at law; I do not intend to retain a reversion in myself."* It should also be noted that drafting a future interest to anyone's heirs, not just the grantor's heirs, is a tricky business. The UPC has a statutory rule of construction that resolves most of the problems. See UPC § 2-711.

(b) No Clear Expression of a Contrary Intent. Judge Cardozo's statement notwithstanding, subsequent decisions have settled the point that the presumption can be rebutted even in the absence of a clear expression of a contrary intention. Indeed, one New York case stated that "the presumption which exists from the use of the common-law doctrine as a rule of construction has lost much of its force since Doctor v. Hughes . . . Evidence of intent need not be overwhelming in order to allow the remainder to stand." See Matter of Burchell (N.Y. 1949).

What evidence of contrary intent, short of a clear expression, has been found to rebut the presumption? The presumption is usually rebutted if the grantor reserves a power of appointment over the future interest, so that the future interest created in the grantor's heirs is in the form of a gift-in-default of appointment; the theory is that if the grantor thought he or she had a reversion, the grantor would not have needed a power of appointment. Another ground for holding the presumption rebutted is the complexity and completeness of the disposition of corpus on the grantor's death. As noted in (*a*) above, the future interest in the grantor's heirs seldom comes first in order of priority, but rather comes second or third. There is some indication in the cases that this type of scheme might alone counter the presumption on the theory that such complexity and completeness shows that the grantor gave the matter more than casual thought, and meant what he or she said. Beyond these points, there are several factors unique to individual cases that have rebutted the presumption, but many of the cases are difficult and probably impossible to reconcile. The result in a given case can be quite unpredictable. For further discussion, see Powell on Real Property ¶ 381; Simes & Smith on Future Interests § 1611; Restatement 2d of Property § 30.2 cmt. a; Restatement of Property § 314 cmt. e.

§ 12.6.   The   Worthier   Title   Doctrine   in Operation

(*a*) *General Consequences of Applying the Doctrine*. If the presumption is not rebutted, and the worthier title doctrine applies, the grantor owns the reversionary interest. This reversionary interest need not be a reversion, though it usually is. Because the worthier title doctrine applies to executory interests as well as remainders, and because the prior estate can be a defeasible fee simple (§ 12.4(a)), the grantor's reversionary interest can be a possibility of reverter. For example, suppose *G* conveys land "to *A* and his heirs so long as *A* never allows liquor to be sold on the land, and upon *A*'s allowing liquor to be sold on the land, the land goes to my (*G*'s) heirs." The executory interest purportedly granted *G*'s heirs presumptively becomes a possibility of reverter in *G*.

Whatever the exact nature of the grantor's reversionary interest, several further consequences are obvious. During the grantor's lifetime, the grantor owns the reversionary interest; the grantor's heirs-apparent have no interest, only an expectancy. Accordingly, the grantor (not the grantor's heirs-apparent) has an alienable interest, and the grantor's creditors (not the creditors of any of the grantor's heirs-apparent) can subject the reversionary interest to the payment of their claims. Further, if the grantor dies still owning the interest, it passes by will to the grantor's devisees (usually under the grantor's residuary clause) rather than to the grantor's heirs; it passes to the grantor's heirs only if the grantor dies intestate.

(b) Trust Termination. The worthier title doctrine enables the grantor of an inter-vivos trust to revoke the trust and get the property back even when the grantor did not retain a power to revoke in the trust instrument. Under trust law, a trust can be terminated prematurely, and the trust property distributed to the beneficiaries, if the grantor and all possible beneficiaries join in a petition so requesting. See Restatement 2d of Trusts § 338.

EXAMPLE 12-1. *G* conveyed property to a trustee, in trust, directing the trustee to pay the income to *G* for life, and on *G*'s death to pay the corpus of the trust to *G*'s heirs. The trust instrument did not empower *G* to revoke the trust. Some time after the trust was created, *G* changes her mind and wants the trust property returned. *G*'s child *A* is at that time *G*'s heir-apparent.

If *G*'s trust created a remainder in her heirs, the trust cannot be terminated. Even if *A* joins in *G*'s petition, *A* does not own the full remainder interest. See supra § 9.2. Consequently, *G* and *A* are not the only possible beneficiaries of the trust. Because *G*'s actual heirs are as yet unascertained, and potentially include persons as yet unborn, there is no way to obtain the consent of all possible beneficiaries of the trust.

If, however, the doctrine of worthier title applies, *G* can terminate the trust. She is the sole beneficiary, owning both the income interest for life and the reversion that follows it.

Three of the jurisdictions that have abrogated the worthier title doctrine have nevertheless granted relief to grantors like *G*. New York enacted a statute that provides that, *for trust termination purposes only,* *G*'s heirs have no beneficial interest. N.Y. Est. Powers & Trusts Law § 7-1.9. By court decision in the District of Columbia and by statute in California, a guardian ad litem can consent to the trust's premature termination on behalf of the grantor's unascertained heirs. See Hatch v. Riggs Nat'l Bank (D.C. Cir.

1966); Cal. Prob. Code § 15405. A difference between these solutions should be noted. Under the worthier title doctrine and under the New York statute, *G* is entitled to regain full ownership of the entire trust corpus. Under the guardian ad litem method, the whole corpus is not necessarily returned to *G*; part of it (presumably an amount approximating the actuarial value of the remainder interest) may be held aside for future distribution to *G*'s actual heirs upon her death.

Still another solution to the trust termination problem might be noted. Legislation in some states makes *all* inter-vivos trusts revocable unless the trust expressly states otherwise. This reverses the usual rule that all inter-vivos transfers, including those in trust, are irrevocable unless expressly made revocable. Legislation like this operates in a much broader range than the worthier title doctrine, the New York legislation, or the guardian ad litem method.

(c) Federal Estate Tax Consequences. Application of the worthier title doctrine can cause unexpected estate tax consequences. First, if the grantor's reversion is not divested upon the grantor's death, its value is includible in his or her gross estate under I.R.C. § 2033. Secondly, even if the reversion is divested upon the grantor's death, the doctrine might bring into his or her gross estate the value of the interest of a transferee who can obtain personal possession or enjoyment of the property only by surviving the grantor; this amount could equal the

value of the entire corpus. This would arise under I.R.C. § 2037 when the value of the reversion immediately before the grantor's death exceeds 5 per cent of the value of the corpus if, in addition, certain other requirements are met. Of course, in many of the cases in which the doctrine of worthier title has been applied the value of the entire corpus would be includible anyway under I.R.C. § 2036, because the grantor retained an income interest for life. See generally Stanley M. Johanson, Reversions, Remainders, and the Doctrine of Worthier Title, 45 Tex. L. Rev. 1, 16-27 (1966).

§ 12.7. Present Status of the Worthier Title Doctrine

The inter-vivos branch of the doctrine of worthier title is presumptively part of the jurisprudence of most jurisdictions as a rule of construction, though there is no strong authority one way or the other in many of these states. See Restatement 2d of Property § 30.2, Reporter's Note 3. In a few jurisdictions, older cases exist applying the inter-vivos branch as a rule of law. See *id.*, Reporter's Note 4. Whether these decisions would be followed today is problematical.

The doctrine was abolished in England in 1833. The doctrine is abolished by statute in Arkansas,

California, Illinois,[1] Massachusetts, Minnesota, Nebraska, New York, North Carolina, Tennessee, Texas, and West Virginia. Statutes in a few other states provide that "heirs" means children (e.g., Ga. Code § 44-6-23). See Restatement 2d of Property § 30.2, Statutory Notes 1 & 5.

The doctrine was abrogated by judicial decision in the District of Columbia. See Hatch v. Riggs Nat'l Bank (D.C. Cir. 1966). Astonishingly, the recently promulgated Restatement 2d of Property states that the doctrine continues as a rule of construction. ☹ See Restatement 2d of Property § 30.2(1). This prompted the drafters of the UPC to insert a section abrogating the doctrine. ☺ See UPC § 2-710.

§ 12.8. The Worthier Title Doctrine as an Instrument of Social Policy

Like the destructibility rule and the Rule in Shelley's Case, the worthier title doctrine can be viewed as an instrument of social policy: It promotes alienability by untying the fetters purportedly imposed on the property by the grantor's earlier disposition. If the original conveyance was of a legal interest in

---

[1] But see Stewart v. Merchants Nat'l Bank (Ill. App. Ct. 1972), where the court seems to have held that the statute only abrogates the doctrine as a rule of law, but not as a rule of construction. A subsequent decision of the Illinois Supreme Court, however, referred to Illinois's "1955 statutory abolition of the doctrine." See Harris Trust & Savings Bank v. Beach (Ill. 1987).

land, the doctrine enables the grantor subsequently to transfer a fee simple absolute estate. If the original conveyance was in trust, the doctrine enables the grantor to revoke the trust, freeing the grantor to transfer the trust property in fee simple absolute.

Seen as an instrument that promotes alienability of property, however, the worthier title doctrine operates in a very narrow range and its benefits are dwarfed in comparison to its costs. The court in Hatch v. Riggs Nat'l Bank (D.C. Cir. 1966), in refusing to recognize the worthier title doctrine while at the same time having sympathy enough with the trust termination problem to fashion an alternative solution to it, said it as well as any:

> We see no reason to plunge the District of Columbia into the ranks of those jurisdictions bogged in the morass of exploring, under the modern doctrine of worthier title, "the almost ephemeral qualities which go to prove the necessary intent." The alleged benefit of effectuating intent must be balanced against the resulting volume of litigation and the diversity and difficulty of decision. We are not persuaded that the policy of upholding the intention of creators of trusts is best effectuated by such a rule of construction, with its accompanying uncertainty.

Perhaps modern courts will view Hatch v. Riggs Nat'l Bank as just as persuasive as earlier courts viewed Doctor v. Hughes. If so, there is hope for the doctrine's demise even without abrogating legislation, at least in those jurisdictions that, like the District of Columbia, have no strong precedents previously accepting the doctrine.

§ 12.9.   Summary Comparison of the Basic Requirements of the Destructibility Rule, the Rule in Shelley's Case, and the Doctrine of Worthier Title

A table comparing the three feudally-based rules should provide a helpful summary at this point.

Destructibility Rule	*Rule in Shelley's Case*	*Inter-vivos Worthier Title*
A legal contingent remainder in land is destroyed if it has not vested by the time of the termination of the preceding freehold estate	A remainder in land that is purportedly created in the life tenant's heirs or the heirs of the life tenant's body, and that is of the same quality as that of the life estate, is held by the life tenant	When a transferor, by an inter-vivos conveyance, purports to create a future interest in the transferor's own heirs, the transferor is presumed to intend to retain a reversionary interest
Feudal basis: livery of seisin	Feudal basis: forcing land to pass by descent rather than by purchase	Feudal basis: forcing land to pass by descent rather than by purchase

Destructibility Rule	*Rule in Shelley's Case*	*Inter-vivos Worthier Title*
Rule of law	Rule of law	Rule of construction by majority view
Merger is one way of causing destructibility; merger, if it takes place, precedes the application of the Rule	Merger, if it takes place, and it usually does, applies after the operation of the Rule, not before	Merger is not relevant
Inter-vivos and testamentary transfers	Inter-vivos and testamentary transfers	Inter-vivos transfers only
Only to land	Only to land	Land and personalty
Applicable only to remainders	Only to remainders	Remainders and executory interests
Applicable only to legal contingent remainders	Applicable to legal and equitable remainders, but the remainder and the preceding estate must be of the same quality	No similar requirements; applicable to equitable as well as legal future interests; can be of different quality from prior estate

Destructibility Rule	*Rule in Shelley's Case*	*Inter-vivos Worthier Title*
Identity of the remainderperson irrelevant so long as remainder is contingent (preceding estate must be a freehold)	Remainder must purportedly be created in the heirs or heirs of the body of the ancestor who is given the preceding freehold estate	Remainder must purportedly be created in the heirs of the transferor if land, the next of kin of the transferor if personalty
Abolished in over half the states. Statutory abolition is commonly not retroactive; crucial date is when the prior freehold terminated.	Abolished in over three-fourths of the states. Statutory abolition is commonly not retroactive; crucial date is effective date of deed or death of testator.	Abolished in only a few states. Statutory abolition is commonly not retroactive. Crucial date is effective date of deed.

Chapter 13

THE RULE AGAINST PERPETUITIES

The remainder of the book—consisting of four chapters—is devoted to the Rule Against Perpetuities. Under modern law, the most important consequence of classification concerns the Rule Against Perpetuities (the Rule). Classifying the future interests in a disposition sorts out which interests, if any, are subject to the Rule.

The present chapter explains the common-law Rule Against Perpetuities (common-law Rule). Although the common-law Rule is the principal focus of many first-year Property courses, the common-law Rule is a minority rule in the United States today. ☺ More than half the states have reformed the common-law Rule in one way or another and, as of this writing, forty percent of the states have enacted the Uniform Statutory Rule Against Perpetuities (1986) (Uniform Rule).[1] Chapter 14 explains the various reform

[1] Throughout this chapter, footnotes identify jurisdictions that have replaced the common-law Rule with the Uniform Rule subsequent to the decision cited in text.

measures, with special emphasis on the Uniform Rule. The final three chapters, Chapters 15, 16, and 17, explain how the common-law Rule and the Uniform Rule apply to special areas—class gifts, powers of appointment, charitable gifts, and commercial transactions.

§ 13.1.   Statement of the Common-Law Rule

As formulated by Professor John Chipman Gray, the common-law Rule provides:

> ☞ *No [nonvested property] interest is [valid] unless it MUST vest, if at all, not later than twenty-one years after some life in being at the creation of the interest.*

Gray on Perpetuities § 201.

No single-sentence formulation of so complex a body of law as perpetuities law could be entirely complete and accurate. Gray's formulation is no exception. Nevertheless, Gray's formulation is considered to be the classic statement of the common-law Rule, and it provides a good starting point for analysis. We will have to fill a few gaps and add some qualifications before we are through.

The first step in considering the validity of an interest is to determine whether the interest is subject to the Rule. Only an interest that is subject to the Rule can violate it.

§ 13.2.   Interests Subject to the Rule

(a) Future Interests in Property. The sole concern of the common-law Rule is whether a future interest in *property* is certain to vest or fail to vest (terminate) within the time allowed (the perpetuity period). If a transaction creates a future interest in property, it makes no difference whether the interest is legal or equitable; nor does it make any difference whether the subject matter is land or personalty: The Rule potentially applies.

Legal relationships that do not create future interests in property are not subject to the Rule. Thus contracts—even long-term contracts—are generally exempt. For example, optional modes of settlement for the payment of life-insurance proceeds and annuity contracts are exempt, even though future payments may be subject to uncertainties that might not be resolved within the perpetuity period. See Holmes v. John Hancock Mutual Life Ins. Co. (N.Y. 1942); Doyle v. Massachusetts Mutual Life Ins. Co. (6th Cir. 1967).

(b) Contingent Remainders and Executory Interests. The types of future interests in property to which the Rule applies are contingent remainders and executory interests. The Rule does not apply to reversions (because they are always vested), vested remainders (whether or not subject to defeasance), possibilities of reverter, or rights of entry.

(c) The Special Case of Class Gifts. Class gifts are subject to the Rule, and are treated specially. The early English decision of Leake v. Robinson (Ch.

1817) established the following rule for class gifts:

> ☞ *If the interest of* ANY *potential class member* MIGHT *vest beyond a life in being plus 21 years, the* ENTIRE *class gift is invalid.*

The rule of *Leake* is called the "all or nothing" rule. Under this rule, a class gift is either *completely* valid or *completely* invalid. The "all or nothing" rule does not allow the interest of each class member to be treated separately. The rule makes it impossible for some class members to have valid interests if other class members have invalid interests.

The interests of unborn (or unadopted) class members are subject to the Rule because they are executory interests that are contingent on birth (or adoption). See supra § 7.3. If the interests of living class members are vested subject to open, the "all or nothing" rule subjects their interests to the Rule and renders them invalid if the interests of other class members are invalid. This is an area, therefore, that we must explore more fully later on. See infra § 15.2. In this chapter, we will accept the "all or nothing" rule without questioning its justification.

§ 13.3.   The "Perpetuity Period"

The common-law perpetuity period is the period of time produced by the lifetime of a person in being at the creation of the interest plus 21 years. In common usage, the period is described in short-hand form as a "life in being plus 21 years." The period can be extended by one or more periods of gestation, *but only when an actual pregnancy makes the extension necessary*. In other words, the period of gestation is not automatically part of the perpetuity period in all cases. See Cadell v. Palmer (H.L. 1883).

(a) The Life-in-Being Part of the Period. The person who serves as the life in being is traditionally called the *measuring life*. The measuring life must be a person who was "in being" at the creation of the interest. This means that the measuring life must have been alive or in gestation when the interest was created. The measuring life must also be a human being. A corporation, plant, or animal cannot be used. See Simes & Smith on Future Interests § 1223.

There are no additional restrictions. Theoretically, any human being in the world who was alive or in gestation when the interest was created can be the measuring life. As a practical matter, though, it is not this simple, as we shall see infra § 13.5, when we address the problem of searching for a measuring life in actual cases.

(b) The 21-Year Part of the Period. Although the 21-year part of the perpetuity period is described by Gray as coming *after* the death of the measuring life, and it is often referred to as the *tack-on* 21-year period, the 21-year part of the period need not be preceded by a measuring life. It can stand on its own. Thus a testamentary transfer "to my grandchildren who are living 21 years after my death" would be valid.

Although only sparse authority exists on the question, it seems to be agreed that the 21-year part cannot come first, followed by a life that is in being 21 years *after* the creation of the interest. The measuring life must be in being *at* the creation of the interest. To give an example, suppose a testator devises property in trust "to pay the income to the testator's children for 21 years, then to pay the income to the testator's then-living grandchildren for life, and on the death of the survivor of those grandchildren, to pay the corpus of the trust to the testator's descendants then-living by representation." If the testator is survived by one or more children, the remainder interest in the corpus of the trust violates the common-law Rule and is invalid.

It may appear that invalidating the remainder interest is proper in policy because the testator seems to be attempting to manipulate the situation to measure the length of the trust by the lives of very young persons, thus elongating the period more than should be allowed. This is not the case, however, for a testator can select very young persons as the measuring lives anyway, so long as they are alive at death, and can tack on a 21-year period at the end. See infra § 13.16. Thus the testator's scheme is not one of improper manipulation, and might have been utilized for a valid family purpose—to avoid disinheriting any grandchildren.

(c) The Period of Gestation. As noted above, a child in gestation when the interest was created can be a measuring life because the child is considered

then to be "in being." The perpetuity period can also be expanded at its ending point to account for an actual period of gestation, if necessary. See infra Example *13-1*.

§ 13.4.   The Requirement of Initial Certainty

(a) The Meaning of "Must Vest If At All." The common-law Rule does not (and could not) require a guarantee that an interest will vest within the perpetuity period. What the Rule requires, to use Gray's terminology, is that the interest, when created, must be guaranteed to vest *if at all* within the perpetuity period. The phrase "if at all" means that the contingencies must be guaranteed to be finally resolved within the perpetuity period. Thus the Rule prohibits interests that might *remain* contingent beyond the perpetuity period. Conversely, the Rule validates interests that must vest or terminate within the perpetuity period.

(b) Statement of the Requirement of Initial Certainty. The common-law Rule is, in reality, a rule that requires initial certainty. Reformulated in terms of the requirement of initial certainty, the common-law Rule states:

☞ *In order for a contingent remainder or an executory interest to be valid, there CANNOT be ANY possible chain of post-creation events that would permit the interest to remain nonvested beyond a life in being plus 21 years.*

(c) A Person Qualifies as the "Measuring" Life Only if that Person Validates the Interest. The term "measuring life" is misleading. It suggests that the law "measures" a "perpetuity period" for each case. It suggests a two-step procedure: (1) identify a particular person as *the* life in being in each case; (2) then test the interest to see if it might remain nonvested beyond 21 years after that person's death.

This is not the procedure, however. The common law does *not* measure a perpetuity period for each case. No person qualifies as the "measuring life" unless that person *validates* the interest. Thus:

☞ *Valid interests have a "measuring life."*

☞ *Invalid interests have no "measuring life."*

Invalid interests fail because there is no measuring life to make them valid—not because they might remain nonvested beyond 21 years after the death of an identified person.

The search for a "measuring life" is therefore a search for a *validating life*. In the interest of clarity of thought, this book—from here on—uses the term "validating life" when referring to the common-law measuring life.

(d) There is No "Perpetuity Period" at Common Law. To get at the above points from a slightly different angle, note that the common-law Rule tests the validity of an interest as of the point of its creation. Testing the validity of an interest as of the

point of its creation means that validity turns on a projection regarding the various times in the future when the interest *might* vest or terminate. Validity at common law does not depend on when in the future the interest *does* vest or terminate. Consequently, the common law has no need to measure off a "perpetuity period." A perpetuity period would only be necessary if validity turned on the timing of *actual* vesting or termination.

For interests for which there is *no* validating life, there is no need to measure off a perpetuity period because the interest is invalid no matter what happens; such an interest is given no chance to become valid by vesting within a certain period of time.

Even for interests for which there *is* a validating life, there is no need to keep track of that person to see when he or she dies. The time of that person's death is immaterial because, by definition, the interest cannot possibly vest or terminate beyond 21 years after that person's death. That person's longevity does not matter. For valid interests, in other words, the common law uses the life-in-being-plus-21-years "period" in a way that does not require measuring off an actual period of time by tracing the lifespan of the so-called "measuring (validating) life."

§ 13.5.   How to Search for a Validating Life

(a) Goal of the Search: To Find One Person For Whom There Is No Invalidating Chain of Possible Post-Creation Events. The Official Comment to § 1

of the Uniform Rule sets forth the following guidance
for solving common-law perpetuities problems:

> The process for determining whether a
> validating life exists is to postulate the death of
> each individual connected in some way to the
> transaction, and ask the question: Is there with
> respect to this individual an invalidating chain of
> possible [post-creation] events? If one individual
> can be found for whom the answer is No, that
> individual can serve as the validating life. As to
> that individual there will be the requisite causal
> connection between his or her death and the
> questioned interest's vesting or terminating no
> later than 21 years thereafter.

Note that the converse is also true: If no person can
be found for whom there is no invalidating chain of
possible post-creation events, there is no validating
life; an interest for which there is no validating life is
invalid. Note one other point: You only need to
identify one invalidating chain of possible post-
creation events to disqualify a candidate from being
a validating life. There may, in fact, be several
invalidating chains of events that would disqualify
that candidate, but you need not identify them all.
One is enough.

(b) Only Insiders Need to be Considered. In
searching for a validating life, there is no formal rule
forbidding the testing of anyone in the world to see
if he or she has the causal connection demanded by

the requirement of initial certainty. There is, for example, no law against testing your favorite movie star or rock star in each case, if you want to do that. But experience has shown that no outsider will pass the test.

You can, therefore, safely limit the persons you test to insiders—those who are connected in some way to the transaction. Only insiders have a chance of supplying the causal connection demanded by the requirement of initial certainty. The insiders to be tested vary from situation to situation, but would always include the transferor, if living, the beneficiaries of the disposition, including but not restricted to the taker or takers of the challenged interest, the objects and donee of a power of appointment, persons related to the foregoing by blood or adoption, especially in the ascending and descending lines, and anyone else who has any connection to the transaction. If there is any doubt about whether a particular person is an insider, no harm is done by subjecting that person to the test. Usually it takes no more than an instant to determine whether a person on the fringe of the transaction validates the interest.

There is, however, no point in testing complete outsiders—persons selected at random from the world at large who are clearly unconnected to the transaction—just because the outsider happened to be in being at the creation of the interest. No outsider can possibly be the validating life because there will always be a chain of possible post-creation events that will disqualify every outsider who might be proposed. By definition, no outsider's time of death can have any effect on vesting.

> **EXAMPLE 13-1.** *G* devised land "to my son *A* for life, remainder to *A*'s children who live to age 21."
> The interest in question is the contingent remainder in *A*'s children. To determine whether that interest is valid, you must test the insiders in this transaction to see if any one of them satisfies the requirement of initial certainty. If there is any such person, that person is the validating life and the interest is valid.
> Because only insiders need to be tested, the obvious candidate to test first is *A*. *A* satisfies the requirement of initial certainty because no possible chain of post-creation events disqualifies him. None of his children can reach 21 (or die under 21) beyond 21 years after his death. Because *A* satisfies the test, and is a validating life, there is no need to test any of the other insiders, such as *A*'s wife[2] or any of *A*'s children who

---

[2] The facts of the example do not indicate whether *A* was married at *G's* death. If he was, his current wife would not satisfy the requirement of initial certainty. An invalidating chain of possible post-creation events that disqualifies her is that she might die immediately after *G's* death and that *A* might then have a child (by another women) who would reach 21 or die under 21 more than 21 years after the death of *A*'s current wife. Note also that the mother of *A*'s new child cannot serve as the validating life either because she might be born after *G's* death. See infra § 13.15.

were alive or in gestation at *G*'s death.[3]

But what about the possibility that *A*'s wife will be pregnant when *A* dies? Does this possibility not disqualify *A*? At *G*'s death, we do not know whether this will happen or not, but we do know that it might happen. Were it to happen, the child obviously could not reach 21 within 21 years after *A*'s death. The common law does not allow this possibility to be disqualifying, however. The common law provides that, *if this were to happen*, the "perpetuity period" would be extended to include *the period of gestation of A's child*. See supra § 13.3(c).[4]

What about another possibility, the possibility that *A*'s wife will become pregnant from artificial insemination of *A*'s sperm *after A*'s death? The added period of gestation does not solve this problem, for sperm and ova banks make it possible for men and women to have "post-death" children. So far, no case has addressed that question, but the common law will almost certainly not allow this possibility to be

[3] The facts of the example do not indicate whether *A* had any children who were alive or in gestation at *G*'s death. If he did, none of them would satisfy the requirement of initial certainty. A chain of possible post-creation events that disqualifies them is that all of them could die immediately after *G*'s death and *A* could later have other children who could reach 21 more than 21 years later.

[4] Recall, however, that a period of gestation is not an automatic part of the perpetuity period. Thus if *G*'s devise had been "to *A* for life, remainder to such of *A*'s children as are living 21 years and 9 months after *A*'s death," the remainder would have been invalid.

disqualifying either. See Am. L. Prop. § 24.22 (Supp. 1977) (suggesting that the "lifetime" of the validating life should be extended to include any period of post-death reproductive capability); 3 Restatement 2d of Property, intro. note to ch. 26, at 131 (arguing that post-death children are presumptively excluded from class gifts "because of the practical considerations of providing assurance for an indefinite period of time that a share in the class gift will be available for such after-born persons."). Section 1(d) of the Uniform Rule takes care of the problem (and the more conventional problem of A's wife being pregnant when A dies) by providing that, for perpetuity purposes, "the possibility that a child will be born to an individual after the individual's death is disregarded." The Uniform Rule takes no position on whether post-death children are presumptively included in or excluded from class gifts.

In Example *13-1*, A happened to be a devisee, but he is not the validating life for that reason.

EXAMPLE *13-2*. G devised land "to my daughter B for life, remainder to A's children who live to age 21."

The obvious insiders to test first in this case are A and B. Although B is the life tenant, she does not satisfy the requirement of initial certainty. A chain of possible post-creation events that disqualifies her is that A might have a child who reaches 21 (or dies under 21) more than 21 years after her death. A does satisfy the requirement of initial certainty, however, even though he is not a devisee. As explained supra

> Example *13-1*, he is the validating life and the interest
> is valid because the law assumes that his death
> terminates the possibility that he will have additional
> children.

The validating life not only need not be a devisee;
he or she need not even be mentioned in the
instrument. See infra Example *13-3*.

(c) Survivor of Group. The validating life need not
be narrowed down to one individual, but can be a
later-to-be-determined member of a group of
individuals. It is common in these cases to say that
the members of the group are the validating live*s*.
This is acceptable, as long as it is recognized that the
true meaning of the plural is singular, i.e., that the
validating life is the life of the member of the group
who turns out to live the longest. As the court said in
Skatterwood v. Edge (K.B. 1697), "for let the lives
be never so many, there must be a survivor, and so
it is but the length of that life . . . ."

> EXAMPLE *13-3*. G devised land "to my grand-
> children who live to age 21." Some of G's children
> are living at G's death.
>
> The grandchildren's springing executory interest
> does not violate the common-law Rule. The validating
> life is that one of G's children who turns out to live
> the longest. It is impossible for any of G's grand-
> children to reach 21 or die under 21 more than 21
> years after the death of G's last surviving child.
>
> Note the following points about this example: (1) It
> would commonly be said that G's children are the

validating lives; (2) G's children are not devisees; and (3) G's children are not even mentioned in the instrument.

(d) Recipient of the Interest as the Validating Life.
A well established but sometimes overlooked point is that the recipient of an interest can sometimes be his or her own validating life. See, e.g., Rand v. Bank of California (Or. 1964).[5] This point sometimes validates an interest that is contingent on the recipient's reaching an age exceeding 21 or is contingent on the recipient's surviving a particular point in time that exceeds or may exceed 21 years after the interest was created or after the death of a person in being at the date of creation.

EXAMPLE 13-4. G devised land "to A's children who are living 25 years after my death." A predeceased G. At G's death, A had three living children.

The executory interest created in A's children does not violate the common-law Rule. A's children are their own validating lives. Each child will either survive the 25-year period or fail to do so within his or her own lifetime. To say this another way, we will know no later than at the death of each child whether or not that child survived the required period.

---

[5] Oregon subsequently replaced the common-law Rule with the Uniform Rule. See infra § 14.2.

EXAMPLE 13-5. G devised land "to *A*'s children who live to age 25." *A* predeceased *G*. At *G*'s death, *A* had three living children, all of whom were younger than 25 and some of whom were younger than four years of age.

The executory interest created in *A*'s children does not violate the Rule. *A*'s children are their own validating lives. Each child will either reach age 25 or fail to do so within his or her own lifetime. To say this another way, we will know no later than at the death of each child whether or not that child survived to the required age.[6]

(e) Multiple Interests. Dispositions of property sometimes create more than one interest that is subject to the Rule. When this happens, you must test the validity of each interest separately. A life that validates one interest might or might not validate the other interests. Consequently, you must search for a validating life for each interest.

EXAMPLE 13-6. G devised the residue of his estate in trust, directing the trustee to pay the income "to *A* for life, then to *A*'s children for the life of the survivor, and upon the death of *A*'s last surviving child, to pay the corpus of the trust to *A*'s

---

[6] Note that if all of *A*'s children had been older than four years of age (but younger than 25) at *G*'s death, each class member's interest would be valid on an alternative basis—each class member's interest would be guaranteed to vest or terminate within 21 years after *G*'s death.

grandchildren." G was survived by A and by A's two children, X and Y.

There are two interests in this disposition that are subject to the Rule—the remainder interest in the income created in A's children and the remainder interest in the corpus created in A's grandchildren.

Income. Because the remainder interest in the *income* created in A's children is a class gift, it is subject to the Rule. See supra § 13.2(d). To determine whether this interest is valid, you must test the insiders to see if any of them satisfies the requirement of initial certainty. The obvious insider to test first is A. A satisfies the requirement of initial certainty because no possible chain of post-creation events disqualifies A. All of A's children will be born, or at least conceived, during A's lifetime. Thus this interest is valid.[7]

Corpus. The remainder interest in the *corpus* created in A's grandchildren is also subject to the Rule because it is a class gift. The validating life for the remainder interest in the income—A—does not qualify as a validating life for the remainder interest in the corpus. A is disqualified because it is possible that A will have a child (Z) who is conceived and born after G's death and it is possible that that child will have a child (a grandchild of A) who is born (i.e., his or her contingent interest will vest) more than 21 years after the death of A.

The only other apparent insiders to test are X and

---

[7] Note that A's children have a remainder interest for the life of the survivor of A's children, not for each child's own respective lifetime. Thus there are no cross remainders in the income in this case to worry about.

Y, the two children of *A* who were alive at *G*'s death. Neither *X* nor *Y* qualifies as a validating life either, however, because it is possible that *Z*'s child will be born more than 21 years after the deaths of *X* and *Y*. Since there is no validating life for the interest of this grandchild, the "all or nothing" rule invalidates the entire class gift in corpus created in *A*'s grandchildren. The invalid remainder interest in the corpus is replaced by a reversion in *G*. *G*'s reversion passed by intestacy to his heirs at his death. See infra § 13.9.

(f) Executory Interests Following Defeasible Fees. An executory interest following a defeasible fee is subject to the common-law Rule and will be invalid unless there is a validating life.

> *EXAMPLE 13-7.* *(1)* *G* devised land "to *A* and his heirs so long as liquor is not sold on the land, and upon liquor's being sold on the land, the land goes to *B*."
>
> *(2)* *G* devised land "to *A* and his heirs on condition that no liquor be sold on the land, but if liquor is sold on the land, the land goes to *B*."
>
> In both cases, *A* and *B* survived *G*.
>
> The interest in question is *B*'s executory interest. The interest is invalid in both cases[8] because there is no validating life. The obvious insiders to test in both cases are *A* and *B*, but neither satisfies the requirement

[8] The consequences of invalidity may differ, however, as between Variations *(1)* and *(2)*. See infra § 13.9.

of initial certainty. *B* is not in possession of the land and cannot control its use. Although *A* is initially in possession and controls its use, he can transfer his defeasible fee to someone born after *G*'s death. This afterborn devisee, heir, or grantee of *A* might allow liquor to be sold on the land more than 21 years after the death of either *A* or *B*. Because there is no other insider to test, the executory interest is invalid.

If the dispositions were changed so that the contingency could only happen during the lifetime of *A* or *B*, *B's* executory interest would be valid. See infra Examples *13-8* and *13-9*.

EXAMPLE 13-8. *G* devised land "to *A* and her heirs so long as *A* does not allow liquor to be sold on the land, and upon *A*'s allowing liquor to be sold on the land, the land goes to *B*."

B's executory interest is contingent on *A's personally* allowing liquor to be sold on the land. Consequently, *A* satisfies the requirement of initial certainty and is the validating life. As of *G*'s death, it is certain that *B*'s executory interest will either vest or terminate during the lifetime of *A*. If *A* should die without allowing liquor to be sold on the land, *A*'s possessory estate will ripen into a fee simple absolute and *B*'s interest will terminate.

EXAMPLE 13-9. *G* devised land "to *A* and his heirs so long as liquor is not sold on the land, and upon liquor's being sold on the land, the land goes to *B* if *B* is then living."

B satisfies the requirement of initial certainty and is the validating life for her own interest. If no liquor is sold on the land during *B*'s lifetime, *B*'s executory interest will be extinguished. If liquor is sold on the land after *B*'s death, irrespective of who allowed the liquor to be sold, *A*'s fee simple will terminate, but the person who received the possibility of reverter from *G* is the one who will then become entitled to possession, not *B*. Since possibilities of reverter are exempt from the Rule Against Perpetuities (supra § 13.2(b)), the possibility of reverter is valid even though it might vest beyond a life in being plus 21 years.

§ 13.6.   Time of Creation

In analyzing a perpetuity question, the time of creation of the property interest in question is crucial. The creation point fixes the time when the validating life must be "in being." The creation point also limits the facts and circumstances that can be taken into account in determining validity. Under the common-law Rule, an interest is valid only if, at the point of its creation, with the facts and circumstances then existing taken into account, the interest is certain to vest or terminate within a life in being plus 21 years. The facts that *actually* occur from that time forward, including the post-creation facts that are known at the time of the lawsuit, are disregarded—with one exception concerning interests created by the exercise of, or in default of the exercise of, certain powers of appointment (see infra § 16.5(b)-(c)).

(a) Testamentary Transfers. Property interests created by will are created when the testator dies, not when the testator signs the will. Thus the validating

life for testamentary transfers must be a person who was alive (or in gestation) when the testator died, and the facts and circumstances that are relevant to the validity of an interest created by will are those existing at the testator's death.

(b) Inter-Vivos Transfers. Property interests created by inter-vivos transfer are created when the transfer becomes effective for purposes of property law generally. This would ordinarily be the date of delivery of the deed or the funding of the trust. Thus the validating life for inter-vivos transfers must be a person who was alive (or in gestation) when the transfer became effective, and the facts and circumstances that are relevant to the validity of an interest created by inter-vivos transfer are those existing at that time.

(c) Postponement Principle. The general rules stated above are subject to exceptions in certain cases when an interest is subject to a power. These special rules are explained infra § 13.7.

(d) Facts and Circumstances. The facts and circumstances existing at creation can be just as important in determining the validity of an interest as the contingencies attached to that interest. Examples *13-5* and *13-6* illustrate the point. By varying the facts existing on *G*'s death in each of these examples, the remainder interest created in *A*'s grandchildren could be made valid in *13-6*, and the executory interest created in *A*'s children who reach 25 in *13-5* could be made invalid.

EXAMPLE 13-10. The same disposition as in Example *13-6* (*G* devised the residue of his estate in trust, directing the trustee to pay the income "to *A* for life, then to *A*'s children for the life of the survivor, and upon the death of *A*'s last surviving child, to pay the corpus of the trust to *A*'s grandchildren"). *G* was survived by *A*'s two children, *X* and *Y*, but, unlike Example *13-6*, *A* predeceased *G*.

A's death before *G* validates the grandchildren's remainder interest in the corpus. Since *A* was dead at *G*'s death, *X* and *Y* are the only children *A* will have. All of *A*'s grandchildren will therefore be born or at least conceived during the lifetime of the survivor of *X* and *Y*. Thus *X* and *Y* constitute the validating lives for the grandchildren's interest.

The facts and circumstances existing at creation not only include the facts as such but also the rules of law or construction that those facts trigger. A rule of construction that figures in many perpetuities cases is the *rule of convenience*. See infra § 15.1(c). The rule of convenience plays a crucial role in the next three examples.

EXAMPLE 13-11. The same disposition as in Example *13-5* ("to *A*'s children who live to age 25"). At *G*'s death, *A* had three living children, all of whom were younger than 25, but, unlike Example *13-5*, *A* survived G.[9]

The executory interest created in A's children who reach 25 is invalid. Before explaining why, it will be helpful to develop a little further the reason why their interest was valid under the facts as originally set forth. The key to the validity of the children's interest when A predeceased G was that, at G's death, it was impossible for any additional children of A to be born and become members of the class. The class was closed naturally upon A's prior death. The fact that the class was closed by the time of G's death allowed A's children to be their own validating lives. It was certain that all of A's children were "in being" at the creation of their interest.

Under the altered facts, however, additional children can be born to A after G's death. Such after-born children can become class members, for the class of potential takers is not closed artificially at G's death by the rule of convenience. (The class is not then closed artificially because none of A's children is then entitled to possession; none has yet reached 25.) Thus more children can be born to A, and those conceived before the class closes (when A dies or when one of his children reaches 25, whichever happens first) will be potential members of the class. This is what makes the entire class gift invalid: It is

[9] In Example *13-5*, some of A's under-25 children were younger than four years of age. Recall that if all of A's under-25 children had been older than four years of age, there would have been an alternative basis for validating the remainder interest. See supra note 6. Because, in Example *13-11*, above, A survived G, the ages of A's under-25 children are irrelevant.

possible, looking at the situation as of *G*'s death, that a child of *A* will be conceived and born after *G*'s death but before the class closes and it is possible that this after-born child will reach age 25 more than 21 years after the death of the survivor of the four insiders connected to the transfer who were "in being" at the creation of the interest—*A* and the three children of *A* who were living when *G* died.

EXAMPLE 13-12. The same disposition as in Example *13-5* ("to *A*'s children who live to age 25"). Unlike Example *13-5*, *A* survived *G* and *A*'s eldest child had reached 25 by the time of *G*'s death.

Unlike Example *13-11*, the fact that *A* survived *G* does not invalidate the executory interest created in *A*'s children who reach 25. Although *A*'s survival of *G* makes it possible for *A* to have additional children after *G*'s death, such after-born children will not be class members. Under the rule of convenience, the fact that *A*'s eldest child had reached 25 by the time of *G*'s death closes the class artificially at *G*'s death. Thus the three children who were living at *G*'s death constitute their own validating lives, just as they did under the original facts of *13-5*.

EXAMPLE 13-13. *G* devised land "to *A* for life, then to *A*'s children who live to age 25." *A* survived *G*. By the time of *G*'s death, *A*'s eldest child had reached 25.

The remainder interest created in *A*'s children who reach 25 is invalid. Unlike Example *13-12*, the rule of convenience does not close the class at *G*'s death, despite the fact that one child had then reached 25. The reason is that *A*'s preceding life estate postpones distribution. Thus this class will not close until *A* dies. This leaves open the possibility that *A* will have a child shortly before his death who will be a member of the class and who will reach 25 more than 21 years after the deaths of *A* and those of *A*'s children who were alive at *G*'s death. This possibility renders the entire class gift invalid under the "all or nothing" rule.

§ 13.7. Postponement Principle

As explained supra § 13.6(c), the general rule is that property interests are created when the transfer becomes effective for property law purposes—at the date of the testator's death for testamentary transfers and at the date of delivery of the deed for inter-vivos transfers.

(a) Revocable Trusts. A handful of decisions has held that, for perpetuity purposes, the time that property interests are created in *revocable* inter-vivos transfers, typically in trust, is postponed to the time when the power to revoke expires. A power to revoke expires at the death of the settlor, unless the power was released or fixed to expire earlier. In one of the leading decisions on this question, Cook v. Horn (Ga. 1958),[10] the court stated the basis for the postponement principle:

So long as the settlor of an inter vivos trust has the absolute right to revoke or terminate the trust

---

[10] Georgia subsequently replaced the common-law Rule with the Uniform Rule. See infra § 14.2.

for his own exclusive personal benefit, there is no tying up of property and no restraint upon the alienability of the property in the trust fund . . .

While the authorities embracing this principle are not numerous, there are no contrary decisions and the principle is widely regarded as a settled part of perpetuity law. The principle is codified in § 2 of the Uniform Rule.

> *EXAMPLE 13-14.* G conveyed property in trust, directing the trustee to pay the income to herself (*G*) for life, then to *G*'s son *A* for his life, then to *A*'s children for the life of the survivor of *A*'s children who are living at *G*'s death, and upon the death of such last surviving child, the corpus of the trust to be distributed among *A*'s then-living descendants, by representation. *G* retained the power to revoke the trust.
>
> The interest in question is the remainder interest in the corpus created in *A*'s then-living descendants. The postponement principle validates this interest. Under the postponement principle, the remainder interest is created at *G*'s death, not at the creation of the trust. Treating the remainder interest as created at *G*'s death allows *A*'s children who are living at *G*'s death to be the validating lives.
>
> If the creation of the remainder interest had not been postponed, the interest would have been invalid. A child of *A* might have been conceived and born between the date when the trust was created and *G*'s death, such after-born child might have turned out to

be the last surviving child of *A* who was alive when *G* died, and such child might have lived more than 21 years beyond the deaths of all the insiders connected to the transfer who were "in being" when the trust was created—*G*, *A*, and *A*'s then-living children. And, of course, the same can be said of all outsiders—every other person in the world who was "in being" when the trust was created.

(b) *Other Interests Subject to a Power.* Does the postponement principle extend beyond revocable trusts? Court authority on this question is sparse if not non-existent, but the commentators believe that it does. See Simes & Smith on Future Interests § 1252. The Restatement of Property, too, states the principle in broader terms: Under the Restatement, the time of creation is postponed so long as the interest "is destructible, pursuant to the uncontrolled volition, and for the exclusive personal benefit of the person having such a power of destruction." Restatement of Property § 373. Under this statement of the principle, the power need not be a power to revoke and it need not be held by the settlor or transferor. An *unqualified* and *currently exercisable* power held by *any* person *acting alone* to make himself or herself the beneficial owner of the interest in question is sufficient. Section 2(b) of the Uniform Rule codifies this proposition.[11]

For example, under the Restatement and the Uniform Rule, the time of creation of a remainder interest in trust would be postponed if the income beneficiary held a presently exercisable general power of appointment over that remainder interest or if any person held a power to invade the corpus of the trust.

Be sure to notice an important consequence of the idea that a power need not be held by the settlor to postpone the time of creation: It allows postponement even in cases of testamentary transfers.

> *EXAMPLE 13-15.* G devised property in trust, directing the trustee to pay the income "to A for life, remainder to such persons as A shall appoint; in default of appointment, the property to remain in trust to pay the income to A's children for the life of the survivor, and upon the death of A's last surviving child, to pay the corpus to A's grandchildren." A survived G.
>
> If the remainder interest created in A's grandchildren is created at G's death, it is invalid. But if the Restatement view is followed, or if the Uniform Rule applies, the creation of the remainder interest is

---

[11] The Restatement 2d of Property § 1.2 states the postponement principle in unduly narrow terms. The Restatement 2d states that the principle only applies if someone, "acting alone, has a power currently exercisable to become the unqualified beneficial owner of *all* beneficial rights in the property in which the nonvested interest exists." (Emphasis added.)

postponed to the expiration of A's presently exercisable general power (at A's death). The postponement validates the interest.

Since this transaction is equivalent in substance to G's having devised the property to A in fee simple absolute and A's having then devised the property at his or her death in accordance with G's gift-in-default clause, the Restatement view ought to be followed even in jurisdictions that have not codified it.

Note, however, that if G had conferred on A a *nongeneral* power or a general *testamentary* power, there would be no postponement because neither power would be a currently exercisable power to make A the beneficial owner of the remainder interest. Consequently, the remainder interest would have been created at G's death, causing the grandchildren's interest to be invalid.

§ 13.8.   Constructional Preference for Validity

Gray stated that a will or deed should be construed without regard to the Rule Against Perpetuities, and then the Rule should be "remorselessly" applied to the provisions so construed. Gray on Perpetuities § 629. Some courts have adhered to this proposition. See Colorado Nat'l Bank v. McCabe (Colo. 1960);[12] Continental Ill. Nat'l Bank & Trust Co. v. Llewellyn (Ill. App. Ct. 1966). Most courts, however, incline toward the proposition put by the Restatement of Property § 375, which is that where an instrument is

---

[12] Colorado subsequently replaced the common-law Rule with the Uniform Rule. See infra § 14.2.

ambiguous—that is, where it is subject to two or more plausible constructions, one of which causes a Rule violation and the other of which does not—the construction that does not result in a Rule violation should be adopted. Cases supporting this view include Southern Bank & Trust Co. v. Brown (S.C. 1978);[13] Davis v. Rossi (Mo. 1930).

This constructional preference for validity has many proper applications, as we shall see in later sections. It is worth emphasizing, however, that it properly applies only in cases of genuine ambiguity—where the transferor's language is *fairly* susceptible to more than one construction. It is improper to change the clear meaning of the language of an instrument to avoid a perpetuity violation *under the guise of construction,* though on occasion courts have done so. There is another principle—reformation—that allows invalidity-avoiding changes to be made directly, but only a very few jurisdictions adhere to the reformation principle for perpetuities cases. Several jurisdictions that previously adhered to it have replaced it with the Uniform Rule. We will explain the reformation principle infra § 14.4, on perpetuity reform.

---

[13] South Carolina subsequently replaced the common-law Rule with the Uniform Rule. See infra § 14.2.

§ 13.9. The Consequences of Invalidity

When an interest is invalid because it violates the common-law Rule, the invalid interest is stricken from the disposition. Unless the doctrine of infectious invalidity applies (see infra § 13.11), the other interests created by the disposition (assuming that none of them violates the Rule) take effect as if the invalid interest had never been created.

Striking the invalid interest does not have the same consequences in all cases. The consequences depend on whether the invalid interest was a remainder or an executory interest and on whether the invalid interest was the last one in the disposition or an intermediate one.

When the invalid interest is a *remainder interest following a life estate or a term of years* or is an *executory interest following a fee simple determinable*, its invalidity will probably (though not necessarily) cause a gap in the disposition. If the transfer was inter vivos, the gap will be filled by a reversion or a possibility of reverter. If the transfer was by will, the gap will be filled by the residuary clause or, if the invalid interest was created in the residuary clause, by intestate succession.

> *EXAMPLE 13-16. G* devised land "to *A* for life, then to *A*'s children for the life of the survivor, and upon the death of *A*'s last surviving child, to *A*'s grandchildren." *G* devised her residuary estate to her husband, *H*.
>
> Due to the invalidity of the remainder created in

A's grandchildren, the disposition reads as if that remainder interest had never been created: "to *A* for life, then to *A*'s children for the life of the survivor." Since *G*'s devise did not validly dispose of all interests in the land, the undisposed-of interest is a remainder that passes under *G*'s residuary clause to *H*. This testamentary transfer of the remainder to *H* is deemed to have occurred at *G*'s death. With *H*'s remainder added in, the disposition now reads: "to *A* for life, then to *A*'s children for the life of the survivor, then to *H*." Thus when *A*'s last surviving child dies, the land goes to *H* (or *H*'s successors in interest).

If *G*'s original devise had been in her residuary clause, the undisposed-of interest would have been a reversion that passed by intestacy at *G*'s death to her heirs at law.

EXAMPLE 13-17. G devised land "to *A* for life, then for life to *A*'s children who live to age 25, then to *B*."

The remainder for life created in *A*'s children who reach 25 is invalid. The effect of striking it is not to create a gap that must be filled by the residuary clause. Rather it is to accelerate *B*'s remainder. With the invalid interest stricken, the devise reads: "to *A* for life, then to *B*."

EXAMPLE 13-18. G devised land "to *A* and her heirs so long as no liquor is sold on the land, and upon liquor's being sold on the land, the land goes to *B*." *G* devised his residuary estate to *C*. *D* is *G*'s sole heir at law.

B's executory interest is invalid. The phrase "to *B*" is stricken and the gap is filled by the residuary clause. Under conventional analysis, however, the residuary clause confers an executory interest on *C*, not a possibility of reverter. See supra Example *4-5*. If so, *C*'s executory interest is also invalid. The gap caused by striking *C*'s executory interest is filled by intestate succession, which passes a valid possibility of reverter to *D*. Contra, Brown v. Independent Baptist Church (Mass. 1950), which incorrectly held that *G*'s residuary clause conferred on *C* a valid possibility of reverter rather than an invalid executory interest. The *Brown* decision has been criticized. See Lewis M. Simes, Is the Rule Against Perpetuities Doomed?, 52 Mich. L. Rev. 179 n.4 (1953).

When the invalid interest is an *executory interest* (other than one following a fee simple determinable), the effect will not be to create a gap. Rather, the invalidity of the executory interest will cause the condition subsequent to be stricken, too.

EXAMPLE 13-19. *G* devised land "to *A* for life, remainder to *A*'s children, but if none of *A*'s children lives to age 25, to *B*." *G* was survived by *A*, who had two children, *X* and *Y*, both of whom were younger than 25.

B's executory interest is invalid. As a result, the remainder created in *A*'s children is not subject to the condition of divestment in case all die under 25. Rather, while it still is subject to open, it is no longer subject to complete divestment. With the invalid interest stricken, the devise reads: "to *A* for life, remainder to *A*'s children."

§ 13.10. Separability

When an interest is expressly subject to alternative contingencies, the courts have the option of holding that two interests are created in the same person or class. The effect of doing so is that the invalidity of one of the interests does not invalidate the other. This principle was established in Longhead v. Phelps (K.B. 1770), and has been followed in this country. See Simes & Smith on Future Interests § 1257; Am. L. Prop. § 24.54; Restatement of Property § 376.

Suppose, for example, that property is devised "to *B* if X-event or Y-event happens." *B* in effect has two interests, one contingent on X-event and the other contingent on Y-event. If there is no validating life for X-event but there is one for Y-event, the consequence of separating *B*'s interest into two interests is that only the one contingent on X-event is invalid. *B* still has a valid interest—the one contingent on Y-event. Another way of viewing it is that the invalid contingency is stricken or excised. Thus the devise is altered to read "to *B* if Y-event happens." Examples *13-20* and *13-21* illustrate this principle further:

> **EXAMPLE 13-20.** *G* devised the residue of his estate "to *A* for life, then to *A*'s children who survive *A* and live to age 25, but if none of *A*'s children survives *A* or if none of *A*'s children who survives *A* lives to age 25, then to *B*."
>
> The separability principle does not apply to the remainder interest created in *A*'s children who survive

A and live to age 25. That interest is invalid and replaced by a reversion in *G*'s heirs.

What about *B*'s executory interest? The separability principle applies to *B*'s interest and divides it into two interests—one contingent on none of *A*'s children surviving *A* and the other contingent on none of *A*'s children who survives *A* living to age 25. The one contingent on none of *A*'s children surviving *A* is valid, but the one contingent on none of *A*'s children who survives *A* living to age 25 is invalid. Consequently, the language "or if none of *A*'s children who survives *A* lives to age 25" is in effect stricken from the devise. *B* takes only if none of *A*'s children survives *A*. If one or more of *A*'s children survives *A*, *B* cannot take even if none of them lives to age 25.

Because the separability principle saves one of *B*'s executory interests, the reversion in *G*'s heirs is vested subject to divestment in favor of *B* if none of *A*'s children survives *A*.

The principle of separability is applicable only when the transferor has *expressly* stated the contingencies in the alternative. Where alternative contingencies are merely implicit, no separation will be recognized. See Proctor v. Bishop of Bath and Wells (C.P. 1794). In the words of Sir George Jessel, Master of the Rolls, in Miles v. Harford (Ch. 1879), "that is what [the courts] mean by splitting, they will not split the expression by dividing the two events, but when they find two expressions they give effect to both of them as if you had struck the other out of the will."

EXAMPLE 13-21. G devised the residue of his estate "to A for life, then to A's children who survive A and live to age 25, but if none of A's children does so, then to B."

As in Example *13-20*, the separability principle does not apply to the remainder interest created in A's children who survive A and live to age 25. That interest is invalid and replaced by a reversion in G's heirs.

Unlike Example *13-20*, however, the separability principle is also inapplicable to B's executory interest. B has only one interest, and it is invalid. B cannot take even if none of A's children survives A. Thus the reversion in G's heirs is indefeasibly vested and takes effect in possession when A dies.

Examples *13-20* and *13-21* present clear cases. In *13-20*, the separability principle was clearly applicable; in *13-21*, it was clearly inapplicable. There can also be borderline cases, cases in which the courts can go either way. In borderline cases, the courts should use their best judgment in deciding whether to apply the separability principle. The criterion should be whether applying the principle serves the transferor's general dispositive scheme better than not applying it. See Restatement of Property § 376 cmt. f. If, for example, applying the separability principle would result in adverse tax consequences (which it might do in certain cases too complicated to explore in this book),[14] the court should not treat the contingencies as separable.

The fundamental distinction between expressly separated alternative contingencies and implicit ones has been questioned by certain commentators. See Leach, Perpetuities in a Nutshell, 51 Harv. L. Rev. 638, 654-55 (1938); Bergin & Haskell on Estates in Land and Future Interests 214. The distinction is an easy target, of course, for it is obviously based on the form of expression rather than on the substance of the disposition. The substance of the dispositions in Examples *13-20* and *13-21* is the same.

Nevertheless, an abolition of the distinction would have significant consequences. Much more is at stake than just one small corner of perpetuity law. To recognize the separability of alternative contingencies that are implicit as well as those that are explicit would move the jurisdiction into one of the most complicated and dense forms of wait-and-see, a form of wait-and-see that no jurisdiction in this or any other common-law country has adopted. Although we shall argue that the wait-and-see method of perpetuity reform is highly desirable, the clean and uncomplicated form of wait-and-see incorporated into the Uniform Rule is far more attractive than attempting on a case-by-case basis to figure out all

[14] See Mary Louise Fellows, Testing Perpetuity Reforms: A Study of Perpetuity Cases 1984-89, 25 Real Prop. Prob. & Tr. J. 597, 656-59 (1991).

the possible combinations of post-creation events that are implicit in a disposition in order to give effect only to the "valid" ones. On the Uniform Rule's method of wait-and-see, see infra § 14.2.

§ 13.11. Infectious Invalidity

In appropriate cases, the invalidity of an interest may, under the *doctrine of infectious invalidity*, be held to invalidate one or more otherwise valid interests. The question turns on whether the general dispositive scheme of the transferor will be better served by eliminating only the invalid interest or by eliminating other interests as well. This is a question that must be answered on a case by case basis. Several items are relevant to the question, including who takes the stricken interests in place of those designated by the transferor. Some jurisdictions have become noted for a greater willingness to apply infectious invalidity than others. See Simes & Smith on Future Interests § 1262; Am. L. Prop. § 24.48 et seq.; Restatement of Property § 402.

§ 13.12. Technical Violations

The required *certainty* that an interest will vest or terminate within a life in being plus 21 years has invalidated some interests even though they do not violate the *policy* of the Rule. The policy of the Rule is not violated because, realistically speaking, the likelihood that the interest will remain contingent beyond the perpetuity period is either zero or so remote as to be negligible. Such cases fall generally into three categories, which received their names from Professor Leach's article, Perpetuities in a Nutshell, 51 Harv. L. Rev. 638 (1938): (1) the fertile octogenarian (§ 13.13); (2) the administrative contingency (§ 13.14); and (3) the afterborn spouse (§ 13.15).

§ 13.13. Fertile Octogenarians:[15] The Conclusive Presumption of Lifetime Fertility

(a) Standard Fertile-Octogenarian Case. In some of our previous examples, invalidity resulted from the possibility of after-born children entering a class. Let us reintroduce one of those examples, Example *13-6*:

> EXAMPLE *13-22*. The same disposition as in Example *13-6* (*G* devised the residue of his estate in trust, directing the trustee to pay the income "to *A* for life, then to *A*'s children for the life of the survivor, and upon the death of *A*'s last surviving child, to pay the corpus of the trust to *A*'s grandchildren.") *G* was survived by *A* and by *A*'s two children, *X* and *Y*.
>
> In Example *13-6*, the remainder interest in the corpus created in *A*'s grandchildren was invalid because of the possibility that *A* would have a child (*Z*), conceived and born after *G*'s death, who would have a child conceived and born more than 21 years after the death of the survivor of *A*, *X*, and *Y*.

---

[15] The term "octogenarians" is not to be taken literally. The term refers to persons who are infertile, young or old, male or female.

Suppose, however, that when *G* died, *A* was infertile because she had passed the menopause (but see infra § 13.13(b))? Or, suppose that *A* was then infertile for any other reason, such as he had undergone a vasectomy or she a complete hysterectomy or a tubal ligation? Section 13.6(d) emphasized the point that the facts and circumstances existing when the interest is created are to be taken into account. Are *these* facts and circumstances relevant also, so that the possibility of *A* having after-born children is to be disregarded? The answer that the courts have almost universally given is No. For purposes of the common-law Rule, early English decisions, of which Jee v. Audley (Ch. 1787) is the best-known, laid down the proposition that all persons are *conclusively* presumed to be capable of having children throughout their entire lifetimes, regardless of their age or physical condition. In the *Jee* case, Sir Lloyd Kenyon, the Master of the Rolls (and later to become the Lord Chief Justice of England), stated:

I am desired to do in this case something which I do not feel myself at liberty to do, namely to suppose it impossible for persons in so advanced an age as John and Elizabeth Jee [both age 70] to have children; but if this can be done in one case it may in another, and it is a very dangerous experiment, and introductive of the greatest inconvenience to give a latitude to such sort of conjecture.

Only one American common-law decision has squarely rejected Jee v. Audley and held in a perpetuities case that the presumption of lifetime fertility is rebuttable, not conclusive. In that case, Lattouf's Will (N.J. Super. Ct. App. Div. 1965),[16] the court found that the presumption was rebutted because the person in question, a female—although apparently in her normal child-bearing years—had undergone a complete hysterectomy. In contrast to *Lattouf*, there are other contexts in which American courts have held the presumption of lifetime fertility to be rebuttable and in fact rebutted either by the age of the person in question or by the person's physical condition. See Scott on Trusts § 340.1. But *Lattouf* is the only perpetuities case to allow rebuttal of the presumption. The Restatement of Property § 377 squarely supports the conclusive presumption, and there are many perpetuities cases, recent as well as not so recent, that have adhered to it. See, e.g., Turner v. Turner (S.C. 1973)[17] ("The possibility of childbirth," the court said, "is never extinct."); Abram v. Wilson (Ohio Prob. Ct. 1966) ("Obviously," the court said of the testator's 75-year-old brother, "it is clearly possible for [him] to have children . . . .").

---

[16] New Jersey subsequently replaced the common-law Rule with the Uniform Rule. See infra § 14.2.

[17] See supra note 13.

(b) Advances in Reproductive Technology; Possibility of Adoption. Holding the presumption of lifetime fertility to be rebuttable, as the court did in *Lattouf*, would today be of questionable benefit. The problem is that the common-law Rule requires *certainty*; likelihood, no matter how great, is not sufficient. To save a gift requires establishing that the person *cannot* have additional children. Establishing that having additional children is unlikely, indeed extremely unlikely, is not enough.

It might be possible to establish that a given person cannot have natural-born children. Even here, though, advances in reproductive technology might prevent such proof. Can it be held, for example, that a man who has undergone a vasectomy cannot have children, given the possibility of surgical reversal? Can it be established that a post-menopausal woman cannot have children? See Mark V. Sauer et al., A Preliminary Report on Oocyte Donation Extending Reproductive Potential to Women Over 40, 323 N. Eng. J. Med. 1157 (1990) (reporting that women who have passed menopause can still become pregnant by implantation of embryos that are created from eggs donated by younger women and fertilized by sperm from men, typically the older women's husbands).[18]

---

[18] Newspaper accounts are starting to appear that show that the procedure is being put into practice. See, e.g., California Woman, 53, Gives Birth to Twins, N.Y. Times, Nov. 11, 1992, at A9 (reporting that a 53-year-old menopausal grandmother gave

Suppose in a given case that it is established that having natural children is impossible; the complete hysterectomy was regarded as sufficient proof by the *Lattouf* court. Not considered by the *Lattouf* court, however, was the possibility of adoption. Since the trend is strongly toward the inclusion of adopted children in class gifts (see UPC § 2-705), and since even elderly people cannot be excluded from adopting children based on age alone, the possibility of adopting children is seldom extinct. In Rev. Rul. 59-143, 1959-1 C.B. 247, the Internal Revenue Service disregarded the possibility of a 55-year-old woman having a natural-born child, but in Rev. Rul. 74-410, 1974-2 C.B. 187, the Service refused to disregard the possibility of a 60-year-old person adopting a child (see also IRS Priv. Ltr. Rul. 80-10-011). The Service, moreover, was applying a tax-law standard that allowed it to disregard an event whose occurrence was "so remote as to be negligible," a much less rigid standard than the perpetuity-law standard that only allows *impossible* events to be disregarded.

birth to twins; she became pregnant by implantation of embryos created from eggs donated by another woman and fertilized by sperm from the older woman's 32-year-old husband); Pregnant Woman, 62, Raises Eyebrows in Italy, Detroit Free Press, Nov. 30, 1992, at 3A (reporting that Sicilian widow, age 62, is four-months pregnant after implantation of embryos created from donated eggs that were fertilized by the sperm of her late husband, who died a year earlier).

In short, making the presumption rebuttable rather than conclusive might not greatly alleviate the so-called "fertile-octogenarian problem."

(c) Constructional Preference for Validity. The constructional preference for validity discussed in § 13.8 provides a solution to some "fertile-octogenarian" cases. If the possibility of future children was remote when the transferor executed the document, the court could hold that the transferor never intended to include after-born or after-adopted children in the class gift. So construed, the perpetuity standard of absolute certainty is met, and the interest is valid. See, e.g., Bankers Trust Co. v. Pearson (Conn. 1953)[19] (testator meant children in being when his will spoke of the children of his brother, age 55, and his sisters, ages 52 and 57); Joyner v. Duncan (N.C. 1980) (testator meant children in being when his will spoke of the children of his 47-year-old son).

Since the relevant time for determining a testator's intent is the time of *execution* of the will, not the time of death, this construction is ordinarily possible only if the testator knew that the person's age or physical condition realistically excluded further child-bearing (or adoptions) at the time the will was executed. Thus, in Example *13-22*, supra, if *A* were a 25-year-old female in normal physical condition

[19] Connecticut subsequently replaced the common-law Rule with the Uniform Rule. See infra § 14.2.

when *G* executed his or her will, this method of avoiding a common-law Rule violation would not be properly available even if *A* had gone through the menopause when *G* died. Consequently, this approach is not a panacea, but it would alleviate the problem in some cases. Yet some courts, without articulating their reasons, have been unwilling to adopt such a construction even in what seem to be appropriate cases. It may be significant to note, however, that the courts in these cases were able to find other ways of upholding the gift. Perhaps these courts would have adopted the validating construction had the other method not been available. See, e.g., Sears v. Coolidge (Mass. 1952)[20] (gift saved under the second-look doctrine: see infra § 16.5); Second Bank-State St. Trust Co. v. Second Bank-State St. Trust Co. (Mass. 1957)[21] (gift saved under the sub-class exemption: see infra § 15.3).

This constructional device has been rejected outright in England on the ground that class gifts are unambiguous and therefore extrinsic evidence is inadmissible for the purpose sought. See Ward v. Van Der Loeff (H.L. 1924). The Restatement of Property § 377 cmt. c answers this point by stating that invalidity under the common-law Rule provides a basis for finding an ambiguity. Cf. Simes & Smith

---

[20] Massachusetts subsequently enacted the Uniform Rule. See infra § 14.2.

[21] See supra note 20.

on Future Interests § 1289.

It may be noted that occasionally, though not often, there will be cases in which this construction is appropriate without finding that further children were unlikely to be born or adopted as of the time the will was executed.

> *EXAMPLE 13-23.* *G* devised property in trust, directing the trustee regarding the disposition of the income. Regarding the corpus, the trust was to terminate "upon the death of my last surviving grandchild," whereupon the corpus "shall be divided into equal parts, one of which shall go to the issue of each of my twelve grandchildren [naming them] who dies leaving issue then surviving." *G* was survived by three children and the twelve named grandchildren.
>
> The remainder interest in the corpus was held valid in Southern Bank & Trust Co. v. Brown (S.C. 1978).[22] The court conceded that the interest would be invalid if the trust was to terminate on the death of *G*'s last surviving grandchild whenever born. However, the court focussed on the fact that the beneficiaries of the trust corpus were the issue of the twelve named grandchildren, all of whom were living at *G*'s death. The court saved the gift by construing "last surviving grandchild" to mean "last surviving of the twelve named grandchildren." The ages or physical condition of *G*'s children when he or she executed the will were irrelevant in this case.

[22] See supra note 13.

Of course, the two approaches to the "fertile-octogenarian problem" outlined above—allowing the presumption of fertility to be rebutted and construing the class to exclude children born or adopted after the questioned interest is created—are not mutually exclusive. Combined, they would rather substantially alleviate the problem. As the law now stands, though, the vast majority view is that the presumption is conclusive. And, while the constructional preference for validity seems to be quite generally accepted as a conventional procedure, there are cases in which it was not applied even though appropriate.

(d) "Precocious Toddlers." If an elderly person or a person whose physical condition prevents the birth of children is conclusively presumed to be able to have children, are young children themselves, those who have not yet reached puberty ("precocious toddlers," as Professor Leach called them) subject to the same conclusive presumption? Cases raising this problem are rare, and the results have been inconclusive. The best-known is Re Gaite's Will Trusts (Ch. 1949), the facts of which form the basis of Example *13-24*, below.

EXAMPLE *13-24*. *G* devised property in trust, directing the trustee to pay the income "to *A* for life, corpus to *A*'s grandchildren who are living at my death or born within five years thereafter who shall live to age 21." *G* was survived by *A*, a 65-year-old widow, and by *A*'s two children and one grandchild.

Is a child under the age of five conclusively

presumed to be capable of having a child? If so, the questioned interest—the remainder created in A's grandchildren who reach 21—is invalid. Although any grandchild of A's born to A's two children who were living at G's death will either live to age 21 or die younger no later than 21 years after the death of the survivor of these two children (who were "in being" at G's death, and thus potentially were validating lives), the conclusive presumption if applicable would say that it is possible that A will conceive and bear a child who will in turn conceive a child, all within five years after G's death. Such grandchild therefore might reach 21 more than 21 years after the death of the survivor of A and A's two children and one grandchild who were living when G died.

In the *Gaite's Will Trusts* case, the English court avoided the question by deciding that even if A were to have an afterborn child who in turn were to have a child, all within five years after G's death, such grandchild would be "illegitimate" (because under English legislation "a marriage between persons either of whom is under the age of sixteen shall be void") and thus not a class member.

In the United States, where there is a movement toward presuming inclusion of nonmarital children in class gifts (see UPC § 2-705), the device used by the English court to side-step the question might not be so readily available. (Nor is it available in England anymore, for by statute enacted in 1969 nonmarital children are presumptively included in class gift language. See Family Law Reform Act, 1969, § 15.)

As might be expected, the *Lattouf* court, which held
the presumption to be rebuttable rather than conclusive, was willing to indicate that the presumption
would be rebutted by age in the case of a 3-year-and-
10-month-old child. The court's statement was
dictum, and rather cryptic: "Marie Endres [who had
the complete hysterectomy] was not pregnant. She
could not be, nor, of course, could the infant Linda
[a female age 3 years and 10 months]." There have
been other American cases, however, in which a
child shortly after (probable) puberty was
conclusively presumed capable of having children.
An example is Rust v. Rust (Tex. Civ. App. 1948),
where the court assumed that the testator's daughter,
Margene, who was 9 1/2 years old when the testator
died, was able to have a child before her 14th
birthday. (The court found a way to uphold the gift
anyway.)

§ 13.14. The Administrative Contingency
(a) Standard Administrative-Contingency Case.
The term "administrative contingency" refers to the
performance by a fiduciary (an executor, a trustee) of
some administrative function, the completion of
which probably will not but *might* take more than 21
years. Typical examples are the completion of the
probate of a will, the settlement of an estate, the
payment of debts or taxes, the sale of estate assets, or
the delivery of trust corpus on the termination of a
trust.

EXAMPLE *13-25*. *G* devised land "to my grand-children, born before or after my death, who are living upon final distribution of my estate." *G* was survived by children and grandchildren.

The grandchildren's interest is invalid, by the majority view. Though unlikely, there is a possibility that the final distribution of *G*'s estate will not occur within 21 years after *G*'s death. (There have been such instances: see Hostetter, Jr. v. Estate of Hostetter (Ill. App. Ct. 1979) (25 years); Estate of Garrett (Pa. 1953) (23 years); Haddock v. Boston & Maine Ry. (Mass. 1888)[23] (63 years).) This possibility eliminates validating the interest on the basis of the 21-year part of the period. In addition, there are no lives that can validate it. Grandchildren may be conceived and born after *G*'s death, and such after-born grandchildren may survive the final distribution of *G*'s estate (or fail to do so) beyond 21 years after the deaths of *G*'s children and grandchildren who were living at *G*'s death.

(b) Survival of a Period that Might Exceed 21 Years. As Example *13-25* illustrates, the term "administrative contingency" is somewhat misleading. The term does not refer to the possibility that the administrative task will never be completed. If it did, all interests that are to take effect in possession upon the completion of an administrative task would be

---

[23] See supra note 20.

contingent. But in fact, such gifts are upheld.[24] Cases are collected in Am. L. Prop. § 24.23 n. 2. Rather, it is accepted that the task will be completed, presumably because of the fiduciary's legal obligation to do so; the uncertainty is the length of time it might take to finish the job. Thus, as in Example *13-25*, the administrative-contingency problem commonly arises because of a contingency of survival of the completion of the administrative function. In such cases, the problem is really one of survival of a period of time that might exceed 21 years. We have seen *this* problem before—in Example *13-4*. As exemplified by that example, interests that are contingent on survival of a period that might exceed 21 years are not always invalid. They will be valid if the beneficiaries can be their own validating lives. The beneficiaries can be their own validating lives if the questioned interest is created in one or more individual takers or is created in a class that is closed at the testator's death.

[24] Contra, Miller v. Weston (Colo. 1920), where the court held a devise to *A* "on the admission of this will to probate" to be contingent on the probate of the will and invalid because probate "may never happen." The court was unwilling to accept probate as a certainty even if "probate is required by law to be made." The perpetuity standard of absolute certainty did not allow the possibility of the law's being disobeyed to be ignored! Colorado subsequently replaced the common-law Rule with the Uniform Rule. See supra note 12.

EXAMPLE 13-26. *G* devised land "to my children who are living upon final distribution of my estate." *G* is survived by children.

The children's interest is valid. Because no children will be born to *G* after her death, her children are their own validating lives.

(c)   Class Subject to Open for More Than 21 Years. When a class is not closed at the testator's death, the administrative-contingency problem can arise even if there is no condition precedent of survival. Take a variation of Example *13-25* to illustrate this point. Suppose that the gift were created in *G*'s great-grandchildren instead of *G*'s grandchildren. The interest would be invalid even without the condition precedent of survival. A great-grandchild could be conceived and born before the probate of *G*'s estate is completed and more than 21 years after the death of the survivor of *G*'s children and those of *G*'s grandchildren who were living at *G*'s death. Note, however, that the invalidity here is due to the fact that the class of great-grandchildren could not only increase after the testator's death but could also increase after the death of lives in being at the testator's death.

If the class cannot increase after lives in being, the absence of a condition precedent of survival will save a gift created in a class that is not closed at the testator's death. To illustrate this, let us return to the original facts of Example *13-25*, where the gift was created in *G*'s grandchildren. Suppose that no condition precedent of survival was imposed. Omitting the condition precedent of survival would make the grandchildren's interest valid because no new members could join the class after the death of the survivor of *G*'s children, all of whom were of course "in being" at *G*'s death.

(d) The Fiduciary's Obligation. A minority of courts has devised an escape from the administrative-contingency problem. Since the administrative function is to be performed by a fiduciary, these courts hold that the fiduciary's obligation is to complete the task within a "reasonable time." They further hold that a "reasonable time" is less than 21 years. See, e.g., Brandenburg v. Thorndike (Mass. 1885);[25] see also Belfield v. Booth (Conn. 1893);[26] Asche v. Asche (Del. Ch. 1966); cf. In re Taylor (Cal. 1967).[27]

The difficulty with this minority view is that, while there may be an obligation to complete fiduciary tasks expeditiously, it is a fiction to say that the settlement of an estate can *never* take more than 21 years without violating a fiduciary duty. While rare, there can be cases in which protracted and successive litigation over a multitude of issues legitimately ties an estate up for a very long time. See, e.g., the cases

[25] See supra note 20.

[26] See supra note 19.

[27] California subsequently enacted the Uniform Rule. See infra § 14.2.

cited supra Example *13-25*. Even on a case by case basis, it would seem to be impossible to predict, with the certainty required by the common-law Rule, that no such delay will properly arise.

(e) Constructional Preference for Validity. Depending on the dispositive language, the constructional preference for validity described in § 13.8 may be available as a method of avoiding invalidity. For example, if a condition of survival is ambiguous, the condition can be construed to relate to the death of the testator or of the life tenant rather than to the completion of the administrative task. See Restatement of Property § 374 cmt. f. Indeed, some courts have adopted this construction even when the language unambiguously related to an estate's final distribution. See Malone v. Herndon (Okla. 1946). where a will provided that, on the death of the life tenant leaving issue surviving him, the "trust estate shall be paid over, delivered and conveyed to such issue living at the time of said payment, delivery and conveyance." The court construed this clause to require survival of the life tenant, not the time of payment, delivery and conveyance!

(f) Contingencies Relating to an Event External to the Family. Property interests do not necessarily raise the administrative-contingency problem simply because they are geared to the happening of some event external to the family. If no one is legally obligated to make the event happen and if the event might happen more than 21 years later, the invalidity that results may be equally disturbing, but the

solutions employed to deal specifically with the administrative-contingency problem are usually inapposite. An example of such a property interest is an open class gift that is contingent on survival of World War II. See Brownell v. Edmunds (4th Cir. 1953); but cf. Monarski v. Greb (Ill. 1950); Grynberg v. Amerada Hess Corp. (D. Colo. 1972) ("[A]s a matter of practical business judgment," the court said in dictum, "it is difficult to conceive of an oil field which would be operated without realizable profit for 21 years beyond a life in being . . . .").

§ 13.15. The Afterborn Spouse

(a) Standard Afterborn-Spouse Case. The term "afterborn spouse" refers to the fact that an unnamed "widow," "widower," "spouse," or "surviving spouse" of a beneficiary is excluded from serving as the validating life. The beneficiary's "widow," "widower," "spouse," or "surviving spouse" *might* turn out to be someone who was conceived and born after the creation of the interest, no matter how improbable that possibility is. Thus if no other validating life can be located, the questioned interest, if subject to the common-law Rule, is invalid.

> EXAMPLE 13-27. *G* devised land "to my son *A* for life, remainder to his widow for her life, remainder to *A*'s then-living descendants." *G* was survived by *A*, *A*'s wife *W*, and their adult children, *X* and *Y*.
>
> The questioned interest—the remainder created in *A*'s descendants—is invalid. See, e.g., Pound v.

Shorter (Ga. 1989);[28] Easton v. Hall (Ill. 1926); Chenoweth v. Bullitt (Ky. Ct. App. 1928); Restatement of Property § 370 cmt. k & illus. 3. Though improbable, it is possible that A's widow will not be W, but someone who was born after G's death and who will more than 21 years beyond the deaths of A, W, X, Y, and any other person "in being" at G's death.

(b) No Violation if Beneficiaries Can Be Their Own Validating Lives.   The possibility of an afterborn spouse does not create a common-law Rule violation if the beneficiaries of the remainder interest following the spouse's death can be their own validating lives. In Example *13-27*, for example, the beneficiaries of the remainder interest would be their own validating lives if the remainder were created in named individuals (X and Y, perhaps) or a class that was closed at G's death (the children of G's predeceased daughter, B). Furthermore, if the remainder was not contingent on survival, the fact that it was still subject to open at G's death would not invalidate it if the class could not increase beyond lives in being. For example, in the absence of a condition precedent of survival, a remainder created in G's grandchildren would be valid in Example *13-27*. See Lanier v. Lanier (Ga. 1962).[29] But one created in G's great-grandchildren would be invalid,

---

[28] See supra note 10.

[29] See supra note 10.

with or without a condition precedent of survival.

(c) Constructional Preference for Validity. Even when no other validating lives can be located, as in the original facts of Example *13-27,* the constructional preference for validity outlined in § 13.8 can often be employed to avoid the afterborn spouse problem. When the dispositive language fairly allows, some courts have construed G's reference to A's "widow." "widower," "spouse," or "surviving spouse" as only referring to the person to whom A was married when the will was executed or when G died. See Willis v. Hendry (Conn. 1941)[30] (G's will referred to "the wife of my said son"); Friend's Will (N.Y. 1940) (G's will referred to "the widow of my said son Sol"). So construed, A's widow could not be afterborn, and thus the validating life in Example *13-27* would be the survivor of A and W. Note, too, that it should be easier to construe "wife," "husband," or "spouse" as referring to the person's current spouse than "widow," "widower," or "surviving spouse."

§ 13.16. Perpetuity Saving Clauses

(a) Traditional Clauses. The common-law Rule should be, and for the most part is, less fearsome to practicing estate-planning lawyers than it is to law students and law graduates studying for the bar examination. This is not because estate-planning lawyers have found that the Rule becomes more

---

[30] See supra note 19.

understandable with experience, but because they have discovered a secret: They need not be greatly concerned about the technicalities of the Rule. They protect their clients's plans from invalidity by using perpetuity saving clauses.

A typical perpetuity saving clause might provide:

The trust hereby created shall terminate in any event not later than 21 years after the death of the last survivor of my descendants who are in being at the time this instrument becomes effective, and unless sooner terminated by the terms hereof, the trustee shall, at the termination of such period, make distribution to the persons then entitled to the income of this trust, and in the same shares and proportions as they are so entitled.

Formulated and used properly, perpetuity saving clauses mean that no lawyer need ever fear that a trust or other property arrangement he or she drafts will violate the common-law Rule. In addition, unless the trust or other property arrangement is unreasonable—for example, unless it is to continue beyond the death of the last living member of the transferor's youngest descendant living when the trust or other arrangement was created—, the practicing lawyer need not fear that the perpetuity saving clause will have any practical effect other than to save the disposition from a common-law Rule violation. Trusts are routinely created that would violate the common-law Rule were it not for the perpetuity saving clause;

essentially a technicality, a perpetuity saving clause is nevertheless essential.

Perpetuity saving clauses do not typically govern the term of the trust; they operate as a back-stop just in case the actual term of the trust exceeds the time allotted by the saving clause. That part of a perpetuity saving clause that establishes this period of time is called the *perpetuity-period component*. Saving clauses contain another component, called the *gift-over component*. This component expressly creates a gift over that is guaranteed to vest at the termination of the period established in the perpetuity-period component, but only if the interests in the trust or other arrangement have neither vested nor terminated earlier in accordance with their primary terms.

It is important to note that regardless of what group of persons is designated in the perpetuity-period component of the saving clause, the survivor of the group is not necessarily the person who would be the validating life for the questioned interest in the absence of the saving clause. Without the saving clause, the questioned interest might in fact have been invalid because of the existence of an invalidating chain of possible post-creation events with respect to every insider who might be proposed as a validating life. The persons designated in the saving clause, however, become validating lives for all interests in the trust or other property arrangement. The saving clause confers on the last surviving member of the group the requisite causal connection demanded by the requirement of initial certainty. See Norton v. Georgia R.R. Bank & Trust (Ga. 1984) (upholding the validity of a traditional perpetuity saving clause).

It needs to be stressed that a saving clause measures off a true "perpetuity period." In contrast to the validating life determined by the search process described supra §§ 13.4 and 13.5, the validating life who emerges as the survivor of a group designated in a saving clause is also a "measuring life." The persons designated in a saving clause must be kept track of in order to determine when the last surviving member of that group dies.

In most cases, the saving clause not only avoids a violation of the common-law Rule; it also, in a sense, over-insures the client's disposition against the possibility that the gift over will ever take effect. The period of time established by the perpetuity-period component of the clause provides a margin of safety. Almost always, the length of time is sufficient to exceed—usually by a substantial margin—the time when the interests in the trust or other arrangement actually vest (or terminate) by their own terms. The clause, therefore, is usually a formality that validates the disposition without affecting the substance of the disposition at all.

(b) Royal Lives, Dozen Healthy Babies, and Other Ploys. The Restatement 2d of Property § 1.3 cmt. a states that a perpetuity saving clause is ineffective if "the number of individuals specified as the measuring lives . . . is so large that it would be an impossible administrative burden to locate them initially, let

alone determine the death of the survivor. . . ."
Accord Restatement of Property § 374 cmt. *l*;
Uniform Rule § 1 cmt. pt. B (designation of group is
invalid if the group is such "that it would cause it to
be impracticable to determine the death of the
survivor."); Thellusson v. Woodford (Ch. 1805).

One of the broadest groups of designated lives that
has been upheld appeared in the so-called royal-lives
clause in In re Villar (C.A. 1929). In *Villar*, the
testator provided for the vesting of all interests in a
trust "at the expiration of 20 years from the day of
the death of the last survivor of all lineal descendants
of Her Late Majesty Queen Victoria who shall be
living at the time of my death." The court did not
have precise evidence regarding the number or
identity of Queen Victoria's descendants living at the
testator's death in 1926, but did have evidence that
there were at least 120 of them living in 1922. The
Restatement of Property § 374 cmt. *l* states that a
clause like that in *Villar* would be found invalid by
an American court, as would specified similar periods
such as one measured by the lives of "those persons
whose names appear in the City Directory of the City
of X."

Although the royal-lives clause in *Villar* is one of
the widest groups that has ever been upheld, even by

an English court,[31] cases of a trust or saving clause actually being invalidated under this principle are few.[32]

Validity is one thing; discretion and practicability are another. A device sometimes mentioned by commentators is the dozen-healthy-babies ploy, under which the transferor designates a period governed by the life of the survivor of a number of newborn babies in the maternity ward of a specified hospital. A 21-year period is then tacked on after the death of the survivor. Writing in the early 1950's, when average life expectancy at birth was about 68 years, Professor Leach said that the period resulting from this device would "add up to about a century."[33] Although it would seem that his mathematics were a little off (68 + 21 = 89, not 100), Professor Leach undoubtedly understood that a group of newborns will almost certainly include several persons who will outlive average life expectancy. Professor Leach

---

[31] Another candidate for the prize comes from Warren's Will (1961), where the period was measured by the life of the survivor of 194 marital issue of Queen Victoria.

[32] In In re Moore (Ch. 1901), the testator created a trust to endure until "twenty-one years from the death of the last survivor of all persons who shall be living at my death." In a short opinion, the court held the gift void for uncertainty. "It is impossible to ascertain when the last life will be extinguished," the court said. Cases are collected in Reporter's Note No. 3 to § 1.3, Restatement 2d of Property.

[33] W. Barton Leach & Owen Tudor, The Common Law Rule Against Perpetuities, in Am. L. Prop. § 24.16, at 52.

apparently estimated that an additional 11 years or so would account for this.

With the current life expectancy at birth averaging 75 years, the total period of time produced by this device today would average out to a period well in excess of the 96 years calculated by adding 21 to 75. In fact, it would yield an average period of about 115 years.[34] Professor Leach rightly condemned such a practice,[35] but he was probably poking at a strawman. To our knowledge, practicing lawyers do not use the dozen-healthy-babies ploy. They see the task of identifying and keeping track of the lives of a

---

[34] The average life expectancy of the longest-living member of a group of twelve newborn babies, selected at random, is 94.2 years. With the 21-year tack-on period, the dozen-healthy-babies ploy would produce, on average, a period of about 115 years (94 + 21).

The 94-year life expectancy was computed by applying a complicated actuarial formula to the data set forth in Table 80CNSMT, in Fed. Est. & Gift Tax Rep. (CCH) ¶ 6415.301 (1989). Starting with an original cohort of 100,000 newborns, Table 80CNSMT gives the number of people who live to age one (98,740), age two (98,648), and so on to ages 109 (33) and 110 (0).

I would like to express gratitude to Dr. Cecil Nesbitt, professor emeritus of mathematics at the University of Michigan, for deriving the actuarial formula used in the computation; he derived the formula from the principles set forth in N. Bowers et al., Actuarial Mathematics Ch. 16 (1986).

[35] See J. H. C. Morris & W. Barton Leach, The Rule Against Perpetuities 13 (2d ed. 1962).

dozen babies who are wholly unrelated to the client's family as fanciful and impracticable. If they want to extend the period as long as practicable, they can designate the descendants of the transferor's parents or even of the transferor's grandparents rather than the descendants of the transferor. These broader groups of family members are nearly certain to sweep in a number of very young children and, with the 21-year period tacked on after the death of the survivor, produce a period of around 100 years and perhaps longer.

Chapter 14

PERPETUITY REFORM

Largely due to enactments of the Uniform Statutory Rule Against Perpetuities (Uniform Rule), the common-law Rule is no longer the majority rule in the United States. ☺ The need for perpetuity reform is not much in doubt. The common-law Rule is too harsh when it invalidates property interests that are almost but not quite certain to vest if at all within a life in being plus 21 years. The "fertile octogenarians" (supra § 13.13), the administrative contingencies (supra § 13.14), and the afterborn spouses (supra § 13.15) fall into this category. So also do most cases of age contingencies exceeding 21. The Uniform Rule cures the over-invalidating tendencies of the common-law Rule by adopting the wait-and-see method of perpetuity reform.

Until the promulgation of the Uniform Rule in 1986, there was little hope for a unified reform method. Scattered reform measures were proposed, but none attracted more than a few adoptions. In the few years since its promulgation, the Uniform Rule has seized the momentum. Since its promulgation, no state has enacted a different reform method. As of this writing, the Uniform Rule has been enacted in forty percent of the states. The Uniform Rule has been approved by the American Bar Association, on the unanimous recommendation of the Council of the A.B.A. Section of Real Property, Probate and Trust Law. It has also been unanimously endorsed by the Joint Editorial Board for the Uniform Probate Code, the Board of Regents of the American College of Trust and Estate Counsel, and the Board of Governors of the American College of Real Estate Lawyers. The Uniform Rule has been incorporated into the UPC as Part 9 of Article II. As noted, the Uniform Rule has been enacted in forty percent of the states, making it the single most widely adopted method of perpetuity reform to date. It seems to be on its way to becoming the majority rule in the United States.

§ 14.1.   Wait-and-See: General Introduction

The common-law Rule based validity upon the full array of *possible* post-creation events. In its early stages, the perpetuity-reform movement focused on the technical-violation categories (supra § 13.12). Since the post-creation chains of possible events that invalidate those interests are so unlikely to happen, it was rather natural to propose that the basis of validity be shifted from possible to actual post-creation events. Instead of invalidating an interest because of what *might* happen, waiting to see what *does* happen seemed then and still seems now to be more sensible. This approach is known as the wait-and-see method of perpetuity reform.

(a) Validating Side Preserved; Only Invalidating Side Altered. Wait-and-see does not alter the *validating* side of the common-law Rule. Dispositions that would have been valid under the common-law Rule remain valid. Practitioners under a wait-and-see regime can and should continue to use a traditional perpetuity saving clause (supra § 13.16). The wait-and-see element is applied only to interests that fall prey to the *invalidating* side of the common-law Rule. Under wait-and-see, interests that would be invalid at common law are no longer *initially* invalid. They are, as it were, given a second chance: They are valid if they actually vest within the permissible vesting period; they become invalid only if they remain in existence but still nonvested at the expiration of that period.

(b) Saving-Clause Principle of Wait-and-See. Wait-and-see should be thought of as a perpetuity saving clause injected by law. Conversely, the perpetuity-period component of a traditional saving clause should be thought of as a privately established wait-and-see rule. The permissible vesting period under wait-and-see is, or should be, the equivalent of the perpetuity-period component of a well-conceived saving clause.

The saving clause is rounded out by providing the near-equivalent of a gift-over component via a provision for judicial reformation of a disposition in case the interest is still in existence and nonvested when the permissible vesting period expires.

(c) Title in Abeyance. One of the early objections to wait-and-see should be mentioned at this point. It was once widely argued and is still occasionally argued that wait-and-see can cause harm because it puts the validity of property interests in abeyance—no one can determine whether an interest is valid or not. This argument has been shown to be false. Keep in mind that the wait-and-see element is only applied to interests that would be invalid were it not for wait-and-see. These otherwise invalid interests are always *nonvested* future interests. It is now understood by most, and should be understood by all, that wait-and-see does nothing more than subject that type of future interest to an *additional* contingency. To vest, the other contingencies must not only be satisfied; they must be satisfied within a certain period of time. If that period of time—the permissible vesting period—is easily determined, then the additional contingency causes no more uncertainty in the title than if the same time-contingency had been placed in the governing instrument itself. It should also be noted that only the status of the affected future interest is deferred. During the interim, the other interests, such as the interests of current income beneficiaries, are not affected.

(d) The Permissible Vesting Period. The greatest controversy over wait-and-see concerns how to determine the permissible vesting period. (The permissible vesting period is the period of time during which contingencies can be validly satisfied.)

The conventional assumption has always been that

the permissible vesting period should be determined by reference to so-called measuring lives who are in being at the creation of the interest; the permissible vesting period under this assumption expires 21 years after the death of the last surviving measuring life.

But who are the "measuring lives"? The problem arises because the common-law Rule contains no mechanism for identifying measuring lives under wait-and-see. The only mechanism for determining validity that the common law provides is the requirement of initial certainty, which as noted supra § 13.4, is a mechanism for testing the validity of an interest at the point of its creation. The decision is made at the point of creation, with actual post-creation events disregarded. Thus the common law has no cause to mark off a "perpetuity period" during which actual post-creation events are allowed to be taken into account. At common law, there either is or is not a validating life. There is no validating life for invalid interests, hence there is no common-law "perpetuity period" to wait out. A permissible vesting period is necessary only under the wait-and-see method of perpetuity reform.

As we shall see (infra § 14.2(b)), the Uniform Rule breaks with convention and adopts a permissible vesting period of a flat 90 years.

§ 14.2   Wait-and-See Under the Uniform Statutory Rule Against Perpetuities (Uniform Rule)

The National Conference of Commissioners on Uniform State Laws promulgated the Uniform Rule in 1986, and amended it modestly and brought it into the UPC in 1990.[1] So far, the Uniform Rule has been enacted in California, Colorado, Connecticut, Florida, Georgia, Hawaii, Indiana, Kansas, Massachusetts, Michigan, Minnesota, Montana, Nebraska, Nevada, New Jersey, New Mexico, North Dakota, Oregon, South Carolina, and West Virginia.

(a) Basic Operation. The general contour of the Uniform Rule is similar to conventional wait-and-see regimes. The validating side of the common-law Rule is retained but the invalidating side is replaced with wait-and-see and deferred-reformation elements. The major departure is that the Uniform Rule uses a flat 90-year permissible vesting period under its wait-and-see element rather than a period ending 21 years after the death of the survivor of a group of measuring lives.

Section 1(a)(1) of the Uniform Rule codifies the validating side of the common-law Rule and § 1(a)(2) establishes the wait-and-see element:

---

[1] The 1990 amendment added subsection (e) to § 1 (UPC § 2-901(e)).

§ 1(a). A nonvested property interest is invalid unless:

(1) when the interest is created, it is certain to vest or terminate no later than 21 years after the death of an individual then alive; or

(2) the interest either vests or terminates within 90 years after its creation.

The basic operation of the wait-and-see element is illustrated by the following example.

EXAMPLE 14-1. G devised the residue of his estate in trust, directing the trustee to pay the income "to A for life, then to A's children for the life of the survivor, and upon the death of A's last surviving child, to pay the corpus of the trust to A's then-living descendants, by representation.") G was survived by A and by A's two children, X and Y.

Under the common-law Rule, the remainder interest in the corpus created in A's descendants would be invalid. Consequently, the remainder interest would not be initially valid under § 1(a)(1) of the Uniform Rule. But, unlike at common law, the remainder interest would not be initially invalid either. Section 1(a)(2) of the Uniform Rule applies, allowing 90 years for the remainder interest to vest. If A's last surviving child dies within 90 years after G's death, as is very likely, the remainder interest is valid. If A's last surviving child lives beyond the 90-year period, the remainder interest is invalid, but the disposition can be judicially reformed to make it valid. On how it might be reformed, see infra Example *14-2.*

(b) Rationale of the 90-Year Permissible Vesting Period. The most striking feature of the Uniform Rule is that its wait-and-see element uses a flat period of 90 years. The rationale for this step was explained by the Reporter for the Uniform Rule as follows:

[T]he philosophy behind the 90-year period was to fix a period of time that approximates the average period of time that would traditionally be allowed by the wait-and-see doctrine. There was no intention to use the flat-period-of-years method as a means of lengthening the [permissible vesting] period beyond its traditional boundaries. The fact that the traditional period roughly averages out to a longish-sounding 90 years is a reflection of a quite different phenomenon: the dramatic increase in longevity that society as a whole has experienced in the course of the twentieth century. Seen in this light, the 90-year period is an evolutionary step in the development of the wait-and-see doctrine.

[T]he traditional method of delimiting the [permissible vesting] period is to use actual measuring lives plus 21 years. Specifically, under this method, a group of persons—called the measuring lives—is identified. Once the group is identified, the lives of all its members are traced to see which one outlives all the others and when that survivor dies. The [permissible vesting] period extends 21 years beyond the death of that last surviving measuring life.

From its inception, the actual-measuring-lives approach has been plagued by two problems: identification and tracing. The identification problem concerns the method by which the measuring lives are to be chosen. Rival methods have been advanced. Under one method . . . , the measuring lives are identified by testing each disposition to determine the persons whose lives have a "causal relationship" to the vesting or failure of the future interest in question. The actual meaning of causal relationship is in dispute, and the adoption of that method could require front-end litigation to determine the identity of the measuring lives in a given case. Neither the Restatement [2d of Property] nor [the Uniform Rule] adopted the causal-relationship method. The Restatement specifies the measuring lives in a different way. The Restatement uses a list composed, generally speaking, of the transferor, the beneficiaries of the disposition, the parents and grandparents of the beneficiaries, and, in certain cases, the donee of a nonfiduciary power of appointment; of the foregoing, those who are in being at the creation of the interest are the measuring lives. It soon became apparent that the Restatement's list contained ambiguities, at least at the fringes, which could also require front-end litigation to determine the full complement of measuring lives in a given case. The framers of [the Uniform Rule] concluded that an ambiguity-free formulation of the specified-list method would necessitate a complex set of statutory provisions. . . .

The second problem plaguing the actual-measuring-lives approach is that of tracing. No matter how the measuring lives are identified, the lives of those actual individuals must be traced to determine which one is the longest survivor and when he or she died.

The tracing and identification problems are exacerbated by the premise, seemingly accepted under both methods, that the measuring lives cannot always remain a static group, assembled once and for all at the beginning. Instead, individuals who were once measuring lives must be dropped from the group if certain events happen (such as the individual's divorce, adoption out of the family, or assignment of his or her beneficial interest to another); conversely, individuals who were not among the initial group of measuring lives must be included later if certain events happen (such as marriage, adoption into the family, or receipt of another's beneficial interest by assignment or succession) and if they were living when the interest in question was created. This instability within the group of measuring lives heightens the potential for a further round of litigation at one point or another during the running of the [permissible vesting] period.

By opting for a flat period of years, the framers of [the Uniform Rule] eliminated the clutter that has heretofore plagued the wait-and-see strategy—the problems of identifying, tracing, and possibly litigating the make-up of a sometimes-fluctuating group of measuring lives. The expiration of a [permissible vesting] period measured by a flat period of years is litigation free, easy to determine, and unmistakable.

The framers of [the Uniform Rule] considered objections to replacing the actual-measuring-lives approach with a flat period of years, despite the gain in administrative simplicity that would result. One such objection was the idea that the use of actual measuring lives—especially if determined by the causal-relationship method—generates a [permissible vesting] period that self-adjusts to each situation, somehow extending the dead hand no further than necessary in each case. A flat period of years obviously cannot replicate a self-adjusting function. This objection proved unfounded, however, for the actual-measuring-lives approach also fails to perform a self-adjusting function. Although that approach produces [permissible vesting] periods of different lengths from one case to another, it does not generate a [permissible vesting] period that expires at a natural or logical stopping point along the continuum of each disposition, thereby pinpointing the time before which actual vesting ought to be allowed and beyond which it ought not to be permitted. Instead, the actual-measuring-lives approach—under either the specified-list or casual-relationship method—generates a [permissible vesting] period whose length almost always exceeds by some arbitrary period of time the point of actual vesting in cases that are traditionally validated by the wait-and-see strategy. The actual-measuring-lives approach, therefore, performs a margin-of-safety function, a function that can be replicated by the use of a proxy such as the flat 90-year period under [the Uniform Rule].

In standard cases, the rivalry between the causal-relationship and the specified-list methods of identifying actual measuring lives is very little concerned with the length of the [permissible vesting] period. Often, the specified-list method will produce a greater number of measuring lives than the causal-relationship method. In the normal course of events, however, the [permissible vesting] period is not governed by the number of measuring lives, but by the lifetime of the youngest. Unless the additional measuring lives are younger than the others or are clustered in very young age groups, such as under the twelve-healthy-babies ploy, a greater number of measuring lives seldom adds to the length of the [permissible vesting] period. In the normal course of events, the youngest measuring life is the key to the length of the [permissible vesting] period, and no matter which method is used for determining the identity of the measuring lives, the youngest measuring life, in standard trusts, is likely to be the transferor's youngest descendant living when the trust was created. The 90-year period of [the Uniform Rule] is premised on this proposition. Using four hypothetical families deemed to be representative of actual families, the framers determined that, on average, the transferor's youngest descendant in being at the transferor's death—assuming the transferor's death to occur between ages 60 and 90, which is when 73 percent of the population die—is about 6 years old. The remaining life expectancy of a 6-year old is about 69 years. The 69 years, plus the 21-year tack-on period, gives [a permissible vesting] period of 90 years. Although this method may not be scientifically accurate to the nth degree, the Drafting Committee considered it reliable enough to support a [permissible vesting] period of 90 years, given the margin-of-safety function that it performs.

.Lawrence W. Waggoner, The Uniform Statutory Rule Against Perpetuities: The Rationale of the 90-Year Waiting Period, 73 Cornell L. Rev. 157, 162-68 (1988).

(c) Acceptance of the 90-Year Period Under the Federal Generation-Skipping Transfer Tax. In general terms, trusts that were irrevocable on September 25, 1985, are exempt from the federal generation-skipping transfer tax. See Tax Reform Act of 1986 § 1433(b)(2). These trusts are called "grandfathered trusts." Under Treasury Regulations,

"grandfathered trusts" can become ungrandfathered if a nongeneral power of appointment is exercised so as to postpone the vesting of an interest beyond the perpetuity period. See Temp. Treas. Reg. § 26.2601-1(b)(1)(v)(B)(2) (1988). Acting in ignorance of the 90-year period of the Uniform Rule, the original version of this regulation defined the perpetuity period solely in terms of a life in being plus 21 years. After the 90-year period of the Uniform Rule was brought to the attention of Treasury Department officials, the Department issued proposed regulations that accommodate the Uniform Rule's 90-year period. See Prop. Treas. Reg. § 26.2601-1(b)(1)(v)(B)(2) (1992) ("For purposes of this paragraph (b)(1)(v)(B)(2), the exercise of a power of appointment that validly postpones or suspends the vesting, absolute ownership or power of alienation of an interest in property for a term of years that will not exceed 90 years (measured from the date of the creation of the trust) will not be considered an exercise that postpones vesting beyond the perpetuities period.").

(d) Deferred Reformation Under the Uniform Rule. Another feature of the Uniform Rule is deferred-reformation. If an interest becomes invalid because it fails to vest (or terminate) within the 90-year permissible vesting period, § 3 of the Uniform Rule directs a court, upon the petition of an interested person, to reform the disposition within the limits of the 90-year period, in the manner deemed by the court most closely to approximate the transferor's

manifested plan of distribution. The "interested person" who would frequently bring the reformation suit would be the trustee. Deferred-reformation is available in any one of three circumstances.

Seldom will this feature become applicable. Of the fraction of trusts and other property arrangements that are incompetently drafted, and thus fail to satisfy the validating side of the common-law Rule, almost all of them will have terminated by their own terms long before any of the allowable circumstances for reformation arise.

If, against the odds, the right to reformation does arise, it will be found easier than perhaps anticipated to determine how best to reform the disposition.[2] The court is given two reformation criteria: (i) the transferor's manifested plan of distribution and (ii) the 90-year permissible vesting period. Because governing instruments are where transferors manifest their plans of distribution, the imaginary horror of courts being forced to probe the minds of long-dead transferors will not materialize.

The theory of the Uniform Rule is to defer the right to reformation until reformation becomes truly necessary. Thus, the basic rule is that the right to reformation does not arise until a nonvested property interest or a power of appointment becomes invalid;

---

[2] Note that reformation is mandatory, not subject to the discretion of the court. Consequently, the common-law doctrine of infectious invalidity (supra § 13.11) is superseded by the Uniform Rule.

this does not occur until the expiration of the 90-year permissible vesting period. By confining perpetuity litigation to those few cases in which the permissible vesting period actually is exceeded, perpetuity litigation is reduced.

> *EXAMPLE 14-2.* The same disposition as in Example *14-1* (*G* devised the residue of his estate in trust, directing the trustee to pay the income "to *A* for life, then to *A*'s children for the life of the survivor, and upon the death of *A*'s last surviving child, to pay the corpus of the trust to *A*'s then-living descendants, by representation.") *G* was survived by *A* and by *A*'s two children, *X* and *Y*.

As explained in Example *14-1*, the Uniform Rule allows 90 years for the remainder interest to vest. If *A* still has a living child or children on the 90th anniversary of *G*'s death, the remainder interest becomes invalid, but, on the petition of an interested person, the disposition must be judicially reformed to make it valid.

The most appropriate form of reformation would be to vest the remainder interest in *A*'s descendants who would take if *A*'s last surviving child had died on the 90th anniversary of *G*'s death. This would not cut short the income interest of *A*'s living child or children. The remainder interest in *A*'s descendants would be vested *in interest* as of the 90th anniversary of *G*'s death, but not vested in possession. Possession would still be postponed until the actual death of *A*'s last surviving child.

In certain cases, the Uniform Rule grants the right to reformation *before* the 90-year period runs out. The Uniform Rule grants a right to early reformation when it becomes necessary to do so or when there is no point in waiting the 90-year period out. Thus the Uniform Rule grants a right to early reformation whenever the share of any class member is entitled to take effect in possession or enjoyment, even though the class gift is not yet but still might become invalid under the wait-and-see element.

> *EXAMPLE 14-3. G* devised property in trust, directing the trustee to pay the income "to *A* for life, then to *A*'s children"; the corpus of the trust is to be equally divided among *A*'s children who reach the age of 30. *G* was survived by *A*, by *A*'s spouse (*H*), and by *A*'s two children (*X* and *Y*), both of whom were under the age of 30 when *G* died. After *G*'s death, another child (*Z*) was born to *A*. Although unlikely, suppose that at *A*'s death (prior to the expiration of the 90-year period), *Z*'s age was such that he could be alive but under the age of 30 on the 90th anniversary of *G*'s death. Suppose further that at *A*'s death *X* and *Y* were over the age of 30.

> The criteria for early reformation are met: (1) *X* and *Y* are entitled to possession of their shares as of *A*'s death; and (2) under the "all or nothing" rule applicable to class gifts (supra § 13.2(c); infra § 15.2), the class gift might become invalid because *Z* might reach 30 beyond the 90-year period following *G*'s death.

The most appropriate form of reformation would be to make Z's interest contingent on reaching the age Z can reach if Z lives to the 90th anniversary of G's death. This reformation makes Z's interest valid under the Uniform Rule and validates the entire class gift. X and Y, therefore, are immediately entitled to receive their one-third shares. If Z's interest later vests, Z would receive the remaining one-third share. If Z fails to reach the required age under the reformed disposition, the remaining one-third share would be divided equally between X and Y or their successors in interest.

The Uniform Rule also grants the right to early reformation in one other situation. The right to early reformation under this provision arises if a nonvested property interest can vest but not before the 90-year period expires. Though unlikely, such a case can theoretically arise. If it does, the interest—unless it terminates by its own terms earlier—is bound to become invalid eventually. There is no point in deferring the right to reformation until the inevitable happens. Thus the Uniform Rule provides for early reformation in such a case, just in case it arises.

EXAMPLE 14-4. G devised property in trust, directing the trustee to divide the income, by representation, among G's descendants living from time to time, for 100 years. At the end of the 100 years, the trustee is to distribute the corpus to G's then-living descendants, by representation.

Because the remainder interest to *G*'s descendants living 100 years after *G*'s death can vest but not before 90 years, the Uniform Rule grants a right to early reformation. The most appropriate form of reformation would be to reduce the 100-year period to 90 years.

§ 14.3. Earlier Versions of Wait-and-See

The Uniform Rule was preceded by various other versions of wait-and-see. These antecedents followed the conventional approach of measuring the permissible vesting period by actual measuring lives plus 21 years. All these earlier versions suffered from the same difficulty: None provided a satisfactory and predictable means of identifying the "measuring lives." Nevertheless, some of these earlier versions are still in effect in a few states.

(a) Pennsylvania-Style Statutes. Enacted in 1947, the Pennsylvania statute (20 Pa. Cons. Stat. Ann. § 6104(b)) was the first wait-and-see statute. The statute mistakenly presupposes that there is a common-law perpetuity period, and so it contains no method of determining the permissible vesting period for wait-and-see. The statute provides:

Upon the expiration of the period allowed by the common law rule against perpetuities as measured by actual rather than possible events, any interest not then vested and any interest in members of a class the membership of which is then subject to increase shall be void.

Pennsylvania-style statutes are also in effect in Ohio, South Dakota, Vermont, and Virginia. The only case ever to apply the Pennsylvania statute or a Pennsylvania-style statute is Pearson Estate (Pa. 1971), a decision universally condemned for not explaining who the measuring lives were and how they were to be identified under the statute. See, e.g., Lawrence W. Waggoner, Perpetuity Reform, 81 Mich. L. Rev. 1718, 1762-76 (1983).

(b) Massachusetts-Style Statutes. Enacted in 1954, the Massachusetts-style statute expressly measures the permissible vesting period by the period of one or more life estates created in persons in being at the creation of the interest:

> In applying the rule against perpetuities to an interest in real or personal property limited to take effect at or after the termination of one or more life estates in, or lives of, persons in being when the period of said rule commences to run, the validity of the interest shall be determined on the basis of facts existing at the termination of such one or more life estates or lives. In this section an interest which must terminate not later than the death of one or more persons is a "life estate" even though it may terminate at an earlier time.

Massachusetts-style statutes are in effect in Maine and Maryland. Until 1989, this type of statute was also in effect in Connecticut and Massachusetts; it was repealed when Connecticut and Massachusetts enacted the Uniform Rule.

Choosing to restrict the permissible vesting period to one or more life estates created in persons in being at the creation of the interest does not even reverse the invalidity in a standard administrative-contingency case, nor does it provide appropriate relief in age-contingency-exceeding-21 cases. The statutes, in fact, further provide that if at the end of the restricted vesting period, an interest would be invalid because it is "contingent upon any person attaining or failing to attain an age in excess of twenty-one, the age contingency shall be reduced to twenty-one as to all persons subject to the same age contingency." In Second Nat'l Bank v. Harris Trust & Savings Bank (Conn. Super. Ct. 1971), this latter provision was held inapplicable to a trust that was created by the exercise of a general testamentary power of appointment and that provided for the income to go to the testator-donee's daughter, Mary, for 30 years, remainder to Mary, but if she was not then living, to her descendants, per stirpes. The court held that the executory interest created in Mary's descendants violated the Rule Against Perpetuities and was invalid; the effect was to render Mary's remainder interest absolute. As for the age-contingency provision of the statute, the court said: "It seems too clear for argument that the remainder to Mary's children is not 'contingent upon any person attaining or failing to attain an age in excess of twenty-one.'"

(c) Kentucky-Style Statutes. Enacted in 1960, the Kentucky statute (Ky. Rev. Stat. § 381.216) adopts a permissible vesting period measured by the life of persons who have a "causal relationship" to the vesting or failure of the interest in question:

> In determining whether an interest would violate the rule against perpetuities the period of perpetuities shall be measured by actual rather than possible events; Provided, however, the period shall not be measured by any lives whose continuance does not have a causal relationship to the vesting or failure of the interest.

Kentucky-style statutes are also in effect in Alaska and Rhode Island. Until 1987 and 1992, respectively, this type of statute was also in effect in Nevada and New Mexico; it was repealed when Nevada and New Mexico enacted the Uniform Rule.

The meaning of "causal relationship to the vesting or failure of the interest" is much in dispute.

> *EXAMPLE 14-5. G* deeded real property "to *A* and his heirs, but if the property is used for nonresidential purposes, to *X* and her heirs."
>
> Although it would seem that *A* is the only person whose life bears a causal-relationship to whether *X*'s interest vests, the architect of the causal-relationship formula and the principal drafter of the Kentucky statute believes that *X* is the only permissible measuring life in this example! See Jesse Dukeminier, Perpetuities: The Measuring Lives, 85 Colum. L. Rev.

1648, 1705-06 (1985) (arguing that X has a causal-relationship to vesting because X is the beneficiary of the nonvested interest; and arguing that, although A does have a causal-relationship to the vesting of X's interest, A must be excluded because he might transfer his possessory interest to unknown successors in interest).

EXAMPLE 14-6. G died in 1921, survived by his son A and A's daughter, X. G left a will that created a testamentary trust, under which the trustee was to pay the income from a portion of his residuary estate to A for life, then to A's children for life, and on the death of each of A's children, to pay to "the child or children of such deceased child . . . , per stirpes and not per capita, his [or] her proportionate share of this trust estate, as an estate vested in fee simple, discharged of all trust."

After G's death, several additional descendants were born. Among them were A's son, Y, and X's three children and Y's two children. After A's death in 1935, each of his children began receiving a proportionate share of the trust income. Y died in 1985, survived by his two children and by his sister, X, and her three children.

Applying the Rhode Island causal-relationship statute, the Supreme Court of Rhode Island upheld the remainder interest of Y's children in half the trust corpus. Fleet Nat'l Bank v. Colt (R.I. 1987). The court identified the testator's granddaughter, X, as the causal-relationship measuring life. At the time of Y's death, X was the only one of A's children who was alive at G's death. The court reasoned:

[X] is thus a life in being and an acceptable measuring life. She is causally connected not only to the vesting of the remainder in her own children, but also to the life estate of her siblings and thus to the remainder in her sibling's children. If, for example, [X] had predeceased her father [A], the income that [A] had been receiving as a first life tenant would have been divided [into fewer shares]. Thus, the amount of [Y]'s share, and consequently the amounts of his children's shares, were dependent upon the survival of [X].

The court's reasoning has been criticized on the ground that, "[a]t most, [X] was related to the resolution of only the first uncertainty—the division of shares at [A]'s death. Even here, [A]'s life, not [X]'s, is the defensive life. The fact that a class member, such as [X], happened to be alive at the effective date, is not significant. If, however, we see [X] as significant at [A]'s death, nevertheless she serves no useful function thereafter, and her continued life thereafter should be unusable." Robert L. Fletcher, Perpetuities: Basic Clarity, Muddled Reform, 63 Wash. L. Rev. 791, 832 n.57 (1988).

Despite the obvious uncertainties in identifying causal-relationship measuring lives, the Supreme Court of Mississippi *judicially* adopted the wait-and-see method of reform using "causal-relationship" lives. Estate of Anderson (Miss. 1989).

(d) Restatement 2d of Property (1983). In adopting the wait-and-see method of perpetuity reform, the Restatement 2d of Property adopted a different method of determining the wait-and-see measuring lives. The Restatement uses a predetermined list of lives. Under § 1.3(2), the permissible vesting period expires 21 years after the death of the survivor of:

(a) The transferor if the period of the rule begins to run in the transferor's lifetime; and

(b) Those individuals alive when the period of the rule begins to run, if reasonable in number, who have beneficial interests vested or contingent in the property in which the non-vested interest in question exists and the parents and grandparents alive when the period of the rule begins to run of all beneficiaries of the property in which the non-vested interest exists, and

(c) The donee of a nonfiduciary power of appointment alive when the period of the rule begins to run if the exercise of such power could affect the non-vested interest in question.

If a property interest is still in existence but nonvested at the expiration of the permissible vesting period, § 1.5 provides that "the transferred property shall be disposed of in the manner which most closely effectuates the transferor's manifested plan of distribution and which is within the limits of the rule against perpetuities."

So far, the Restatement's version of wait-and-see has not been directly adopted by any common-law court, nor has it been legislatively enacted by any state. A statute enacted in Iowa was influenced by the Restatement, however; the Iowa statute designates as the measuring lives the beneficiaries and "the grandparents of all such beneficiaries and the issue of such grandparents. . . ." Iowa Code § 558.68(2)(b)(2) (enacted in 1983).

§ 14.4. The Immediate-Reformation Method of Perpetuity Reform

Although wait-and-see is the method of perpetuity reform that has attracted the most following by far, it is not the only method that has attracted any following. One of the other methods that has some (but declining) following is called "immediate reformation." Under this method, a court is authorized or, in some legislation, directed to cure any violation of the common-law Rule by reforming the disposition to make it valid. Unlike the *deferred*-reformation element of most wait-and-see statutes, including the Uniform Rule, the immediate-reformation method allows reformation at any time.

The Oklahoma statute (Okla. Stat. tit. 60, § 75) is representative of legislation adopting immediate reformation:

Any interest in real or personal property that would violate the rule against perpetuities shall be reformed, or construed within the limits of the rule, to give effect to the general intent of the creator of that interest whenever that general intent can be ascertained. This provision shall be liberally construed and applied to validate such interest to the fullest extent consistent with such ascertained intent.

Similar statutes are in effect in Missouri and Texas.[3] Until 1991, California had a similar statute, but repealed it when it enacted the Uniform Rule. Without the benefit of legislation, a few courts have judicially adopted the immediate-reformation method. See Edgerly v. Barker (N.H. 1891); Carter v. Berry (Miss. 1962); In re Chun Quan Yee Hop (Hawaii 1970); and Berry v. Union Nat'l Bank (W. Va. 1980). Hawaii and West Virginia, however. subsequently enacted the Uniform Rule, effectively displacing the *Hop* and *Berry* decisions for post-effective-date transfers.

Although these judicial decisions and statutes authorize or direct reformation of the defective instrument in a way that comes as close as possible to the transferor's intent without violating the common-law Rule, the cases have all been of a similar type—an age contingency or a period in gross exceeding 21. In each of the above cases, the court

---

[3] The Texas statute seems to have been unnecessarily limited to charitable gifts. See Foshee v. Republic Nat'l Bank (Tex. 1981).

reformed the disposition by lowering the age contingency or period in gross to 21.

A method of reformation more faithful to the transferor's intention would have been to insert a saving clause into the governing instrument. See Olin L. Browder, Jr., Construction, Reformation, and the Rule Against Perpetuities, 62 Mich. L. Rev. 1 (1963); Lawrence W. Waggoner, Perpetuity Reform, 81 Mich. L. Rev. 1718, 1755-59 (1983); John H. Langbein & Lawrence W. Waggoner, Reformation of Wills on the Ground of Mistake: Change of Direction in American Law?, 130 U. Pa. L. Rev. 521, 546-49 (1982). Recently, the Supreme Court of Mississippi adopted this method of reformation. Unfortunately, the court revealed a degree of misunderstanding by also purporting to adopt the wait-and-see method of perpetuity reform without seeming to realize that immediate reformation and wait-and-see are mutually inconsistent. See Estate of Anderson (Miss. 1989) (court upheld testamentary trust that was to last for 25 years from the date of admission of the will to probate, the income to be used for the education of the descendants of the testator's father, and the corpus at the end of the 25-year period to be paid over to the testator's nephew, Howard Davis, or if Howard was not then living, to the heirs of Howard's body; by inserting a saving clause and by adopting wait-and-see, the court validated the trust without reducing its term to 21 years).

§ 14.5.　Specific-Statutory-Repair Method

Since the over-invalidating tendencies of the common-law Rule largely manifest themselves in the technical-violation categories (supra § 13.12), a few states have enacted precise legislative provisions directed specifically at these categories.

This method, the specific-statutory-repair method, is in effect in two jurisdictions—Illinois, where it is combined with wait-and-see for trusts, and New York. Until 1988, this method was also in effect in Florida, but was repealed when Florida enacted the Uniform Rule. Until 1991, California had a statute aimed at the afterborn spouse category, but not the other categories of technical violation, but repealed it when it enacted the Uniform Rule.

(a) The Fertile-Octogenarian Problem. The Illinois statute alleviates the fertile-octogenarian problem (supra § 13.13) by providing that persons above 65 and below 13 are deemed incapable of having a child; that evidence is admissible regarding the incapacity of having a child by a living person who is under 65; and that the possibility of having a child or more remote descendant by adoption shall be disregarded. New York has a similar provision.

(b) The Administrative-Contingency Problem. The Illinois statute alleviates the administrative-contingency problem (supra § 13.14) by presuming that the probate of a will, the appointment of an executor, administrator, or trustee, the administration of an estate, the payment of debts, the sale or distribution of property, the determination of tax

liabilities, or any other administrative contingency must happen, if at all, within the perpetuity period. New York has a similar provision.

(c) The Afterborn-Spouse Problem. The Illinois statute alleviates the afterborn-spouse problem (supra § 13.15) by presuming that an interest in the "widow," "widower," or "spouse" of another person was intended to refer to a person who was living at the date that the Rule commences to run. New York has a similar provision.

(d) Age Contingencies Exceeding 21. The Illinois statute provides that where an interest would be invalid because it depends upon any person attaining or failing to attain an age exceeding 21 years, the age shall be reduced to 21 regarding every person to whom the age contingency applies. Such a statute can be categorized as constituting a form of the immediate-reformation method of perpetuity reform described supra § 14.4. However, because its application is narrow and because the nature of the reformation is specified and is required by the statute, rather than discretionary with the court, it is listed here as part of the specific-statutory-repair method. New York has a similar provision.

§ 14.6.   Abolition of the Rule

The ultimate method of perpetuity reform is abolition of the Rule. In 1969, Wisconsin enacted legislation that abolished the common-law Rule Against Perpetuities and rendered a related rule, the rule against the suspension of the power of alienation, inapplicable "if the trustee has power to sell, either expressed or implied, or if there is an unlimited power to terminate in one or more persons in being." Wis. Stat. § 700.16. See also S.D. Codified Laws Ann. § 43-5-8. Compare Idaho Code Ann. § 55.111.

Chapter 15

CLASS GIFTS UNDER THE RULE AGAINST PERPETUITIES

This chapter contrasts the common-law Rule Against Perpetuities (common-law Rule) with the Uniform Statutory Rule Against Perpetuities (Uniform Rule) regarding class gifts.

§ 15.1. A Primer on Class Gifts

(a) What is a Class Gift? A class gift is a gift of property to a group of persons identified by a group label, such as "children," "grandchildren," "issue," "descendants," "brothers," "sisters," "nieces," "nephews," or "first cousins." Not all gifts to a group of persons are class gifts, however. To be a class gift, the number of persons in the group must be able to increase or decrease. That is, the group must be described in a way that allows persons to be added to or dropped from the group as events (such as births, adoptions, or deaths) unfold in the future, so that the property is divided among the group as its membership is constituted at some future time. See Restatement of Property § 279. A gift to a static group is a not a class gift; it is a series of separate gifts of a fractional share of the property to each

member of the original group.

Generally speaking, then, the following rules of thumb determine whether a gift is or is not a class gift:

☞ *A gift is likely a class gift if the group members are ONLY identified by a group label (such as "to my children").*

☞ *A gift is likely NOT a class gift, although the takers are identified by a group label, if the group members are also identified by name (such as "to my children, A, B, and C") or by number ("to my three children") or by both name and number ("to my three children, A, B, and C"). Gifts like these are gifts of a fixed fraction to each of the designated individuals—in this case, a gift of one-third to A, of one-third to B, and of one-third to C.*

Although the law treats these rules as *presumptions* that can be rebutted by a contrary intent "found from additional language or circumstances,"[1] see Restatement of Property § 280, the case law shows that the presumptions are seldom rebutted. Because of the infrequency of actual rebuttal, the examples in this chapter assume that the above rules have not been rebutted.

---

[1] Hence the word "likely" in the above formulations.

The distinguishing feature of a class gift therefore is the ability of the group to fluctuate in number. Fluctuations in number can come about through an *increase* in the number of takers (caused by births or adoptions), and/or through a *decrease* in the number of takers (caused by deaths).

The ability to fluctuate in number does not continue forever. Births, adoptions, or deaths can cause fluctuations only if they occur within a finite period of time. As a general proposition, once the time of possession has arrived, fluctuation comes to an end. However, as we shall see, this is only a general proposition, and the time limit on increase and the time limit on decrease are not always identical. That is, the ability of a given class gift to increase might expire before its ability to decrease expires, and vice versa. Indeed, some class gifts might never be able to increase, only decrease, and vice versa. The point is that the time limit on the increase feature and the one on the decrease feature must be analyzed separately in each case. Identifying these time limits is a crucial preliminary step toward determining the validity of a class gift under the common-law Rule, for as we shall see, a class gift violates the common-law Rule if it is subject to increase or decrease beyond a life in being plus 21 years.

(b) Decrease in Class Membership. A class is subject to decrease if the gift is subject to a requirement of survival. Unless a specific provision is explicitly added to the dispositive language (such as "any class member who enrolls in law school loses

his or her share"), classes do not decrease after the time to which survival is required. The prior—but *not subsequent*—death of a person otherwise entitled to share in the class gift property causes a decrease in the class.

To note, however, that a class member who fails to fulfill a requirement of survival drops out of the class—i.e. loses his or her right to participate—is to describe only part of the decrease feature inherent in the idea of a class gift. The other part is that the deceased class member's lost share is added to the shares of those other members of the class who do become entitled to participate. This is the part that is unique to class gifts—the built-in or implicit *gift over* to the other members of the class.

In the case of all *testamentary* transfers of property, only devisees who survive the testator are entitled to take. This implicit requirement of survival of the testator is imposed by the common law, and applies to class gifts and individual gifts alike. The difference between a class gift and individual gifts arises from the fact that there is no built-in gift over to the other takers in the case of individual gifts.

> *EXAMPLE 15-1.* *G* devised land "to my children in equal shares." When the will was executed, *G* had three children (*A*, *B*, and *C*). *A* predeceased *G*, but *B* and *C* survived her.
>
> Because *G*'s will created a class gift, *B* and *C* each take an undivided one-half interest in the devised land, probably as tenants in common.

If, on the other hand, *G*'s will had created individual gifts of a one-third share to each of *G*'s three children (suppose, for example, that the dispositive language had been "to my three children, *A*, *B*, and *C*"), the result would have been different. *A*'s lost one-third share would not have been added to the shares of *B* and *C*; their shares would have remained constant. *A*'s lost one-third share would have gone to *G*'s residuary devisees or, in the unlikely event that there was no residuary clause, to *G*'s heirs by intestate succession.

Because a class gift such as the one in Example *15-1* is an immediate testamentary gift in fee simple absolute, it is subject to decrease between the time of the execution of the will and of the testator's death. See Restatement of Property § 279 cmt. d. Once the testator has died, the ability to decrease comes to an end. Thus if, after *G*'s death, *B* dies survived by *C*, *B*'s one-half interest would not be divested in favor of *C*.

Suppose, however, that the class gift is a *future* interest rather than an immediate one in fee simple absolute. Here the question of whether the ability to decrease continues beyond the testator's death depends on whether a condition of survival is attached to the class gift.

> EXAMPLE *15-2*. *G* devised land "to *A* for life, remainder to *A*'s children." *G* was survived by *A* and by *A*'s three children, *X*, *Y*, and *Z*. *Z* died during *A*'s lifetime, but *X* and *Y* survived *A*.

The class (consisting of X, Y, and Z as of G's death) is not allowed to decrease beyond G's death. The reason is that no express condition of survival was attached to the children's remainder interest.[2] Consequently, upon A's death, X, Y, and Z (i.e., Z's successor in interest) each take an undivided one-third possessory estate in the devised land in fee simple absolute. Z, in other words, does not drop out of the class because of her death between the deaths of G and A.

If, on the other hand, G's will had expressly imposed a condition of survival (suppose, for example, that the dispositive language had been "to A for life, remainder to A's children who survive A"), then the class would have continued to be subject to decrease beyond G's death. Z therefore would have dropped out of the class. Z's lost one-third share would have been added to the shares of X and Y. So, upon A's death, X and Y would each have taken an undivided one-half possessory estate in the devised land in fee simple

---

[2] This analysis is based on the common-law rule that a future interest is not subject to a condition of survival of the life tenant unless one is expressly imposed. This rule may be changed by statute. UPC § 2-707, for example, presumptively makes all future interests *in trust* subject to a condition precedent of survival and provides that the deceased person's surviving descendants take the share that the deceased person would have taken had he or she survived; thus, under this statute, had G's devise been in trust, Z's one-third share would be divided among Z's descendants who survived A, and would only go to X and Y if Z left no such descendants.

absolute.[3] The ability to decrease in size would have come to an end on *A*'s death, however, so that if, after *A*'s death, *X* died survived by *Y*, *X*'s one-half interest would not have been divested in favor of *Y*.

(c) Increase in Class Membership: Class Closing and the Rule of Convenience. The ability of the takers to increase in number is unique to class gifts. The following example develops the difference between class gifts and individual gifts on this point.

> EXAMPLE 15-3. *G* devised land "to my children." When the will was executed, *G* had two children (*A* and *B*). Subsequently, *G* had a third child (*C*). *G* was survived by *A*, *B*, and *C*. No children were in gestation at *G*'s death.
>
> Because *G*'s will created a class gift, *A*, *B*, and *C* each take an undivided one-third interest in the devised land.
>
> If, on the other hand, *G*'s will had created individual gifts (suppose, for example, that the dispositive language had been "to my two children, *A* and *B*"), the result would have been different. The shares of *A* and *B* would not have been decreased to one-third each by *C*'s birth and survival of *G*; the shares of *A* and *B* would have remained constant at

---

[3] This analysis is based on the common law. Had *G*'s devise been in trust, UPC § 2-707 provides that *Z*'s one-third share would be divided among *Z*'s descendants who survived *A*, and would only go to *X* and *Y* if *Z* left no such descendants. See supra note 2.

one-half each. Not being a class gift, the devise would not have been subject to increase, and *C* would not have been entitled to share in the devised land.[4]

A class can increase (the class is "subject to open") as long as new entrants can join the class. The possibility of new entrants is cut off—i.e., the class "closes" to further increase—at the *earlier* of two events: (1) the physiological or natural closing of the class; or (2) the artificial or premature closing of the class brought about by application of the so-called *rule of convenience.*

The physiological closing of a class occurs when the possibility of births (or, if adopted members are within the class description, adoptions) becomes extinct. In Example *15-3,* supra, the class gift created in the testator's children physiologically closed when the testator died. A class gift created in a transferor's grandchildren would physiologically close when the transferor's last surviving child dies.

A class may close earlier, however. When this happens, it is obvious that the class closes artificially or prematurely. Artificial closing is governed by the

---

[4] This analysis is based on the common law. Under UPC § 2-302, *C* would take an equal share in the devised land unless it is proved that *G* intentionally excluded *C.* Under statutory law in nearly all non-UPC states, *C* would take an intestate share unless it is proved that *G* intentionally excluded *C; C*'s intestate share would ordinarily be paid out of *G*'s residuary estate rather than out of the devised land.

rule of convenience. The rule of convenience is a rule of construction rather than a rule of law, which means that it yields to a contrary intent. In practice, however, a contrary intent can seldom be shown, and consequently the results dictated by the rule of convenience typically prevail. The ensuing discussion assumes that the rule of convenience has not been rebutted.

Once a class is closed by the rule of convenience, new entrants are cut off. Subsequently conceived or adopted persons cannot join the class even though they otherwise fit the class label. New entrants can join a class, therefore, only if they are conceived or adopted while the class is still open. In addition, it is important to keep in mind that each time a new entrant joins a class, the shares of the existing class members are reduced.

When does a class close under the rule of convenience?

☞ *Under the rule of convenience, a class closes when the property must be distributed.*

The rule of convenience is based on the following reasoning: Although the basic intent of the transferor is to keep the class open until it closes physiologically, the "inconveniences" that would arise from keeping the class open beyond the time of distribution would cause most transferors to prefer to close the class prematurely or artificially in order to avoid those inconveniences. Keeping a class open beyond the time of distribution would "inconvenience" the distributees by causing them to receive a defeasible possessory estate, not an absolute estate. A possessory estate that is defeasible is less marketable and, if personalty, requires some device such as the posting of security to protect the interests of unborn (or unadopted) class members.

As indicated above, the rule of convenience comes into play only when the class did not close physiologically by the time of distribution. An immediate testamentary gift created in the children of the testator, as in Example *15-3*, does not require premature closing, nor ordinarily does a postponed gift created in the children of the life tenant. Similarly, a class gift created in the children of a person other than the testator or the life tenant does not close prematurely if the parent predeceases the time of distribution.

If the parent is still living at the time of distribution, however, the rule of convenience is applied. When at least one member of the class is in existence, an immediate class gift closes at the date the gift becomes effective, and a class gift taking effect in possession at the termination of a life estate closes at the death of the life tenant.

EXAMPLE 15-4. *G* devised land "to my grandchildren." When *G* executed her will, her only son *A* had a child (*X*). Subsequently, but before *G*'s death, *A* had a second child (*Y*). *G* was survived by her son *A* and by her two grandchildren, *X* and *Y*. No grandchildren were in gestation at *G*'s death.

Under the rule of convenience, the class remains open until *G*'s death but closes when *G* died even though *A* is still alive and therefore is deemed to be capable of having more children. *X* and *Y* each take an undivided estate in one-half of the devised land in fee simple *absolute*. In other words, their estates are not subject to partial divestment in favor of any later born (or later adopted) child of *A*.

Let us vary the facts slightly. Suppose that at *G*'s death, *A*'s wife was pregnant, and that after *G*'s death *G*'s third grandchild (*Z*) was born viable.[5] The law considers *Z* to have been "in being" at *G*'s death, making *Z* a class member. So, *X*, *Y*, and *Z* would each take an undivided one-third possessory estate in the devised land in fee simple absolute.

Take another variation of the facts. Suppose that, at *G*'s death, *A* and his wife were seeking to adopt a child (*V*). Under applicable state law, adopted children are presumptively deemed to have the same status as birth children for purposes of class gifts in private instruments. Is *V* entitled to share in *G*'s class gift? *V* is if the effective date of the order of adoption

[5] See Ebbs v. Smith (Ohio Ct. C.P. Prob. Div. 1979) for the proposition that *Z* must be born viable—i.e., capable of sustaining life outside the womb—in order to be a class member. See also Note, Recent Developments, 70 Mich. L. Rev. 729, 735 (1972). Compare Restatement 2d of Property § 26.1 cmt. c & § 26.2 cmt. c (stating merely that "a child in gestation must be born alive"). Under UPC § 2-108, an intestacy section that is made applicable to class gifts by UPC § 2-705, *Z* would have to live 120 hours or more after birth in order to be a class member.

preceded *G*'s death. If, however, the adoption did not become effective until after *G*'s death, *V* might be excluded even though *V* had been born or at least conceived before *G*'s death. See Estate of Markowitz (N.J. Essex County Ct. P. Div. 1973) ("Born when?. . . . Regardless of the time when an adopted child is physically born, he or she does not come into existence as a child of the adoptive parent until the effective date of the order of adoption."); but see Restatement 2d of Property §§ 26.1 cmt. d & 26.2 cmt. d ("By analogy to a child in gestation, a child who is in the process of being adopted is regarded as an adopted child during the period the adoption is in process.").

There is an exception to the rule that an immediate class gift by will closes at the testator's death. If at that time there are *no* class members "in being," the class does not close prematurely; rather, it remains open until it closes physiologically.

    EXAMPLE 15-5. G devised land "to my grandchildren." At *G*'s death, *G*'s daughter *A* was still alive, but *A* had no living children and she was not pregnant.

    In this case, the rule of convenience does not close the class at *G*'s death. Rather, the class remains open until the death of *A*. All after-born grandchildren, if any, are entitled to participate. The only feasible alternatives to keeping the class open until *A* dies would be to nullify the class gift entirely or to allow *A*'s first born child to have the whole property in fee simple absolute. It is thought that few testators would desire either of these results, and so the rule of convenience holds the class open until it closes physiologically.

Note, however, that if *A* had been pregnant at *G*'s death, and if *A*'s child was subsequently born viable, then the rule of convenience would close the class on *G*'s death, resulting in that child taking the whole property in fee simple *absolute*.

How does the rule of convenience apply to class gifts in which possession is postponed—i.e., to *future interests* created in a class? (For a review of the classification of future interests that are subject to open, see supra §§ 7.3 and 7.6.) As indicated above, the basic principle of the rule of convenience is that the class closes when a distribution of the property must be made. This principle holds true for postponed class gifts.

☞ *In cases in which a class gift is preceded by a life estate, the general rule is that the class closes on the life tenant's death.*

EXAMPLE 15-6. *G* devised land "to *A* for life, remainder to *B*'s children." *G* was survived by *A*, *B*, and *B*'s child (*X*). *B* had a second child (*Y*) during *A*'s lifetime. *B* survived *A*. *B* had a third child (*Z*) after *A*'s death.

The class continues to be subject to increase beyond *G*'s death and during *A*'s lifetime. It closes on *A*'s death even though *B* is still alive and is deemed to be capable of having more children. *X* and *Y* are clearly entitled to participate. Z will also be entitled to participate if Z was in gestation at A's death, but if Z was conceived after A's death, Z will be excluded.

Let us vary the facts. Suppose that by the time of A's death, no children had been born to B and that none was then in gestation. This situation is analogous to the one in Example *15-5*, and is treated consistently. The class in this situation would not close at A's death but rather would remain open until it closes physiologically—at B's death.

The immediate class gifts and the postponed class gifts considered above had one feature in common: The distribution of the class gift property was to occur all at once, either at the testator's death or at the death of the life tenant. Sometimes, however, a class gift involves sequential distributions. Regarding this type of class gift, the rule of convenience holds that the class closes as soon as *one* class member becomes entitled to receive his or her share. Two examples illustrate the way the rule of convenience is applied to sequential-distribution class gifts.

> *EXAMPLE 15-7.* G bequeathed $90,000 "to my grandchildren who live to age of 21." (Such a bequest would probably be in trust, and it might provide either for the accumulation of the income until distribution, or for the payment of the income to the grandchildren until that time.)
>
> If one grandchild reached 21 before G's death, the class would close when G died.
>
> If no grandchild reached 21 before G's death, the

class would remain open, but only until one grandchild arrives at the age of 21. Closing the class when one grandchild reaches 21 is necessitated by the desire to give that first grandchild (*X*) an indefeasible interest. If, when *X* reaches 21, there are two other grandchildren alive but not yet 21 (*Y* and *Z*), *X* receives one-third of the fund indefeasibly. Later, upon attaining 21, *Y* receives one-half of the remaining fund. Later still, when *Z* attains 21, *Z* receives all the fund that is left. Any grandchildren born (or adopted) after *X* reaches 21 are excluded. If *Y* dies under 21, one-half of the portion *Y* would have received is distributed to *X*, and the other half is paid over to *Z* when *Z* reaches 21. Should *Z* later die under 21, the entire fund is given to *X*.

EXAMPLE 15-8. *G* bequeathed $90,000 in trust "to pay the income to *A* for life, then to distribute the corpus to my nieces and nephews who live to age 21." (Again, the income after *A*'s death but before distribution of the corpus might be either accumulated or paid out.)

If one or more of the nieces or nephews reached 21 prior to *A*'s death, the class closes at *A*'s death, not when the first reached 21. But if none reached 21 by the time of *A*'s death, the class closes as soon as a niece or nephew reaches 21. Any niece or nephew born (or adopted) after the closing of the class is excluded.

§ 15.2.   General Rule: "All or Nothing"

With the above background in mind, we can now consider how the common-law Rule and the Uniform Rule apply to class gifts. As noted earlier (supra § 13.2(c)), and as seen in several examples in chapter 13, class gifts pose a special problem in perpetuity law.

(a) Common-Law Rule. Under the common-law Rule, a class gift stands or falls as an inseparable unit. This all-or-nothing rule, usually attributed to Leake v. Robinson (Ch. 1817), is commonly stated as follows:

☞ *If the interest of* ANY *potential class member* MIGHT *vest beyond a life in being plus 21 years, the* ENTIRE *class gift is invalid.*

Another way of stating the same rule, which you may or may not find more helpful, is set forth in the Restatement of Property §§ 371, 383, and 384:

☞ *A class gift is* ENTIRELY *invalid if its membership* MIGHT *continue to increase or decrease[6] (or both) beyond a life in being plus 21 years.*

---

[6] The word "decrease" refers to a class gift that is subject to a condition *precedent* of survival; it does not refer to a condition subsequent of survival.

Regardless of how the all-or-nothing rule is formulated, it is an offshoot of the separability doctrine discussed supra § 13.10. Because the transferor did not *expressly* separate the interests of the class members as individuals, they cannot be treated separately. Some class members cannot have valid interests if other class members have invalid interests. If *any* potential class member has an invalid interest, the interests of *all* class members are invalid (including those that are certain to vest or terminate within a life in being plus 21 years).

The all-or-nothing rule has been upheld and applied in numerous cases.[7] See, e.g., Beverlin v. First Nat'l Bank (Kan. 1940); Thomas v. Citizens & Southern Nat'l Bank (Ga. 1968); In re Lattouf's Will (N.J. Super. Ct. App. Div. 1965) (court rejected the conclusive presumption of lifetime fertility (supra § 13.13(a)), but applied the all-or-nothing rule). Also, no American statute abrogates the rule.

Should the all-or-nothing rule be abrogated, so that a class gift could at least be saved *in part*? The goal of modern perpetuity law should be to accommodate as much of the transferor's intent as is consistent with perpetuity policy. Abrogating the all-or-nothing rule would give some but not other class members valid

---

[7] Only one American decision, Carter v. Berry (Miss. 1962), has rejected the all-or-nothing rule, and close analysis of that decision reveals that the rejection was dictum. See Lawrence W. Waggoner et al., Family Property Law: Wills, Trusts, and Future Interests 1060 n. 71 (1991).

interests, in effect closing the class earlier than it would otherwise close. This would further intent only in cases in which the saved part turns out to cover *all* the *actual* class members and the part that was not saved turns out to cover merely *potential* class members. If the potential class members whose interests are not saved actually come into existence, then the transferor's intent might be better served by invalidating the entire class gift, so that the class-gift property would filter down by succession to the ultimate benefit of a broader segment of the class. Perhaps the most attractive solution *under the common-law Rule* would be to abrogate the all-or-nothing rule but use the doctrine of infectious invalidity (supra § 13.11) to invalidate the entire class gift when that would better carry out intent.

(b) Uniform Rule. Although the Uniform Rule does not abrogate the all-or-nothing rule, its sting is substantially eliminated by the application of the wait-and-see element. Furthermore, the Uniform Rule does a far better job of carrying out the transferor's intent than abrogating the all-or-nothing rule would do, for in almost all cases it validates the interests of *all* the *actual* class members.

The Uniform Rule treats class gifts as follows:

☞ *Although the interest of one or more potential class members might vest beyond a life in being plus 21 years, the class gift is not initially invalid; rather, the class gift is valid if the interests of all class members vest within 90 years. If the interests of some class members do not vest within 90 years, the disposition can be reformed to validate the interests of all class members who are conceived (or adopted) before the 90-year mark.*

(c) Illustrations. Three examples are given below to illustrate how the all-or-nothing rule meshes with the common-law Rule and with the Uniform Rule: Example *15-9* illustrates a class gift that might decrease beyond a life in being plus 21 years, Example *15-10* illustrates a class gift that might increase beyond a life in being plus 21 years, and Example *15-11* illustrates a class gift that might increase and decrease beyond a life in being plus 21 years.

> EXAMPLE *15-9.* *G* devised land "to *A* for life, then to *A*'s children who live to age 25." *G* was survived by *A*, and by *A*'s two children, *X* and *Y*. *X* had reached 25 at *G*'s death, but *Y* was under 25.
>
> *Common-Law Rule:* The class gift in *A*'s children who reach 25 is invalid. See supra Example *13-13*. The membership of the class might *decrease*, though not increase, beyond a life in being plus 21 years. (Were the all-or-nothing rule to be abrogated, the interests of *X* and *Y* would be valid despite the invalidity of the interests of *A*'s children who might be

born after *G*'s death.[8])

Uniform Rule: The class gift is not initially invalid. Rather, the class gift is valid if, within 90 years after *G*'s death, all of *A*'s children (including children born after *G*'s death) either live to age 25 or die younger, as is very likely. In the very unlikely event that 90 years after *G*'s death, *A* is alive, or is dead but has a child who is alive but younger than 25, the disposition can be reformed to make the class gift valid. The appropriate method of reformation would be to vest the remainder interest in *A*'s children who, 90 years after *G*'s death, had already reached 25 (whether then living or not) or were then living but younger than 25. See supra § 14.2(d).

EXAMPLE 15-10. *G* devised property in trust, directing the trustee to pay the net income "to *A* for life, then to *A*'s children for the life of the survivor, and upon the death of *A*'s last surviving child to pay the corpus of the trust to *A*'s grandchildren." *G* was survived by *A* and by *A*'s two children, *X* and *Y*.

Common-Law Rule: The class gift in *A*'s grandchildren is invalid. See supra Example *13-6*. The membership of the class might *increase*, though not decrease, beyond a life in being plus 21 years. (Were the all-or-nothing rule to be abrogated, the outcome is not certain. Probably, the interests of the children born

---

[8] *X*'s interest would be valid because it was already vested as of *G*'s death. *Y*'s interest would be valid because *Y* is her own validating life. See supra § 13.5(d). There is no validating life for *A*'s afterborn children, however, so their interests would be invalid.

to *X* and *Y* (whether born before or after *G*'s death) would be valid[9] but the interests of the children born to any of *A*'s after-born children, if any, would be invalid.)

Uniform Rule: The class gift in *A*'s grandchildren is not initially invalid. Rather, the class gift is valid if *A*'s last surviving child dies within 90 years after *G*'s death, as is likely. In the unlikely event that, 90 years after *G*'s death, *A* has a living child, the disposition can be reformed to make the class gift valid. The appropriate method of reformation would be to close the class of *A*'s grandchildren as of the 90-year mark. See supra § 14.2(d).

EXAMPLE 15-11. Same facts and disposition as Example *15-10*, except that the remainder upon the death of *A*'s last surviving child was created in "*A*'s *then-living* grandchildren."

Common-Law Rule: The class gift in *A*'s then-living grandchildren is invalid. The class might *increase* beyond a life in being plus 21 years and, due to the addition of the condition precedent of survival of *A*'s last surviving child, it might also *decrease* beyond a life in being plus 21 years. (Were the all-or-nothing rule to be abrogated, probably the interests of the children of *X* and *Y* who were living at *G*'s death

---

[9] *X* and *Y* would be the validating lives for the interests of their own children.

would be valid[10] but the interests of any after-born grandchild, including those born to X and Y, would be invalid.)

Uniform Rule: The class gift in A's then-living grandchildren is not initially invalid. Rather, the class gift is valid if A's last surviving child dies within 90 years after G's death, as is likely. In the unlikely event that, 90 years after G's death, A has a living child, the disposition can be reformed to make the class gift valid. The appropriate method of reformation would be to close the class of A's grandchildren as of the 90-year mark and vest the remainder interest in A's grandchildren who were then living. See supra § 14.2(d).

§ 15.3. Two Exemptions from the All-or-Nothing Rule

Two types of class gifts are exempt from the all-or-nothing rule: (1) specific-sum class gifts and (2) gifts to sub-classes. These special types of class gifts are exempt because the underlying rationale of the all-or-nothing rule does not apply to them. In both cases, the interest of each taker (or group of takers) is *expressly* separated by the transferor, and the share of each taker (or group of takers) is, or is certain to become within a life in being plus 21 years, unaffected by the total number of takers (or the total number of groups of takers).

---

[10] The interests of these grandchildren would be valid because they would constitute their own validating lives. See supra § 13.5(d).

The significance of exempting these two types of class gifts from the all-or-nothing rule is that each class member's or sub-class's interest can be judged separately. Thus, under the common-law Rule, some class members or sub-classes can have valid interests even though other class members or sub-classes have invalid interests. Under the Uniform Rule, the class members or sub-classes that would have valid interests under the common-law Rule are valid and the class members or sub-classes that would have invalid interests under the common-law Rule are valid if they vest within 90 years.

(a) Specific-Sum Class Gifts. The all-or-nothing rule does not apply to specific-sum class gifts—class gifts that give a specific sum of money to each class member. Specific-sum class gifts are to be distinguished from conventional class gifts, under which a sum of money or item of property is to be divided proportionally among however many members of the class there turn out to be. The specific-sum exemption was established in Storrs v. Benbow (Ch. 1853), and has been followed in this country. See Restatement of Property § 385; Simes & Smith on Future Interests § 1266.

> *EXAMPLE 15-12.* G bequeathed "$10,000 to each child of A, born before or after my death, who lives to age 25." G was survived by A and by A's two children, X and Y. X but not Y had already reached 25 at G's death.
>
> If the phrase "born before or after my death" had

been omitted, the rule of convenience (supra § 15.1(c)) would close the class at *G*'s death, and the entire gift would have been valid even if the all-or-nothing rule applied. The inclusion of the "before-or-after" phrase, however, means that *G* intended to include afterborn children.

Common-Law Rule: The interests of the afterborn children are invalid, but the interests of *X* and *Y* are valid because they were living at *G*'s death. The interest of *X*, the child who already had reached 25 on *G*'s death, is valid because it is vested. The interest of *Y*, the other child, is valid because *Y* himself is his own validating life. See supra § 13.5(d).

Uniform Rule: As under the common-law Rule, the interests of *X* and *Y* are valid. The Uniform Rule, however, saves the interests of any of *A*'s children who are born (or adopted) within the 90-year period following *G*'s death, which would undoubtedly include all of *A*'s children.

The rationale for separate treatment was explained by the Lord Chancellor in Storrs v. Benbow:

It would be a mistake to compare [specific-sum class gifts] with [conventional class gifts], for the difficulty which [arises with respect to conventional class gifts] as to giving it to some and not giving it to others does not apply here. The question of whether or not the . . . after-born [children] shall or shall not take, has no bearing at all upon the question of whether . . . an existing [child] takes: the legacy given to him cannot be bad because there is a legacy given under a similar description to a person who would not be able to take because the gift would be too remote.

The justification for separate treatment emerging from this quotation is that: (1) the interest of each child was *expressly* separated from the interests of the other children; and (2) no child had a contingent interest in the share of any other child.

(b) Gifts to Sub-Classes. For similar reasons, the all-or-nothing rule does not apply to gifts to sub-classes. In order for this exemption to apply, two requirements must be met:

(1) The takers must be described as a group of sub-classes; and

(2) The share going to each sub-class must be certain to be finalized within a life in being plus 21 years.

The sub-class exemption is derived from Cattlin v. Brown (Ch. 1853) and is followed in this country. See American Security & Trust Co. v. Cramer (D. D.C. 1959); Restatement of Property § 389.

EXAMPLE *15-13.* G devised property in trust, directing the trustee to pay the income "to *A* for life, then in equal shares to *A*'s children for their respective lives; on the death of each child, the proportionate share of corpus of the one so dying shall go to the children of such child." G was survived by A and by A's two children, X and Y. After G's death, another child (Z) was born to A. A has now died survived by X, Y, and Z.

Both of the requirements of the sub-class rule are met. The takers are described as a group of sub-classes rather than as a single class: "children of the child so dying," as opposed to "grandchildren." The share going to each sub-class is certain to be finalized within a life in being plus 21 years: As of A's death, who is a life "in being," it is certain to be known how many children she had surviving her; since in fact there were three surviving children, each sub-class's share is one-third of the corpus, neither more nor less.

Common-Law Rule: As a consequence of the sub-class rule, the remainder in X's children and the remainder in Y's children are valid. X is the validating life for the one, Y for the other. The remainder in Z's children, however, is invalid. Z was not a life "in being," and he could have children more than 21 years after the deaths of A, X, and Y.

One final point: In a case like this, where there was an afterborn child (Z), a court might apply the doctrine of infectious invalidity (supra § 13.11) to invalidate the remainders in the children of X and Y. To do so would probably better carry out G's overall intent. See Estate of Morton (Pa. 1973); Restatement of Property § 389 cmt. f.

Uniform Rule: As under the common-law Rule, the remainders in X's children and in Y's children are valid. The Uniform Rule, however, almost certainly saves the remainder in Z's children also. If Z dies within the 90-year period following G's death, which is very likely, the remainder in Z's children is valid.

The rationale for separate treatment of the share of each sub-class is the same as that which supports the specific-sum exemption. The basis in Cattlin v. Brown for distinguishing Leake v. Robinson was stated by the Vice-Chancellor as follows:

[This case] is in reality the case of Storrs v. Benbow, substituting a given share for a given sum of money . . . [It] is free from the difficulty which [arose in Leake v. Robinson] . . . . [N]o person out of the prescribed limits [i.e., beyond a life in being plus 21 years] could possibly take the whole of [X's] or [Y's] share, and the exact amount of each share is finally ascertained within the legal limits; and from the time that it is so ascertained no party without the legal period can possibly acquire the least interest in it, so as to divest or diminish it; nor can any party whose interest is so ascertained within the period . . . acquire any interest in the shares of such other parties so as to augment it.

In other words, the interests of the members of each sub-class were *expressly* separated from the interests of the members of the other sub-classes; and, no sub-class had a contingent interest in the share of any other sub-class that might vest beyond a life in being plus 21 years.

Example *15-13*, supra, is a typical sub-class case. It should be compared with Example *15-10*, supra, where the sub-class exemption was not applicable. In both examples, the gift was created in A's grandchildren. One difference between the two examples that may be helpful in spotting a sub-class case is that in Example *15-10*, the grandchildren's interest was to become possessory only on the death of A's last surviving child, whereas in Example *15-13* above, possession was to occur as each child died. This feature—possession of a proportionate share of corpus occurring as each income beneficiary dies—is characteristic of a sub-class case. Such a disposition falls rather naturally into compliance with the first requirement of the sub-class rule: The takers are virtually forced into being described as a group of sub-classes. And, as long as the preceding income interests are valid—i.e. they are created in a class that cannot increase or decrease beyond a life in being plus 21 years—and as long as the amount of corpus going to each sub-class is certain to be finalized within a life in being plus 21 years, then the second requirement will also be met.

This does not mean, however, that the sub-class exemption can never apply where possession is postponed until the last surviving income beneficiary dies. The exemption would still apply in Example *15-13* if merely possession of the shares of the children of each of A's children was postponed until the death of A's last surviving child, as long as the shares themselves were fixed at the death of each child and there was no contingency of survival of the last surviving child. Such a disposition would, of course, be unusual.

To explore this matter a bit further, consider the following example, which is a modified form of the facts in Second Bank-State St. Trust Co. v. Second Bank-State St. Trust Co. (Mass. 1957).[11]

EXAMPLE 15-14. G devised property in trust, directing the trustee to pay the income "to A for life, then to A's children for the life of the survivor, and upon the death of A's last surviving child to pay the corpus of the trust to A's descendants per stirpes."

G was survived by A and by A's two children, X and Y. A had no additional children. A died, survived by X and Y. Shortly after A's death, X died survived by his only child, M. Y is still living.

Common-Law Rule: In the *Second Bank-State St. Trust* case, the court applied the sub-class rule and held that, since A did not have any after-born children, the interests of *all* of the descendants were valid.

Was the sub-class rule really applicable? Although possession was postponed until the death of A's last surviving child, the court concluded that the first requirement of the sub-class rule was satisfied. G's will expressly separated the takers into sub-classes, the court held, because the division of the corpus on the death of A's last surviving child was to be made per stirpes, not per capita. Since a per-stirpes division

---

[11] Massachusetts subsequently enacted the Uniform Rule.

requires that an equal amount be divided among the descendants of each of A's children, the court's conclusion on this point seems plausible.

What of the second requirement? The court pointed out that "the maximum number of [A's] children and, consequently, the maximum number of separate shares, of course, would inevitably be settled at [A's] death." True enough, but this does not alone satisfy the requirement. The requirement is that the share of each sub-class must be certain to be finalized within a life in being plus 21 years. Since in another part of the opinion, the court made it clear that there was "no possibility of any interest returning to [G's] estate," it becomes clear that the court construed the disposition in such a way that the share to which each sub-class would ultimately be entitled was not certain to be determined within a life in being plus 21 years. The share of each sub-class depended upon how many of A's children left surviving descendants. If it should turn out that Y has no descendants, X's descendants will take the whole corpus, not just the one-half share to which at A's death it appeared they would be entitled. This possibility raises no perpetuity problem, of course, because at the death of X or Y, who are measuring lives, the matter would be settled. It should be noted that the court held that the descendants' interests were contingent on survival of the child of A who was their ancestor, but not on survival of A's last surviving child. But, a third child of A might have materialized (Z) and it might have turned out that Z had no descendants surviving him, in which case the share of Z's descendants would vest in X's and Y's descendants, increasing their share from one-third to one-half each. Thus, the shares of each sub-class were subject to fluctuation right up to the time of termination of the trust, which might have been beyond a life in being plus 21 years. The case therefore does not fit within the sub-class rule because the contingent interests of the descendants of X and Y in the shares of the descendants of A's after-born children might vest beyond a life in being plus 21 years, and this contingent interest was not expressly separated from but was an implicit part of the original shares of the descendants of X and Y.

Oddly, the Restatement of Property § 389 cmt. g, recognizes that the sub-class rule is inapplicable to a case such as this, but states that there is an "analogous rule," the terms and rationale of which are unspecified, by which the validity of the share of each sub-class is determined separately anyway.

Uniform Rule: Abstruse discussions like that above would largely disappear under the Uniform Rule. If all of A's children die within 90 years after G's death, which is likely, all interests that would be validated by the sub-class rule would be validated by the 90-year rule even if the sub-class rule were inapplicable. Consequently, there would be no need to litigate the sub-class question.

Only if A had any children still living 90 years out would the sub-class question possibly be litigated. The reason is that, if the sub-class rule were held to apply, the interests that would be validated by the sub-class rule—the interests of the descendants of X and of the descendants of Y—would not need to be reformed, while the interests that would not be validated by the sub-class rule—the interests of the descendants of A's afterborn children, if any—would be reformed to make them valid. If the sub-class rule were held to be inapplicable, however, then the interests of the descendants of X and Y, as well as the interests of the descendants of A's afterborn children, if any, would be reformed to make them valid (by vesting them at the 90-year mark).

Chapter 16

POWERS OF APPOINTMENT UNDER THE RULE AGAINST PERPETUITIES

This chapter contrasts the common-law Rule Against Perpetuities (common-law Rule) with the Uniform Statutory Rule Against Perpetuities (Uniform Rule) regarding powers of appointment.

§ 16.1.   A Primer on Powers of Appointment

(a) What is a Power of Appointment? A power of appointment is generally defined as the authority, held by a nonowner, to designate recipients of beneficial interests in or powers of appointment over the appointive property. See Restatement 2d of Property § 11.1.

The *appointive property* is the property or property interest subject to a power of appointment. The property interest subject to appointment need not be an absolute-ownership interest. In fact, powers of appointment frequently authorize appointment of only a remainder interest in the property, as in the following example.

> EXAMPLE 16-1. *G* transferred property in trust, income to *A* for life, remainder in corpus to those of

A's descendants as *A* shall by will appoint; in default of appointment, to *X-Charity*.

A subsequently dies, leaving a will that appoints the remainder interest to her adult child, *B*.

(b) Parties. The parties connected to a power of appointment are identified by a special terminology:

• *Donor*. The donor is the person who created the power of appointment—*G* in Example *16-1*.

• *Donee*. The donee (powerholder) is the person upon whom the power of appointment was conferred—*A* in Example *16-1*.

• *Objects*. The objects (permissible appointees) are the persons to whom the power can be exercised—*A*'s descendants in Example *16-1*. The donor determines who the objects are by expressly designating them in the instrument creating the power. If the donor does not expressly designate objects, the donee is free in almost all states to appoint to anyone in the world, including the donee, the donee's estate, the donee's creditors, or the creditors of the donee's estate.

• *Appointee*. The appointee is the person the donee appoints—*B* in Example *16-1*. The appointment makes the appointee the owner of the appointed property interest.

• *Takers in Default*. The taker in default is the person who takes the appointive property to the extent the power is not effectively exercised—*X-Charity* in the above example. The taker in default has a property interest that is subject to the power of appointment. Upon *A*'s death, *X-Charity*'s property interest was divested in favor of the appointee, *B*.

In all cases, there is a donor, a donee, and someone in whose favor an appointment can be made. The other parties are not indispensable. The donee is under no duty to exercise a power of appointment and, therefore, appointees might not always exist. Also, the donor need not expressly designate takers in default.

Powers of appointment are personal to the donee. If the donee dies without having exercised the power, the power expires. Upon the donee's death, an unexercised power is not and cannot be passed along to the donee's successors in interest.

(c) Different Kinds of Powers of Appointment. Powers of appointment are differentiated in a variety of ways. Two of the most important distinctions are between presently exercisable and testamentary powers; and between general and nongeneral powers. Both of these distinctions relate to the scope of the donee's authority. An extremely important, overarching principle, set forth in Restatement 2d of Property § 12.2, and followed in almost all states, is that the scope of the donee's authority is presumptively unlimited—that is, the donee's authority regarding appointees and the time and manner of appointment is limited only to the extent the donor effectively manifests an intent to impose limits.

• *Presently Exercisable Powers/Testamentary Powers.* When a living donee can exercise a power only in the donee's will, the power is called *testamentary*.

When a living donee can presently exercise a power, the power is called *presently exercisable*. Some presently exercisable powers are exercisable either in an inter-vivos instrument or in the donee's will, and some are exercisable only in an inter-vivos instrument. The latter type of power is sometimes described as a power *exercisable by deed alone*, although technically the power can be exercised by any instrument or act that is formally sufficient under applicable law to accomplish an inter-vivos transfer. Testamentary exercises of powers to appoint a remainder interest are rarely prohibited, but some powers, such as powers to revoke or amend a trust, or to invade the corpus of a trust, are generally thought to be inherently restricted to inter-vivos exercises.

• *General Powers/Nongeneral Powers.*[1] A general power is one that is exercisable in favor of the donee, the donee's estate, the donee's creditors, or the creditors of the donee's estate. See Restatement 2d of

---

[1] Under an older terminology, adopted by the Restatement of Property § 320, but abandoned by the Restatement 2d of Property, there were three types of powers. *General* powers were defined as powers exercisable wholly in favor of the donee or the donee's estate. *Special* (or limited) powers were defined as powers exercisable only in favor of persons, not including the donee, who constitute a group not unreasonably large. All other powers were called *hybrid* powers.

Property § 11.4; I.R.C. §§ 2041(b), 2514(c). In accordance with the overarching presumption of unlimited authority, the absence of express language excluding the donee, the donee's creditors, the donee's estate, or the creditors of the donee's estate, indicates a general power.[2]

A nongeneral power is one in which the donee, the donee's estate, the donee's creditors, or the creditors of the donee's estate are excluded as objects. See Restatement 2d of Property § 11.4 cmt. b.

The following examples illustrate the overarching presumption of unlimited authority:

> *EXAMPLE 16-2. G* transferred land "to *A* for life, remainder to such person or persons as *A* shall appoint; in default of appointment, remainder to *B.*"
>
> *A*'s power is a presently exercisable general power. It is presently exercisable because the donor, *G*, did not expressly restrict the exercise of the power to a will. The power is general because the donor did not forbid *A* from exercising the power in *A*'s own favor.[3]

[2] In at least one state, however, Maryland, the donee is authorized to appoint to the donee, the donee's estate, the donee's creditors, or the creditors of the donee's estate only if there is express language affirmatively authorizing such an appointment. See, e.g., Frank v. Frank (Md. 1969).

[3] In Maryland, however, the absence of such a restriction is not sufficient to authorize the donee to appoint to himself or herself; the language would have to say something like: "remainder to such person or persons, *including A or A's estate*, as A shall appoint." See supra note 2.

EXAMPLE 16-3. G transferred land "to A for life, remainder to such of A's descendants as A shall by will appoint; in default of appointment, remainder to B."

A's power is a nongeneral testamentary power. It is testamentary because of the donor's insertion of the phrase "by will." Thus any purported inter-vivos exercise of this power by A would be invalid. A's power is nongeneral because A is authorized to appoint only among her own descendants, a group that does not include A.[4]

EXAMPLE 16-4. G transferred land "to A for life, remainder to such person or persons except A, A's estate, A's creditors, or the creditors of A's estate, as A shall by will appoint; in default of appointment, remainder to B."

In accordance with the Restatement 2d's categories, A's power is in the same category as A's power in Example *16-3*, supra—a nongeneral testamentary power.[5]

(d) The General Theory of Powers of Appointment: The Doctrine of "Relation Back." As a technical matter, the donee of a power of

---

[4] This power would be classified as a *special* power under the older nomenclature because the objects are reasonable in number.

[5] The older nomenclature would classify this as a *hybrid* power, not a special power, because the donor did not identify objects that are reasonable in number.

appointment is not recognized as the owner of the appointive property. The conventional distinction between beneficial ownership and a power is stated in Restatement 2d of Property § 11.1 cmt. b:

> The beneficial owner of an interest in property ordinarily has the power to transfer to others beneficial rights in the owned interest. This power is an incident of the owned interest and the transfer is directly from the owner to the beneficiary of the transfer. A power, however, is the authority to designate beneficial interests in property other than as an incident of the beneficial ownership of the property. When the power is exercised, it is the completion of the terms of a transfer that started with the creator of the power.

Upon exercise of a power of appointment, the notion is that the appointed interest passes directly from the donor to the appointee. This is called the doctrine of "relation back": The donee's appointment is deemed to relate back to and become part of the donor's original instrument. The donee is viewed as the donor's agent, as it were; an appointment retroactively fills in the blanks in the original instrument.

> EXAMPLE 16-5. G transferred property in trust, income to A for life, remainder to such of A's descendants as A shall appoint. A makes an inter-vivos

appointment to his child, *C*. Under the doctrine of relation back, *A*'s appointment is viewed as changing *G*'s original disposition to read: "income to *A* for life, remainder to *C*."

The relation back doctrine is capable of providing a rather automatic answer to practically every legal question relating to powers of appointment. Unfortunately, however, the specific answers to which this doctrine would lead are sometimes unacceptable and have not been adopted by the courts. This destroys the relation back doctrine as an organizing principle for analyzing every power of appointment question. Yet, at the same time, the doctrine itself is not so thoroughly discredited that it can be ignored completely. In fact, it is often followed. Consequently, its role (at most) is that of providing a starting—but not necessarily an ending—point of analysis.

When relation back is not followed, it is usually because the nature of the power puts the donee's relationship to the appointive property close enough in substance to that of an outright owner that, for the purposes of the particular question involved, the property should be treated as if owned by the donee. The Rule Against Perpetuities follows or rejects relation back on this basis. For perpetuity purposes, as we shall see, the relation back theory is generally followed for nongeneral powers and for general testamentary powers but rejected for presently exercisable general powers.

• • •

With the above background in mind, we can now consider how the common-law Rule and the Uniform Rule apply to powers of appointment. If a power of appointment violates the Rule Against Perpetuities, the power is invalid, and the disposition takes effect as if the power had never been created. If the power itself is valid, some or all of the interests created by its exercise may violate the Rule and be invalid.

§ 16.2.   Presently Exercisable General Powers

(a) Common-Law Rule and Uniform Rule: Validity of the Power. Under the common-law Rule and the Uniform Rule, a general power that is presently exercisable is treated as the equivalent of a *vested* property interest *in the donee* (rejecting relation back) and is therefore not subject to either Rule.

(b) Common-Law Rule: Validity of the Exercise. In determining the validity of an exercise of a general power presently exercisable, the power is also treated as the equivalent of ownership of the property subject to the power. Accordingly, the *donee* is considered to have created the appointed interests. The exercise is treated as if the donee first exercised the power in his or her own favor and then created the appointed interests out of owned property. Consequently, the appointed interests are created, for purposes of the Rule, when the exercise becomes effective, with the possibility of postponement in certain cases under the principles outlined supra § 13.7. See infra Example *16-6.*

(c) Uniform Rule: Validity of the Exercise. The only change effected by the Uniform Rule is that an exercise that would have been invalid at common law is not initially invalid, but instead is subject to the wait-and-see element. The 90-year period applies, in determining the validity of appointed interests that would have been invalid at common law.

(d) Illustration. Example *16-6* illustrates the difference between the common-law Rule and the Uniform Rule regarding the validity of nonvested interests created by the exercise of presently exercisable general powers.

> **EXAMPLE 16-6.** *A* was the income beneficiary of a trust and the donee of a presently exercisable general power over the succeeding remainder interest. *A* exercised the power by deed, directing the trustee after her death to pay the income to *A*'s children in equal shares for the life of the survivor, and upon the death of her last surviving child to pay the corpus of the trust to her grandchildren.
>
> *Common-Law Rule:* Under the common-law Rule, the validity of the appointed interests depends on whether or not *A*'s appointment was irrevocable. If *A* reserved a power to revoke her appointment, the remainder interest is valid. Under the postponement principle (supra § 13.7), the appointed interests are created at *A*'s death. If *A*'s appointment was irrevocable, however, the remainder interest in *A*'s grandchildren is invalid. The appointed interests were created when the deed was delivered or otherwise became effective.

Uniform Rule: Under the Uniform Rule, the outcome is the same, except that if *A*'s appointment was irrevocable, the remainder interest in *A*'s grandchildren is not initially invalid. Instead, it is valid if *A*'s last surviving child dies within 90 years after *A*'s death, which is a near certainty.

§ 16.3. General Powers Not Presently Exercisable Because of a Condition Precedent

If a general power would be presently exercisable but for the fact that its exercise is subject to a condition precedent, the power is treated by both the common-law Rule and the Uniform Rule as the equivalent of a *nonvested* property interest *in the donee* (rejecting relation back). Remember that a power of appointment expires on the donee's death (supra § 16.1(b)), and so a deferral of a power's exercisability until a future time—even a time certain—imposes a condition precedent, the condition precedent being that the donee must be alive at that future time.

(a) Common-Law Rule: Validity of the Power. Under the common-law Rule, a general power not presently exercisable because of a condition precedent is invalid unless the condition precedent must be resolved one way or the other within a life in being plus 21 years.

Consequently, although (as we shall see infra § 16.4) neither a nongeneral power nor a testamentary power can validly be conferred on an unborn person (unless some special restriction is imposed on it forbidding its exercise beyond a life in being plus 21 years), an unborn person can be the recipient of a valid general power that becomes presently exercisable upon the donee's birth. To be valid, of course, the donee's birth must be certain to occur, if it ever occurs, within a life in being plus 21 years.

(b) Uniform Rule: Validity of the Power. Under the Uniform Rule, a general power not presently exercisable because of a condition precedent is initially valid if it satisfies the common-law Rule. If it does not satisfy the common-law Rule, however, the power is not automatically invalid. Instead, the power is valid if the condition precedent actually occurs within the 90-year period; if it does not, the disposition can be reformed to make it valid (supra § 14.2(d)).

(c) Illustration. Example *16-7* illustrates the difference between the common-law Rule and the Uniform Rule regarding the validity of general powers not presently exercisable because of a condition precedent.

EXAMPLE 16-7. *G* devised land "to *A* for life, then to *A*'s first born child for life, then to such persons as *A*'s first born child shall appoint." *G* was survived by *A*, who is childless.

Common-Law Rule: Under the common-law Rule, the general power conferred on *A*'s first born child is valid. The condition precedent—that *A* have a child—is certain to be resolved one way or the other within *A*'s lifetime; *A* is the validating life. If, however, the relevant language had been "then to such persons as *A*'s first born child shall appoint after reaching the age of 25," the age contingency would invalidate the general power, at common law.

Uniform Rule: Under the Uniform Rule, the outcome is the same, except that if the power in *A*'s first born child was contingent on reaching age 25, the power would not be initially invalid. Instead, it would be valid if *A*'s first born child reaches age 25 within 90 years after *G*'s death.

(d) Common-Law Rule and Uniform Rule: Validity of the Exercise. If a general power that was once not presently exercisable because of a condition precedent is valid and becomes presently exercisable, the validity of an exercise is governed by the same principles discussed supra § 16.2(b)-(d).

16.4. Validity of Nongeneral Powers and General Testamentary Powers

(a) Common-Law Rule. To be valid under the common-law Rule, a nongeneral power (whether testamentary or presently exercisable) or a general testamentary power cannot be *exercisable* beyond a life in being plus 21 years.

Underpinning this rule is the theory of relation back (supra § 16.1(d))—the theory that any property interest created by the donee's exercise of a nongeneral power or of a general testamentary power is created by the donor *when the donor created the power*. Because no such property interest can vest until the power is exercised, the common-law Rule requires certainty that the power cannot be exercised beyond a life in being plus 21 years.

(b) Uniform Rule. The Uniform Rule also follows the basic theory of relation back for nongeneral and general testamentary powers. Under the Uniform Rule, a nongeneral power or a general testamentary power that would be valid at common law is valid. The change effected by the Uniform Rule is that a nongeneral or a general testamentary power that would be invalid at common law is not initially invalid. Instead, the power is valid if it is actually exercised within 90 years after it was created.

(c) Illustrations. Examples *16-8* and *16-9* illustrate the difference between the common-law Rule and the Uniform Rule regarding the validity of nongeneral powers and of general testamentary powers.

> EXAMPLE 16-8. *(1) G* devised land "to *A* for life, then to *A*'s first born child for life, then to such persons as *A*'s first born child shall by will appoint"; or
>
> *(2) G* devised land "to *A* for life, then to *A*'s first born child for life, then to such of *A*'s grandchildren as *A*'s first born child shall appoint."
>
> *G* is survived by *A*, who is childless.
>
> *Common-Law Rule:* Under the common-law Rule, the power of appointment conferred on *A*'s first born child—a general testamentary power in Variation *(1)*, a nongeneral power presently exercisable in Variation *(2)*—is invalid. The latest possible time of exercise is at the death of *A*'s first born child, who cannot be the

validating life because he or she was not "in being" at the creation of the power. The lesson under the common-law Rule is that a nongeneral or a general testamentary power cannot validly be conferred on an unborn person, unless a perpetuity saving clause or some other special provision limits the power's exercisability to a life in being plus 21 years.

Uniform Rule: Under the Uniform Rule, the power in *A*'s first born child is not initially invalid. It is valid if *A*'s first born child exercises the power within 90 years after *G*'s death. (Note that a testamentary exercise of a power takes place when the donee dies, not when the donee executes his or her will. Thus, in Variation *(1)*, *A*'s first born child must die within 90 years after *G*'s death in order for the child's power to valid. In Variation *(2)*, *A*'s first born child must also die within 90 years after *G*'s death if the child chooses to exercise the power by will rather than by deed.)

EXAMPLE *16-9*. *G* devised property in trust, directing the trustee to pay the income "to *A* for life, then in equal shares to *A*'s children for their respective lives; on the death of each child, the proportionate share of corpus of the one so dying shall go to such persons as the one so dying shall by will appoint." *G* was survived by *A* and *A*'s two children, *X* and *Y*. After *G*'s death, another child (*Z*) was born to *A*.

Common-Law Rule: Under the common-law Rule, *Z*'s power (and the power of any other after-born child) would be invalid because it might be exercised beyond a life in being plus 21 years. The question is whether the powers can be treated separately or whether they all must be valid for any of them to be valid. If the powers can be treated separately, the invalidity of Z's power would not invalidate X's power or Y's power because X and Y were lives in being and the latest possible time their powers can be exercised is at their deaths. If the powers cannot be treated separately, however, then X's and Y's powers are also invalid.

The Restatement of Property § 390 cmt. f approves of separate treatment. Separate treatment is also stated to be the law in Am. L. Prop. § 24.32 and in J. H. C. Morris & W. Barton Leach, The Rule Against Perpetuities 141-42 (2d ed. 1962). No cases directly on point are cited in support of the proposition, however, though the English case of Slark v. Darkyns (C.A. 1874) tends toward supporting it. The only American case found on point, Camden Safe Deposit & Trust Co. v. Scott (N.J. Eq. 1937), did not even discuss the possibility of treating the powers separately, and consequently held them all to be invalid. In Re Phillips (Ont. 1913), however, the possibility was discussed and rejected. Nevertheless, since all the requirements of the sub-class rule (supra § 15.3(b)) are met, it seems clear that these powers ought to be accorded separate treatment.

Uniform Rule: Separate treatment should be accorded under the Uniform Rule because the Official Comments so state.[6] See Uniform Rule § 1, Cmt. Part H, Ex. 25. Consequently, X's power and Y's power are initially valid and Z's power is also valid if Z exercises it within 90 years after G's death.

---

[6] Official comments to uniform acts are generally accepted by courts as representing legislative intent.

(d) Fiduciary Powers. Discretionary powers held by fiduciaries are nongeneral powers of appointment, for perpetuity purposes. Discretionary fiduciary powers include a trustee's power to invade the corpus of the trust for the benefit of the income beneficiary or a trustee's power to accumulate the income or pay it out or to spray it among a group of beneficiaries. Under the common-law Rule, such powers are invalid if they might be exercised beyond a life in being plus 21 years. Under the Uniform Rule, powers that would have been invalid at common law can be exercised for 90 years.

Purely administrative fiduciary powers, however, are not subject to either the common-law Rule or the Uniform Rule.

> *EXAMPLE 16-10. G* devised property in trust, directing the trustee to pay the income to *A* for life, then to *A*'s children for the life of the survivor, and on the death of *A*'s last surviving child to pay the corpus to *B*. The trustee is granted the discretionary power to sell and to reinvest the trust assets and to invade the corpus on behalf of the income beneficiary or beneficiaries. *G* was survived by *A* and by *A*'s two children, *X* and *Y*.
>
> *Common-Law Rule:* Although all of the property interests of the beneficiaries of the trust are valid, the trustee's power to invade corpus is invalid. It might be exercised beyond a life in being at *G*'s death plus 21 years. The trust can proceed to be carried out, but the trustee has no power to invade the corpus. The trustee's power to sell and reinvest the trust assets,

however, is valid even though it, too, might be exercised beyond a life in being plus 21 years. The reason is that purely administrative powers, as distinguished from discretionary powers to shift beneficial enjoyment, are not subject to the Rule.

Uniform Rule: Under the Uniform Rule, the trustee's power to invade corpus can be exercised for 90 years. Regarding the trustee's power to sell and reinvest the trust assets, the Uniform Rule follows the rule at common law and exempts purely administrative powers from the Rule.

EXAMPLE 16-11. G devised property in trust, authorizing the trustee to accumulate the income or pay it or a portion of it to A during A's lifetime; after A's death, the trustee was authorized to accumulate the income or to distribute it in equal or unequal shares among A's children until the death of the survivor; and on the death of A's last surviving child to pay the corpus and accumulated income (if any) to B. The trustee was also granted the discretionary power to invade the corpus on behalf of the permissible recipient or recipients of the income. G was survived by A, B, and A's two children, X and Y.

Common-Law Rule: The trustee's powers to spray income and to invade corpus were held invalid at common law in Andrews v. Lincoln (Me. 1901); Bundy v. United States Trust Co. (Mass. 1926); and Thomas v. Harrison (Ohio P. Ct. 1962). Dictum in Lyons v. Bradley (Ala. 1910) and in Woodruff Oil & Fertilizer Co. v. Yarborough's Estate (S.C. 1928), however, supports the argument put forward in Gray on Perpetuities §§ 410.1 to 410.5 that the power to spray income is in fact not one power but a series of annual powers over each year's income. Thus, Gray argued that the power to spray income should be exercisable for 21 years after the death of *A* (how about after the death of the survivor of *A*, *X*, *Y*, and *B*?).

Uniform Rule: Under the Uniform Rule, both the power to spray income and the power to invade corpus are exercisable for up to 90 years.

§ 16.5.   Validity of the Exercise of Nongeneral and General Testamentary Powers

If a nongeneral or a general testamentary power is valid, it can be validly exercised. Whether or not the exercise is valid is the next question.

(a) Common-Law Rule and Uniform Rule: When Appointed Interests Created. In discussing the validity of nongeneral powers and general testamentary powers, it was noted that both the common-law Rule and the Uniform Rule apply the theory of relation back. See supra § 16.4. Both the common-law Rule, by the majority view,[7] and the Uniform Rule also apply the theory of relation back in determining the validity of interests created by the exercise of these types of powers. Thus, any property interest created by the donee's exercise is treated as created by the donor *when the donor created the power*.

Once the time of creation is pinpointed, both the

[7] For the minority view, see infra Example *16-13*.

common-law Rule and the Uniform Rule basically apply the same rules to appointed interests as they apply to interests created by an owner of property. At common law, nonvested interests must be certain to vest, if at all, within a life in being (at the creation of the power) plus 21 years. Under the Uniform Rule, nonvested interests that do not satisfy the common-law Rule are valid if they vest within 90 years after the creation of the power.

EXAMPLE 16-12. (1) A was the life income beneficiary of a trust and the donee of a nongeneral power over the succeeding remainder interest.

(2) A was the life income beneficiary of a trust and the donee of a general testamentary power over the succeeding remainder interest.

In both cases, the trust was created by the will of A's mother, G, who predeceased him. A exercised his power by his will, directing the income to be paid after his death to his brother B's children for the life of the survivor, and upon the death of B's last surviving child, to pay the corpus of the trust to B's grandchildren. B predeceased G; B was survived by his two children, X and Y, who also survived G and A.

Common-Law Rule and Uniform Rule: Under both the common-law Rule and the Uniform Rule, A's appointment in Variation (1) and in Variation (2) is valid. The remainder interest in B's grandchildren was created at G's death when the power was created, not on A's death when the power was exercised. Since B was dead at G's death, the validating lives are X and Y.

EXAMPLE 16-13. Suppose that in Example *16-12*, A exercised his power by his will, directing the income to be paid after his death to his own children for the life of the survivor, and upon the death of A's last surviving child, to pay the corpus of the trust to A's grandchildren. Suppose also that at G's death, A had two children, X and Y, and that a third child Z was born later. X, Y, and Z survived A.

Majority Common-Law View: Under the common-law Rule, as applied in nearly all common-law jurisdictions, the remainder interest in A's grandchildren is treated as created by G when she died (Northern Trust Co. v. Porter (Ill. 1938); cf. Restatement 2d of Property § 1.2, cmt. d, illus. 12) and is therefore invalid.

Minority Common-Law View: In Variation *(1)*, where A's power was a *nongeneral power*, a small number of states have non-uniform legislation that provides that, for perpetuity purposes, the appointed interests were created when A exercised his power, not when his mother created his power.[8] See Del. Code Ann. tit. 25, § 501;[9] S.D. Codified Laws § 43-5-5. If this view were followed, the remainder interest in A's

---

[8]   Prior to its adoption of the Uniform Rule in 1987, Florida had a similar statute.

[9]   Delaware recently added a provision allowing trusts to continue for 110 years after exercise of a nongeneral power. Del. Code Ann. tit. 25, § 503. Any such exercise (and, in certain circumstances, the mere possibility of any such exercise) in a "grandfathered" trust under the federal generation-skipping transfer tax would cause the trust to lose "grandfathered" status. See supra § 14.2(c).

grandchildren would be valid. A's children would be the validating lives. No common-law court, however, has accepted this minority view.

In Variation *(2)*, where A's power was a *general testamentary power*, a small number of states have non-uniform legislation that provides, and at least one common-law court has held, that, for perpetuity purposes, the appointed interests were created when A exercised his power, not when his mother created his power.[10] See Industrial Nat'l Bank v. Barrett (R.I. 1966); Del. Code Ann. tit. 25, § 501; S.D. Codified Laws § 43-5-5; Wis. Stat. Ann. § 700.16(c). Again, under this view, the remainder interest in A's grandchildren would be valid. A's children would be the validating lives.

Uniform Rule: Under the Uniform Rule, the remainder interest in A's grandchildren is treated as created when G died, not when A exercised his power. Unlike the rule at common law, however, the remainder interest is not initially invalid. Instead, it is valid if A's last surviving child dies within 90 years after G's death.

(b) The Second-Look Doctrine. Although, for perpetuity purposes, the nearly unanimous view is that interests created by the exercise of nongeneral powers or of general testamentary powers are treated as created when the power was created, the facts existing when the power was exercised can be taken

---

[10] This is also the view in England. See Rous v. Jackson (Ch. 1885); Perpetuities and Accumulations Act § 7.

into account. Taking this "second look" at the facts is a well-established procedure. See, e.g., Warren's Estate (Pa. 1930); Estate of Bird (Cal. Ct. App. 1964).

EXAMPLE 16-14. Same disposition and appointment as in Example *16-13*. (*A* was the life income beneficiary of a trust and the donee of a nongeneral or a general testamentary power over the succeeding remainder interest. The trust was created by the will of his mother, *G*, who predeceased him. *A* exercised his power by his will, directing the income to be paid after his death to his children for the life of the survivor, and upon the death of *A*'s last surviving child, to pay the corpus of the trust to *A*'s grandchildren.) At *G*'s death, *A* had two children, *X* and *Y*, but, unlike Example *16-13*, *A* had no additional children after *G*'s death, and at *A*'s death *X* and *Y* were still living.

Common-Law Rule and Uniform Rule: Under both the common-law Rule and the Uniform Rule, *A*'s appointment is valid. Under the doctrine of relation back, the remainder interest in *A*'s grandchildren is treated as created at *G*'s death.

If only the facts existing at *G*'s death could be taken into account, the remainder interest would be invalid under the common-law Rule and would be allowed 90 years after *G*'s death to vest under the Uniform Rule. However, under the second-look doctrine, the facts existing at *A*'s death can be taken into account. Taking these facts into account saves *A*'s appointment. At *A*'s death, it has become clear that no additional children were born to *A* after *G*'s death.

Thus A's last surviving child will be either X or Y, both of whom were "in being" at G's death and therefore constitute the validating lives.

Note that if, after G's death, a third child (Z) was born to A, this would make the remainder in A's grandchildren invalid if Z survived A (this was the situation in Example *16-13*). If Z predeceased A, however, the grandchildren's remainder would be validated by the second-look doctrine.

The second-look doctrine is a departure from the fundamental principle that only the facts existing when the nonvested property interest was *created* can be taken into account in determining validity. See supra § 13.6. A persuasive justification put forward for this departure is that until the appointment is made the appointed interests cannot be known and their validity cannot be litigated. Thus no useful purpose would be served by holding appointed interests to be invalid because of what might have happened after the power was created but which at the time of exercise can no longer happen. See Am. L. Prop. § 24.35; Restatement of Property § 392 cmt. a.

Another way of understanding and perhaps justifying the second-look doctrine is this. Restricting consideration to the facts existing when the power was created is out of the question. One post-creation fact that must be considered is the nature of the donee's appointment itself. If this fact could not be considered, no appointment, regardless of its terms, could ever be valid under the common-law Rule because of the *possibility* (as of the power's creation) of the donee's making an *invalid* appointment. Thus the nature of the actual appointment must be considered even though it is an event that occurred after the power was created. Although this amounts to taking a second look to determine the terms of the appointment, the process is rarely so described. Rather, if it is discussed at all, it is viewed as part of the fiction that the appointment "relates back" to the date of the power's creation. Some may therefore find it attractive to think of the second-look doctrine as nothing more than viewing the facts existing when the power was exercised as relating back along with the terms of the appointment.

(c) Second-Look for Gifts-in-Default. A few decisions have extended the doctrine of second look to gifts-in-default. Under these decisions, the gift-in-default clause is judged on the facts existing at the time of *non*-exercise.

> *EXAMPLE 16-15.* A was the life income beneficiary of a trust and the donee of a nongeneral power over the succeeding remainder interest. In default of appointment, the income after A's death was to be paid to his children for the life of the survivor, and on the death of A's last surviving child, the corpus was to be paid to A's grandchildren. A's mother, G, who predeceased him, created the trust in her will. At G's death, A had two children, X and Y. A died without having additional children and without exercising his power. A was survived by X and Y.
>
> The gift-in-default was created at G's death.

Nevertheless, a second look at the facts existing on A's death validates the gift-in-default under both the common-law Rule and the Uniform Rule. See Sears v. Coolidge (Mass. 1952); In re Frank (Pa. 1978); Re Edwards (Ont. 1959). The validating lives are X and Y. Without a second look, the remainder interest in A's grandchildren would be invalid under the common-law Rule and subject to the 90-year permissible vesting period under the Uniform Rule. When G died, there was a possibility that A might have an additional child later, that such afterborn child might survive A, and that such child might have a child (a grandchild of A's) more than 21 years after the death of the survivor of A, X, and Y.

§ 16.6.   The Validity of Appointed Powers and Exercises of Appointed Powers

The donee of a power of appointment might exercise it by creating another power of appointment. The validity of the appointed power and the validity of its exercise are governed by a combination of the principles set forth supra §§ 16.2 to 16.5.

EXAMPLE 16-16. G devised land to A for life, remainder to such of A's descendants as A shall appoint. At his death, A exercised his nongeneral power by appointing to his child B for life, remainder to such of B's descendants as B shall appoint. At her death, B exercised her nongeneral power by appointing to her child C for life, remainder to C's children.

A and B were living at G's death. C was born after G's death. A died after C was born, survived by B and C. B then died survived by C.

Common-Law Rule and Uniform Rule—Validity of B's Power: B's power is valid under the common-law Rule and under the Uniform Rule. B is the validating life because B was alive at G's death and cannot exercise her nongeneral power beyond her own death. If B had been born after G's death, however, B's power would have been invalid under the common-law Rule and would have been given 90 years after G's death to be exercised under the Uniform Rule.

Common-Law Rule—Validity of B's Exercise: Although B's power is valid, her exercise is partly invalid under the common-law Rule. The remainder in C's children violates the Rule because it is subject to increase beyond a life in being at G's death plus 21 years. Since B's power was a nongeneral power, B's appointment relates back and is treated as having been made by A. If B's appointment related back no farther than that, of course, it would have been valid because C was alive at A's death. However, A's power was also a nongeneral power, so B's appointment relates back another step. Because B's appointment is now absorbed into A's appointment, it is treated as having been made by G. Since C was not alive at G's death, he cannot be the validating life. And, since C might have more children more than 21 years after the deaths of A and B and any other person who was "in being" at G's death, the remainder in C's children is invalid.

Uniform Rule—Validity of B's Exercise: Under the Uniform Rule, the remainder in C's children is not initially invalid. Instead, it is valid if C dies within 90 years after G's death.

Variations: Note that if either A's power or B's power (or both) had been a general testamentary power rather than a nongeneral power, the above analysis would not change. However, if either A's power or B's power (or both) had been a general power presently exercisable, B's appointment would have been valid under the common-law Rule and under the Uniform Rule. C would have been the validating life. (If A had the general power presently exercisable, the remainder in C's children would be treated as having been created at A's death, when C was alive; and if the general power presently exercisable were held by B, the remainder in C's children would be treated as having created at B's death, when C was alive.)

Chapter 17

CHARITABLE GIFTS AND COMMERCIAL TRANSACTIONS UNDER THE RULE AGAINST PERPETUITIES

This chapter contrasts the common-law Rule Against Perpetuities (common-law Rule) with the Uniform Statutory Rule Against Perpetuities (Uniform Rule) regarding charitable gifts and commercial transactions.

§ 17.1. Charitable Gifts

With one exception, future interests created in charities are subject to both common-law Rule and the Uniform Rule. Both Rules apply to charitable future interests in the same way they apply to future interests created in private parties. Under the common-law Rule, a condition precedent that might not be satisfied within a life in being plus 21 years invalidates the charitable interest. Under the Uniform Rule, a charitable interest that would have been invalid at common law is given 90 years in which to vest.

EXAMPLE 17-1. *G* devised land "to *A* for life, then to *A*'s children who live to age 25, but if none lives to 25, to *X Charity*."

Common-law Rule: Under the common-law Rule, the remainder created in *X Charity* is invalid. (So is the remainder created in *A*'s children who reach 25. See supra Example *15-9*.)

Uniform Rule: Under the Uniform Rule, the remainder created in *X Charity* is valid if all of *A*'s children die before reaching 25 within 90 years after *G*'s death. (The remainder in *A*'s children who reach 25 is valid if, within 90 years after *G*'s death, all of *A*'s children either live to age 25 or die younger. See supra Example *15-9*.)

Charitable interests, like private interests, are not subject to the Rule if they are vested. There is a pronounced tendency in the decisions to construe charitable interests as vested if the dispositive language permits this classification. Many charitable gifts that would have been invalid under the common-law Rule have been saved by this device.

As noted above, there is one formal exception to the principle that charitable future interests receive no preferential treatment under the Rule. Whether or not a charitable future interest is subject to a remote contingency, the future interest is exempt from both the common-law Rule and the Uniform Rule if it was preceded by an interest created in another charity. The rationale for this exemption is that the law allows property to be perpetually tied up for a single charity, so it ought to accord the same treatment to shifts from one charity to another, even though the shift might take place beyond a life in being plus 21 years or, under the Uniform Rule, beyond 90 years.

> **EXAMPLE 17-2.** *G* devised land "to the *X School District* so long as the land is used for school purposes, and upon the cessation of such use, to *Y City*."
> The executory interest created in *Y City* is exempt from both the common-law Rule and the Uniform Rule and is therefore valid.

For further discussion of charitable gifts under the Rule Against Perpetuities, see Simes & Smith on Future Interests §§ 1278-87.

§ 17.2.   Commercial Transactions

Legal relationships that do not create property interests are not subject to the Rule. See supra § 13.2(a). Many such legal relationships arise out of commercial transactions. The Rule Against Perpetuities would seem to be a wholly inappropriate instrument of social policy to use as a control over such arrangements. The period of the Rule—a life in being plus 21 years (or the Uniform Rule's 90-year approximation of that period)—may be suitable as a limit on donative transfers of property, but it is not suitable for bargained-for exchanges. Nevertheless, under our classificatory scheme, some contractual arrangements do create property interests, and the common-law Rule has been applied to certain types of commercial transactions. The perpetuity argument is usually raised by one of the parties who is seeking to avoid performing on his or her part of the contract.

Recognizing the irrelevance of the life-in-being-plus-21-year period to commercial transactions, the Uniform Rule breaks new ground by excluding all commercial transactions from the Rule Against Perpetuities. See Uniform Rule § 4(1).[1] Consequently, under the Uniform Rule, none of the transactions about to be considered would be subject to the Rule. The committee that drafted the Uniform Rule took notice of the fact that some of these commercial transactions do restrain the alienability of property, but thought that their control was not, strictly speaking, a perpetuity question and hence was beyond the scope of their project. The Official Comment notes, however, that these transactions are subject to the common-law rules regarding unreasonable restraints on alienation and, in some cases, marketable title acts.

Another approach is to enact a separate set of statutory provisions limiting the duration of certain commercial transactions to a flat period of years, as has been done in Illinois (Ill. Rev. Stat. ch. 30, §

---

[1] In Juliano & Sons Enterprises, Inc. v. Chevron, U.S.A., Inc. (N.J. Super. Ct. App. Div. 1991), the court extended the exemption for commercial transactions to a right of first refusal that was created prior to the New Jersey enactment of the Uniform Rule.

194(a)) (40-year limit) and Massachusetts (Mass. Gen. Laws Ann. ch. 184A, § 5) (30-year limit).

(a) Options in Gross. An option in gross is a contract right to purchase property held by an optionee who has no possessory interest in the property, such as a leasehold interest. If the subject of an option is land or a unique chattel, the option is specifically enforceable. Specifically enforceable contracts are treated as creating equitable property interests. Since equitable property interests are subject to the common-law Rule, the great majority view at common law is that options in gross are invalid if they are exercisable beyond a life in being plus 21 years.

> *EXAMPLE 17-3. (1) A*, the owner of Blackacre, sells an option to *B* under which *A* obligates himself and his heirs and assigns to convey Blackacre at any time in the future to *B* and her heirs and assigns, for $X.00.
>
> *(2) A*, the owner of Blackacre, sells Blackacre to *B*. As part of the transaction, *B* obligates herself and her heirs and assigns to reconvey Blackacre at any time in the future to *A* and his heirs and assigns, for $X.00.
>
> *Common-law Rule:* The great majority view at common law is that both options are invalid. This means that neither option is specifically enforceable and damages are not recoverable for its breach.
>
> Note that the option in Variation *(2)* was reserved by the transferor of the property. Although reversionary interests are not subject to the Rule (see supra § 13.2(b)), reserved options are not granted the

same immunity. See Woodall v. Bruen (W. Va. 1915);[2] cf. Gange v. Hayes (Or. 1951).[3] Yet the difference between a reserved option and a right of entry may be only a matter of form. For example, suppose that the grant of Blackacre in Variation *(2)* had read: "to *B* and her heirs, but if the grantor or his heirs should ever tender $X.00 to *B*, her heirs or assigns, the grantor or his heirs shall have the right to re-enter and retake the premises." Presumably this change in form would transform *A*'s invalid option into a valid right of entry.

Uniform Rule: Both options are exempt from the Uniform Rule.

Options that automatically expire if they are not exercised within a life in being plus 21 years are valid. The options in Example *17-3* would have been valid at common law if the owner's obligation to sell had been limited to "the lifetime of the survivor of *A* and *B*," or to "the next 21 years," or to some other period within the Rule. Even if not explicitly so limited, a court might construe the language of the option as being so limited. The absence of language such as "his/her heirs and assigns," for example, might lead a court to hold that the option was to last only during the lifetime of either party or only during

---

[2] West Virginia subsequently enacted the Uniform Rule, including its exemption of commercial transactions.

[3] Oregon subsequently enacted the Uniform Rule, including its exemption of commercial transactions.

their joint lives.

(b) Rights of First Refusal (Preemptive Rights).
Unlike options to purchase, rights of first refusal do
not obligate the owner to sell. They only obligate the
owner to offer the property first to the preemptioner
if the owner decides to sell. The preemptioner can
buy or decline. If the preemptioner declines, the
owner is then free to sell to anyone else.

Rights of first refusal have been held to be subject
to the common-law Rule, and void if they are
exercisable beyond a life in being plus 21 years. See,
e.g., Ferrero Const. Co. v. Dennis Rourke Corp.
(Md. 1988).

It has been suggested, however, that preemptive
rights that require merely an offer at the prevailing
market price as opposed to a fixed price ought to be
valid even if of unlimited duration. See Am. L. Prop.
§ 26.67. The argument is that a market-price right of
first refusal effects no restraint on alienation, direct
or indirect.[4] But this idea was rejected in Atchison v.

---

[4] The New York Court of Appeals recently exempted market-
price preemptive rights created in commercial and/or
governmental transactions, but not in family transactions, from
New York's codified version of the common-law Rule. See
Wildenstein & Co. v. Wallis (N.Y. 1992); Morrison v. Piper
(N.Y. 1990); Metropolitan Transp. Authority v. Bruken Realty
Corp. (N.Y. 1986). These decisions also held that such rights are
subject to, but in these specific instances did not violate, the
common-law rules against unreasonable restraints on alienation.

City of Englewood (Colo. 1969),[5] where the court held that the difficulty of ascertaining and locating the preemptioner at an indefinite time in the future constituted a "sufficiently unreasonable restraint upon the transferability of the property as to justify imposition of the rule against perpetuities." In Cambridge Co. v. East Slope Investment Corp. (Colo. 1985),[6] however, the Colorado court exempted a market-price preemptive right because the preemptioners were required to register their mailing addresses.

Influenced by the argument that market-price rights of first refusal do not effect a direct or indirect restraint on alienation, a number of courts have validated such rights by construing them to be limited in duration to a period within the common-law Rule, even though the document creating the right did not specify an expiration date. See, e.g., Continental Cablevision, Inc. v. United Broadcasting Co. (4th Cir. 1989) (limited to 21 years) (applying Massachusetts law[7]); Shiver v. Benton (Ga. 1983)[8] (limited to a reasonable time); Robroy Land Co., Inc. v. Prather (Wash. 1980) (limited to a reasonable

---

[5] Colorado subsequently enacted the Uniform Rule, including its exemption of commercial transactions.

[6] See supra note 5.

[7] Massachusetts subsequently enacted the Uniform Rule, but added a provision limiting the duration of preemptive rights to 30 years.

[8] Georgia subsequently enacted the Uniform Rule, including its exemption of commercial transactions.

time); Hartnett v. Jones (Wyo. 1981) (limited to joint lives of contracting parties plus 21 years).

Rights of first refusal are not necessarily valid even if their duration is limited to a life in being plus 21 years. The focus here has been mainly on preemptive rights other than those that require an offer at the current market price. See Restatement of Property § 413; Restatement 2d of Property § 4.4. Such rights still might be held invalid, not under the common-law Rule, but under the rules concerning unreasonable restraints on alienation. Some courts that have taken this approach hold that fixed-price preemptive rights are invalid no matter how short their duration, while others hold them invalid only if, considering various factors, they work an unreasonable restraint on alienation.

(c) Options Appurtenant to Leasehold Interests. Options to renew a lease are not subject to the common-law Rule. By the majority American view, options to purchase leased property are also exempt when held by the lessee. Thus such options, even those that are exercisable beyond a life in being plus 21 years, are valid. Options appurtenant to leasehold interests do not necessarily deter the lessee from improving the property, and so public policy does not require controlling their duration.

(d) Leases to Commence in the Future. A lease to commence at a fixed time in the future is valid even if the time is beyond a life in being plus 21 years. This is, at least, the view of the commentators (see, e.g., Simes & Smith on Future Interests § 1242) and

the small handful of cases that have decided the question. Such leases are analogous to springing executory interests that are not subject to any contingency. See supra § 7.9 and § 13.2(b).

> *EXAMPLE 17-4.* *(1) A*, the owner of Blackacre, leases the premises to *B* for 30 years. Shortly thereafter, *A* leases the premises to *C* for 10 years commencing on the expiration of *B*'s term.
>
> *(2) A*, the owner of Blackacre, leases the premises to *C* for 10 years commencing 30 years from date.
>
> *Common-law Rule: C*'s lease is valid in both cases.
>
> *Uniform Rule: C*'s lease is exempt from the Uniform Rule.

A lease scheduled to commence in the future is invalid if it is subject to a contingency that might occur beyond a life in being plus 21 years. There has been considerable litigation concerning the validity of so-called "on-completion" leases—leases scheduled to commence when construction of a building is completed. On-completion leases would clearly be valid if the lessor was obligated to complete construction within 21 years, but in the absence of an explicit obligation of this sort, some courts have held the lease to be invalid. See, e.g., Southern Airways Co. v. DeKalb County (Ga. Ct. App. 1960) (rev'd on other grounds).[9] Others courts, though, have upheld such leases on the theory that the lessee's interest was

---

[9] See supra note 8.

vested from the beginning, see, e.g., Isen v. Giant Food, Inc. (D.C. Cir. 1960), or that there was an implicit obligation to complete the building within a reasonable time, see, e.g., Wong v. DiGrazia (Cal. 1963);[10] Singer Co. v. Makad, Inc. (Kan. 1974).[11]

[10] California subsequently enacted the Uniform Rule, including its exemption of commercial transactions.

[11] Kansas subsequently enacted the Uniform Rule, including its exemption of commercial transactions.

INDEX

References are to Pages

CLASS GIFTS

See also Contingent Interests; Rule Against Perpetuities; Vested Interests

Adopted persons, 72, 225-226, 281, 283, 288-292, 295

Defined, 281

Distinguished from individual gifts, consequences compared, 281-288

Rule Against Perpetuities applicable, see Rule Against Perpetuities

Rule of convenience, 205-208, 287-295

Separate treatment of interest of each class member available only when interests are expressly separated, 127-128, 297

Subject to decrease, how long, 283-287

Subject to increase (open), how long, 287-295

Subject to open, how classified, 71-74

CLASSIFICATION OF FUTURE INTERESTS

Changes in, caused by subsequent events,
  Impermissible changes, 28-29
    See also Destructibility Rule
  Permissible changes, 97-99
    See also Merger

Importance of, 11-16

Process of, 16

CONCURRENT ESTATES

See Fragmentation of Ownership

CONDITION PRECEDENT

See Contingent Interests

INDEFEASIBLY VESTED
See Vested Interests

INHERITANCE
Descent of real property, feudal dues exacted, 139, 161-162
Of nonreversionary future interests traced from last purchaser, early law, 105
Of reversionary future interests traced from last person seized, early law, 105
Primogeniture, 142-143

INHERITANCE, WORDS OF
Absence of can cause ambiguity, 46
"And his heirs" no longer necessary to convey fee, 5-6
"Or his heirs," 6
Presence of can resolve ambiguity, 46, 94-95

LAW, RULES OF
See Rules of Law

LIEN OR CHARGE
On future interest, 89-90
On possessory interest, 52

LIFE ESTATE PUR AUTRE VIE
Defined, 23
In trustee, remainder interest legal rather than equitable, 149
Remainder following, if in holder's heirs or heirs of the body, subject to Rule in Shelley's Case, 147-148

LIFE ESTATE SUBJECT TO A CONDITION SUBSEQUENT

Charted, 16
Defined, 22-23
Followed by reversion and right of entry, 43-44

LIFE ESTATE SUBJECT TO A SPECIAL LIMITATION

Also called determinable life estate, 16
Charted, 16
Defined, 22-23
Distinguished from regular life estate, 22-23
Followed by remainder, 60-61
Followed by reversion and possibility of reverter, 44-45
Remainder following, if in life tenant's heirs or heirs of
the body, subject to Rule in Shelley's Case, 147-
148

LIFE ESTATE SUBJECT TO AN EXECUTORY LIMITATION

Charted, 16
Defined, 22-23
Followed by remainder and executory interest, 61

LIFE ESTATES

See also Particular Estates
Can arise even in absence of words "for life," 45-46
Defined, 22
Followed by remainders, 15, 57-59, 90-95, 123-124

LIMITATION

See also Defeasance; Vested Interests
Language of, 18-20, 22-24, 87

RULES OF CONSTRUCTION
See also Class Gifts
Purpose of, distinguished from rules of law, 166-167

RULES OF LAW
See also Destructibility Rule; Rule Against Perpetuities; Rule in Shelley's Case; Worthier Title Doctrine
Purpose of, distinguished from rules of construction, 166-167

SEISIN
See Destructibility Rule

SEPARABILITY OF PROPERTY INTERESTS
See also Destructibility Rule; Rule Against Perpetuities
Property interests classified and treated separately only if expressly separated, 127-129, 217-221, 297, 302, 304-305, 307-308
Deviation from as adopting dense form of wait-and-see method of perpetuity reform, 220-221
Deviation from as emasculating destructibility rule, 134

SHELLEY'S CASE, RULE IN
See Rule in Shelley's Case

STATUTE OF USES
See Executory Interests

ABOUT THE AUTHOR

LAWRENCE W. WAGGONER, the Lewis M. Simes Professor of Law at the University of Michigan Law School, is one of the preeminent authorities on the subject of this *Nutshell*. He holds the two most prominent national law-reform positions in the field. He is the Reporter for the Restatement (Third) of Property, Donative Transfers (in process) and the Director of Research and Chief Reporter for the Joint Editorial Board for the Uniform Probate Code. In the latter capacity, he was the principal architect and draftsperson of the 1990 revisions of Article II of the Uniform Probate Code. He also served as the Reporter for several other uniform acts, including the Uniform Statutory Rule Against Perpetuities (1986), the Uniform Act on Intestacy, Wills, and Donative Transfers (1991) (a freestanding version of Article II of the Uniform Probate Code), the Revised Uniform Testamentary Additions to Trusts Act (1991), and the Revised Uniform Simultaneous Death Act (1991). He is also an Adviser for the Restatement (Third) of Trusts (in process).